$8.95

S0-BZC-697

A38

"A great deal of hard-to-find information on aspects; some have never been set down in book form before.... Tiemey's approach is contemporary and readable. He skillfully blends the practical and the philosophical to provide an in-depth look at each factor under discussion. His approach works; his interpretations produce recognition and understanding in friends, clients, and others when applied to their charts."
— Review in the Journal of The Fraternity for Canadian Astrologers

DYNAMICS OF ASPECT ANALYSIS

New Perceptions in Astrology

Bil Tierney

CRCS PUBLICATIONS
Post Office Box 20850
Reno, Nevada 89515
U.S.A.

Library of Congress Cataloging in Publication Data

Tierney, Bil.
    Dynamics of aspect analysis.

    Rev. ed. of: Perceptions in astrology. c1980.
    Bibliography: p.
    1. Astrology. I. Title.
BF1708.1.T527 1983   133.5   83-7720
    ISBN 0-916360-18-0

© 1983 by Bil Tierney

All rights reserved under International and Pan-American Copyright Conventions. Printed in the United States of America. No part of this book may be used or reproduced in any manner whatsoever (including photocopying) without written permission from the publisher, except in the case of brief quotations embodied in critical or scholarly articles and reviews.

FIRST CRCS EDITION
    [Originally published privately under the title of *Perceptions in Astrology,* this edition contains a few minor changes, various corrections, and a new Introduction.]

INTERNATIONAL STANDARD BOOK NUMBER: 0-916360-18-0
Published simultaneously in the United States and Canada by:
CRCS Publications
Distributed in the United States and internationally by
CRCS Publications
(Write for current list of worldwide distributors.)
Cover Design: Image & lettering both by Sue Gibson.

Contents

Introduction

One of the most frustrating things for me as a beginning student of astrology was trying to understand the "why" behind the meaning of planet-sign, planet-house, and planet-planet combinations in the natal chart. Most texts merely made flat statements, and their accuracy *would* often impress me. But they left me wondering how *I* could learn to interpret such horoscopic factors without always referring to the books. I eventually gained greater insight into the dynamics of astrology once I realized that it was intelligently held together by basic creative *principles*. I now believe that adherence to these principles is vital to all astrologers wishing to tap effectively into the core meaning or true essence of every facet of the chart.

Dynamics of Aspect Analysis is my attempt to highlight these essential life principles as they apply to aspects and multiple configurations in the chart. Far too many texts on aspects fall short by describing observable end-results rather than discussing the primary purpose, function, and overall theme of the factors described. It also is my belief that while we have already established the fundamentals of the signs, houses, and recognized planets, for the most part our understanding of aspects is weak. Are students helped by such statements as "A sextile is half a trine" or "A semi-square is like a square, only weaker?" I think not. For me, each aspect has its own unique characteristics. No aspect is merely a weaker or stronger version of another.

Formerly published as *Perceptions in Astrology* (1975, 1980), this retitled work underscores my feeling that aspects are the most dynamic level of expression of the basic life principles. I believe a thorough understanding of them is a must in order to build a solid foundation for skilled interpretation.

Information provided in this book has not been gleaned

from statistical research. It solely reflects personal theories and observations based upon my fifteen years' experience with astrology. Since authors do not always make it clear whether what they write is considered "gospel" or is new theory still unsupported by the astrological community, let me reiterate that many statements made in this book are my personal views and that they are sometimes unconventional.

References are made herein to well known personalities who have various aspect configurations and other specific astrological features (retrograde planets, hemispheric emphasis, etc.). However, the difficulty in using famous people as examples of astrological principles is that the world usually only recognizes these individuals for their social contributions or professional achievements. Their private lives, in which deeper facets more relevant to the natal pattern operate, are not open to scrutiny. We may get a closer picture of the real person through his or her autobiography, but we cannot always count on a high degree of self-honesty. Consider this fact here and in any other astrological text which attempts to disclose the influence of certain natal patterns in the lives of people in the limelight. Do not be surprised, in other words, if the disclosures sometime contradict the "image" you may have had concerning that personality. I am merely presenting these names for your personal research and investigation.

It has been a purposeful concern on my part to write this book in a manner relatively free from negative bias, dogmatic thinking, absolute statements, or authoritarian attitudes. I at least hope I have succeeded in this regard. The astrology that excites me is what I call the astrology of "potentiality". I am less concerned about the manner in which factors in the natal chart have been shown to manifest (or not manifest) through statistical analysis. I realize there are individuals who need such scientifically objective and irrefutable evidence to begin to accept astrology's influence upon humankind (acceptable proof does not mean unconditional acceptance, of course, but validation to a degree). I am more interested in what *could* be rather than

what is or has been. *Dynamics of Aspect Analysis* consciously was written with this attitude.

May many of the concepts presented herein stimulate you
to become a more creative, adventurous thinker in astrology.
The Age of Aquarius is almost upon us and is destined to
bring astrology to a level of development never before
dreamed of or technically realized. You owe it to yourself to
be as well-rounded in this fascinating field as possible,
whether through astrological literature, classes, lectures, or
workshops. Truth is like a heavily fruit-bearing tree with
many branches extending in all directions. From whatever
branch you choose to pick such fruit, it will all taste as
sweet. All that is required to take the first step on the path of
self-understanding is an open mind and a sincere, loving
heart. Take that first step today.

—Bil Tierney

This book is dedicated to
my fellow colleague and
constant source of inspiration,
Sylvia Carroll.

1
The Principles Behind the Aspects

The proper analysis of aspects is crucial to the interpretation of any horoscope. Aspects weave powerful and purposeful energy patterns connecting the many parts of the chart. They trace out a highly complex, unduplicated montage of force-fields designed for promoting the individualization of each developing human psyche. Yet as important as aspects are, very few students of astrology seem to have a clear grasp of the fundamental principles underlying the aspects frequently used to delineate a natal chart. While modern astrology interprets the conjunction as an aspect emphasizing self-motivation and direct expression of subjective impulse, it is also an aspect linked with diminished objectivity and limited awareness of others. Why is this? Is the sextile, as tradition states, merely a "weaker" trine and thus slightly less "favorable" in its influence? Or does it possess its own unique qualities? What is it about the square that evokes a sense of stress and frustration? Why does its level of tension manifest as threatening to our security and status quo of affairs? On the other hand, why do trines readily channel energy into creative, personally gratifying activities with relative ease, confidence, and spontaneity? And why do our oppositions often involve a need for compromise with others we confront in our lives?

First of all, it is important to realize that aspects, signs, and houses collectively share one common denominator: all involve arc measurements from a designated starting point within a 360° circle. Varying arc measurements from the vernal equinox create the annual circle or cycle of the zodiac signs of tropical astrology. Varying arc measurements from the ascending point create the diurnal circle or cycle of the mundane houses. Likewise, aspects describe varying arc measurements between two planets at any given time in their synodic cycle, beginning at their conjunction point. Regardless of whether one is dealing with signs, houses, *or* aspects, astrological meaning is derived from the nature of the angles that divide each of these circles. For example:

the archetypal significance of a 60° arc can be expressed thru either a sign (Gemini or Aquarius), a house (3rd or 11th), or the sextile aspect....since all are ideally 60° from their respective starting points. The theoretical assumption thus made here is that aspects are an example of still another level of manifestation of basic creative life principles also defined by signs and houses. In other words, the inherent nature of an aspect should also be reflected on some level by its corresponding sign and house. And in an abstract sense, the corresponding sign's ruling planet should also correlate with the aspect under consideration (since a sign and its natural ruler represent the same basic principle). Therefore, like signs and houses, aspects can be seen as defining meaningful phases of relationship, following an orderly sequence within a more encompassing cyclic experience.

When analyzed from this perspective, aspects are seen as being neither "good" nor "bad." Rather than being "fortunate" vs. "unfortunate," they simply indicate how and where opportunities for opening ourselves to a fuller, more intensive dimension of awareness can best be tapped. Admittedly, astrologers recognize that aspect phases such as the square and opposition denote definite trigger points of tension within the cycle. At these particular phases of the cycle are often experienced noticeable amounts of force, pressure, friction, anxiety, and resistance. Nevertheless, their primary function is to mark peak psychological turning-points in consciousness where we are most apt to undergo natural and necessary developmental crises. These critical aspect phases are opportune for furthering our self-understanding, but always *at our own level* of comprehension (which is established by our ability to intelligently use our free-will). Stressful aspects are thus not intrinsically "evil" or "malefic" in their intent to emphasize where we need to become more self-aware, more other-aware, and ultimately more responsible for the quality of our own self-generated actions and reactions in life. Such so-called "hard" angles are actually our best problem-solving aspects and are essential for the full emergence of our total selfhood. Although somewhat difficult, these tensional aspects urge us to resolve problematic life issues rather than avoid or ignore them. And we tend to dramatically grow in character due to the challenge of these aspects. Relatively "easy" aspects such as the sextile and trine provide us with the added sense of confidence and encouragement needed to sustain growth without strain or struggle, due to the creativity, intelligence, vision, and wisdom they provide. But ironically, they lack the sufficient dynamism required for the most productive utilization of our human resources. We thus must consciously make an enduring effort to use the assets of such aspects with a greater sense of assertion and commitment. Otherwise, they tend to instill a general reluctance to face up to challenges and situational obstacles head-on. It is from this attitude that major and minor aspects herein will be reviewed.

The aspect cycle can be divided into two hemicycles. The first half of the cycle, referred to often by leading humanistic astrologers as the *waxing hemicycle*, initially begins at the conjunction point of the two planets involved. It culminates at the opposition point. The nature of the conjunction aspect itself best exemplifies the main theme of this hemicycle. Generally speaking, all waxing aspects are associated with basic *formative* processes urging the individual to build a structure of personal self-image or ego-identity. These aspects help the individual to develop a subjective sense of self-awareness. Here he is urged to *gain* experience of life thru self-related activities enabling him to first and foremost acknowledge himself as an entity separate and distinct from others. Somewhat unconscious, automatic release of energies directed toward exclusively individual needs characterize the orientation of this hemicycle. Self-preservation tends to be accentuated. The dominant theme of this hemicycle concerns the individual's will to impress himself upon the general environment according to his own terms. Waxing aspects impel him to act out his immediate impulses without reflecting upon the probable consequences of his actions and how they affect others. Thus, this hemicycle tends to be highly instinctual and spontaneous in its basic operation. However, it is at the waxing square phase of this hemicycle that the individual starts to develop a budding awareness that his personal needs tend to be in conflict with the external flow of affairs at times, and must be modified for the sake of the greatest whole. And normally, such an elementary challenge to change and adapt to the pressure of the environment here is typically met with blind, defensive resistance and great uncertainty.

The second half of the cycle, called the *waning hemicycle*, begins at the opposition point of the two planets, continuing until the cycle repeats itself once again at a *new* conjunction point (due to the fact that it is a synodic cycle). The nature of the opposition aspect itself best exemplifies the main theme of this hemicycle. Generally speaking, all waning aspects are associated with basic *evaluative* processes concerned with the balance of individual vs. social needs. Here the individual is to reorient personal objectives according to his developing awareness of a coordinated social whole. While this new perspective is most emphatically realized at the opposition point, the individual is normally first stimulated to work towards such an effort at the waxing quincunx phase. One progressively learns throughout the waning hemicycle to *de*personalize needs and desires *if* they interfere with the rights of others. The individual here can at least become more in touch with the greater purpose behind his drives and motivations towards self-expression. And as he focusses more consistently upon interpersonal or inclusive interests, he becomes better able to respond to life with greater objectivity and breadth of scope. In the waning hemicycle, we are to *use* experience initially gained in the waxing hemicycle. Waning aspects challenge us to share, interact, and *consciously* integrate our objectives with others from a more impersonal level of exchange. We can develop a greater sense of responsibility for our own actions in the more encompassing world around us. Constructively, this hemicycle encourages us to release to our community of fellow-beings valuable life directives based upon a more ideal concept of wholeness and unification.

While self-concern and instinctual impulse characterize the waxing hemicycle, self-reflection and deliberation are more emphasized in the waning hemicycle. Once beyond the opposition point, aspect phases become more complex, less under the direct control of our self-will, and thus seemingly appear more fated or destined than aspects of the waxing hemicycle (which normally allow for more personal volition). Waning aspects enable us to grow thru an awareness of duality, contrast, and diversity, which usually is experienced thru external agents more often than internal forces. If our perspective gained at the opposition phase has failed to stimulate the level of awareness it was intended to, then the "hard" waning aspects tend to generate maladjustment, disenchantment, and alienation within the social sphere. Yet these aspects, like the "soft" aspects of this hemicycle, can constructively be used to urge the individual to reform or reconstruct elements within his existing environment. Waning aspects urge us to cultivate humane values, tolerant outlooks, extended social vision, and altruistic aspirations when put to their best use.

Any aspect will always involve a faster-moving planet and a slower-moving one. Note that it is not the actual rate of motion of a planet at the time of birth, but its natural orbital cycle that determines its rate of motion in this context (which should answer the question about retrograde planets). In my opinion, the slower-moving planet describes the main objective of an aspect at any phase of the cycle. This planet thus represents the aspect's 0° or "home base" point. The quicker-moving planet will therefore either move away or move towards that slower planet. I interpret this as indicating that the faster-moving planet must mobilize itself in an effort to test out its own basic urges according to those experiences determined by the more dominant life principles symbolized by the slower-moving planet. The slower-moving planet becomes the conditioning agent for the necessary development of the faster-moving one. For example: in all VENUS-URANUS aspects, it is Uranus that stimulates the social drives of Venus, and often in a manner that evokes a notable degree of uniqueness, excitement, emotional magnetism, experimentation, and an above-average level of intuitional rapport in a wide range of interpersonal affairs. The Venus principle is normally easier for most individuals to identify with, since it represents a more personally developed, conscious urge. Uranus thus acts as an evolutionary stimulus for Venus, regulating that planet's psychological orientation and guiding it along experiences that allow for an expanded, albeit unstable, capacity for emotional response. How *we* handle this combination of planetary forces will determine whether such aspects become disruptive, chaotic, unsettling, and separative...or whether they manifest as enlightening, insightful, and emotionally liberating. For the most part, I view the slower-moving planet as providing me with the key to determining what the faster-moving planet must further assimilate for its own development in consciousness.

THE CONJUNCTION

An exact conjunction occurs when two planets are positioned at the same degree of longitude on the ecliptic. They are thus 0° apart. The conjunction aspect therefore corresponds with the 0° point of the sign *Aries*, operating thru the *Aries dwad* in the *Aries decanate* of this sign. This aspect is thereby also associated with the *ASC-1st house* and the planet *Mars*.

Since the conjunction aspect is 0 degrees, it technically makes no arc. Because of this, it does not fall into the category of either a standard waxing *or* waning aspect. If anything, the conjunction becomes an aspect partly shared by both hemicycles (since it designates the transitional point at which any cycle officially ends, only to reinstate itself anew). However, since few actual natal conjunctions are partile, they are normally found to be either *applying* or *separating*.

Separating conjunctions tend to operate somewhat like a *waxing* aspect, yet with the utmost subjectivity. The inclination is to gather energies together and *begin* to project them outward towards the environment. On the other hand, applying conjunctions function more like *waning* aspects if anything, since the faster-moving planet is still traversing thru the waning hemicycle. The inclination here is to withdraw back into the self, somewhat unconciously, and consolidate energies for the purpose of *complete* assimilation before initiating them upon a new level. Nevertheless, the conjunction is not concerned with either the gaining *or* usage of experience, but simply provides us an introduction to two planetary forces whose direct blending initiates pure activity, without any real sense of *defined* inner or outer focus.

Due to its correlation with the *ASC-1st house* and *Mars*, the conjunction represents an aspect prompting an intense need for self-relatedness. Symbolic of the inauguration of the aspect cycle, the conjunction urges the blending or merging of planetary energies. The planets involved in conjunction aspect are compelled to pull together and operate as one singular unit for better or worse. Unlike the more objective, give-and-take nature of the opposition, the conjunction does not motivate us to act out its energies with any sense of interpersonal sharing or mutual, reciprocal exchange. Instead, it is highly self-contained and is driven to act out its urges exclusively and independently. It resists external influences. Being less able to evaluate and reflect (unlike the opposition), the conjunction normally has difficulty compromising or adjusting to needs beyond its immediate, self-generated ones. This may explain why individuals with several conjunctions in the chart often appear unaffected by their environment or even oblivious of others from time to time while acting out their impulses. Due to the lack of perspective associated with this aspect, the conjunction tends to represent a blind-spot in one's character. The individual is often too subjectively wrapped up with traits described here to recognize the manner in which the self is presented to the world, even though others often easily observe these traits. Because energies here are so personally identified with, the conjunction appears to operate directly thru behavioral traits rather than thru circumstantial affairs. Unlike the opposition or square, a natal conjunction does not normally tend to project its energies onto people or situations.

Since planets in conjunction aspect dynamically consolidate their power, this is apt to be the strongest aspect of the entire cycle in terms of intensity, concentration, focus, and impact. The fact that the planets are committed to draw their forces together and synthesize gives the conjunction a high degree of solidarity and cohesion. What is basically represented here are newly stirred urges (defined by the principles of the planets) requiring total personal interest and effort if they are to be developed and experienced in the manner they were meant to be. If the planets are able to integrate effectively, then singleness of purpose and strength of direction results, fostering the self-sufficiency required to initiate enterprising activity autonomously. This can support positive self-development by instilling a more well-defined sense of identity and individualism. But if they blend poorly, the more maladjusted planet (typically the faster-moving one) is likely to function awkwardly or in a strained manner in its attempt to synchronize with the other planet. It is pressured to act out its natural impulses according to the more dominant, insistent influence of that other planet. Whether or not they can smoothly work together depends upon the inherent temperaments of both planets. Obviously, Venus and Jupiter share more common denominators than do Saturn and Uranus. So while planets in conjunction must always unite together in action, they won't always feel coordinated at all times (and this is especially the case with the dissociate or "out-of-sign" conjunction, due to the fact that the planets also fall in two different signs). It is not surprising, thus, that the traditional "good" vs. "bad" school of astrology has labelled the conjunction as being a "variable" aspect.

As planets in conjunction aspect are beginning a cycle of relationship, they urge us to plunge into activities that often bear our personal stamp of individuality in some prominent manner. But like the sign Aries, a strongly aspected and/or angular Mars, or 1st house emphasis, many conjunctions studded in a birthchart can disclose an individual who can be markedly self-absorbed or overly preoccupied with personal interests. If the chart does indicate a definite overload of conjunction aspects (as would be found in charts with stelliums), the individual will have to be careful not to let his unconscious "me-first" attitude get out of hand, since such determined self-interest can have a separative effect in relationships due to a general reluctance to cooperate, compromise, or yield to the needs of others. Conjunctions often reveal attitudes we express in a head-strong, one-tracked, and sometimes overbearing manner. So when they dominate the chart (particularly when operating thru fire signs or the fixed quality), the individual can have an exaggerated sense of self-reliance; he usually insists on always having his way and doing everything for himself. Thus, he tends to have a problem sharing himself with others or receiving their advice and assistance. He'd rather learn to know life thru first-hand experience. His biggest stumbling block tends to be his limited perspective of issues at hand (and especially when they involve others). Since the conjunction creates a momentum of forces seeking to irrepressibly thrust out towards the environment, the individual is propelled to express himself thru self-motivated activity. Yet he often does not give due consideration to the consequences or end-results of his actions.

In general, conjunctions highlight, accentuate, emphasize, and give prominence to the planetary principles represented. Constructively, an abundance of properly utilized conjunctions increase the drive to forge ahead with self-initiated projects of personal value. They also help to further the development of strength of character, application of will, inner confidence, self-assurance, and healthy assertiveness. It describes the self-made individualist who displays much initiative and who is usually allowed to live a life that enables him to pursue personal goals without much interference from others. But as ne learns to take full charge of his own life, he also needs to be careful not to diminish the importance of other people's influence. Otherwise, he can become the socially out-of-tune lone wolf.

Few natal conjunctions, or even none at all, suggests that the individual is less prone towards being self-driven. He is less determined to act on his own behalf but is more prone to seek out the support and backing of others. Self-reliance may be lacking in his approach to many areas of his life. He needs to become more one-pointed in his aims and able to

directly execute his plans of actions without hesitation or
vacillation. While he is apt to be readily influenced by the
attitudes of others, he could benefit himself immensely by
becoming more intimately in touch with his own personal
needs. Nevertheless, he may have a more objective view of
life and a broader perspective of others. Still, he should
strive to find time for himself to do things alone and to
value his moments of solitude. By learning to become more
self-involved, he will have less inclination to draw others
into his personal activities. Note that a lack of conjunctions
is often compensated for by significant Aries placements
(Sun or ASC, for example), a prominent Mars, or 1st house
emphasis. In general, conjunctions involving Mars, the
ASC, or Aries placements further underscore the dynamics
of this aspect.

THE SEMI-SEXTILE

An arc of 30° from the 0° Aries stationary point moving
counterclockwise correlates with the sign *Taurus*, and the
sign *Pisces* moving clockwise. The semi-sextile aspect is
thus symbolic of both Taurus/2nd house *and* Pisces/12th
house principles. It all depends upon whether one is dealing
with a waxing or *lower* semi-sextile, or whether one is
referring to a waning or *upper* semi-sextile. But how does
one differentiate between a lower and upper aspect?

The rule is simple: two planets are considered to be in their
waxing or lower aspect phase when the faster planet is
approaching the opposition point of the slower planet
according to the natural sequence of signs. Visually in the
chart, the quicker planet would always be found to be
located on the right-hand (dexter) side of the slower one.
Example: Mercury at 3° Pisces is exactly semi-sextile
Jupiter at 3° Aquarius. Jupiter has its opposition point at
3° Leo. Mercury in Pisces is obviously still moving towards
3° Leo. Thus, Mercury is in *lower* semi-sextile aspect to
Jupiter.

Two planets are considered to be in their waning or upper
aspect phase when the faster planet is *separating* from the
opposition point of the slower planet and is heading towards

a reconjunction with that planet. Visually in the chart, the quicker planet would always be found to be located on the left-hand (sinister) side of the slower one. Example: Mercury at 3° Aquarius is exactly semi-sextile Jupiter at 3° Pisces. Naturally, Jupiter has its opposition point at 3° Virgo. Mercury, therefore, has at some previous point in time started to move away from the opposition point in Virgo, and now is soon to reconjunct Jupiter. Thus, Mercury is in *upper* semi-sextile aspect to Jupiter.

I prefer to use Grant Lewi's terminology of "upper" and "lower" aspects, since they are visually suggestive of the actual placement of the faster-moving planet. Since a waxing aspect must occur anywhere between the conjunction and opposition phase, the faster planet must occupy the lower half of the cycle. Likewise, the faster planet of a waning aspect must occupy the upper half of the cycle beyond the opposition point. The traditional terms "dexter" and "sinister" are quite archaic and not very definitive, especially since the word sinister is also associated with evil and malevolence (the left-handed path in occultism) and thus carries with it negative connotations. The terms "waxing" and "waning" offer me no *immediate* visual image of where the faster planet is located. If nothing else, the "upper" and "lower" terminology is at least my personal preference.

The semi-sextile corresponds to both an *earth* and a *water* sign, and thus can be interpreted as an aspect of a receptive, internalizing nature. Both these elements are stabilizing, conserving, and preserving. It is natural for them to carefully attend to the form-building potential of life. The intake of energy is more characteristic of these elements than is the output. Thus, the semi-sextile phase deals with the *attraction* of resources that need further development. The Taurus factor inclines us to focus upon the productive assemblage of material resources that are practical, self-sustaining, and able to manifest as tangible power thru concrete application. They require our steady nurturance, consistent attention, and ability to organize at least on an elementary level. The Pisces factor represents resources that are comparatively more abstract, intangible, and idealistic in their application. Taurus seeks to firmly secure worldly assets for strictly personal usage and gratification, while Pisces seeks spiritual goods that can eventually be released back into the world for the ultimate betterment of all. In both instances, the semi-sextile attempts to supply us with something of value.

Normally, the semi-sextile is not able to generate enough force to stimulate us to dynamically utilize these potential resources in our daily interactions. Thus, they often remain as untapped, latent abilities. Since the energy level here tends to be insufficient for the activation of full potential, semi-sextiles seem mildly frictional and require some measure of personal exertion and determination if we are to spur them into resourceful activity (these aspects tend to be inertia-prone). In addition, the combination of principles involved lacks the easy facility characteristic of the full sextile, due to the adjustments required by the interplay of two signs of different element and quality structure. This is another reason why the semi-sextile can be felt as slightly tensional at times.

Astrologers have traditionally categorized the semi-sextile as a minor aspect. This should not imply that it is any less significant than the commonly used major aspects. I find it more helpful to interpret minor aspects as portraying subtler life principles representing less obvious nuances of personality. In general, minor aspects function upon a less event-oriented level (or at least manifest in ways less noticeable). They are more prone to indirectly express thru attitude rather than circumstance. Thus, for the most part, the semi-sextile can be very subliminal in its influence. It tends to make us evaluate and inwardly reflect upon situations we attract but do not directly involve ourselves with. Being still close to the conjunction point, the semi-sextile is a very subjective aspect of internal reaction.

The *lower semi-sextile* correlates with the sign *Taurus*, operating thru the *Taurus dwad* in the *Taurus decanate*. It thereby also associates with the *2nd house* and the planet *Venus*. This aspect works as a gentle stimulant, prompting us to develop an instinctual awareness of how and where values suitable for our growth can be built into our nature. It enables us to test out our capacity to productively work with the laws of physical attraction and magnetism in the three-dimensional world. The lower semi-sextile allows us the initial drawing power to attract benefits on a smaller scale which can eventually become constructive personal assets. Resources here represent supportive opportunities in the making. However, due to the natural passivity of this aspect, we seldom apply the effort and drive required to do anything really significant or eventful with these potentials. Until they can be more objectively and intelligently utilized (which normally is more apt to occur at the lower sexile phase), waxing semi-sextiles probably operate upon the level of unconsciousness survival instincts, facilitating necessary physical functioning and comfort. They may tie in with our ability to be receptive to sensation stimuli, the mechanics of which are almost exclusively beyond the threshold of normal waking consciousness. Regardless, more awareness thru life experience is still needed before the true worth of potentials here is recognized, understood, desired, and subsequently assimilated. The lower semi-sextile coaxes us to fertilize those budding interests and attractions that can result in creative self-expression. Here we are provided with workable elementary materials that must be further nurtured and cultivated if they are to bear fruit. We need to apply ourselves in these areas with consistency, patience, and stability.

The *upper semi-sextile* correlates with the sign *Pisces*, operating thru the *Pisces dwad* in the *Pisces decanate* of this sign. It thus also relates to the *12th house* and the planet *Neptune*. This aspect stimulates us to activate latent resources that have stored up within the deeper levels of the psyche. The upper semi-sextile represents perhaps the most delicate and other-worldly of all aspect phases. Here we are put into subtle and somewhat elusive contact with unconscious assets that were likely developed during a previous cycle of experience (i.e., past incarnations, pre-natal consciousness). This aspect enables us to draw from the hidden facets of our innerself. Soul goods here may manifest as creative imagination, visualization power, psychic impressionability, and mystical experience. Upper semi-sextiles have transcendental undertones and can be more fully brought into active expression once we have consciously aspired towards altruistic, collective goals (an urge typically evoked by the upper sextile phase which precedes it in the cycle). The upper semi-sextile symbolizes the final creative phase of the entire aspect cycle, and therefore deals with experiences that require the least amount of ego-involvement (its expression dramatically contrasts the conjunction in this respect). Constructive activation in this area, however, may first entail confronting "unfinished business" from the past requiring the relinquishment or dissolution of self-will before potential here can be actualized. Any ultimate benefit provided by the upper semi-sextile is easier realized once we adopt a genuine concern for selflessly serving humanity. Otherwise, expect it to be inoperative. Being quincunx to the opposition point of the cycle, the upper semi-sextile implies the need to make social adjustments beyond the usual level of give-and-take in relationships. Values developed here are based upon compassionate concern and the willingness to sacrifice temporal desires for a greater social cause. Much refinement in consciousness must take place before this aspect can be effectively utilized. Unlike the more sense-oriented lower semi-sextile, the upper phase denotes spiritual possessions that we can share with others in a charitable, benevolent manner. And in this manner, we also replenish ourselves with sustenance of a transformative nature which we can use to give birth to a higher level of self-awareness (symbolized at the spiraling reconjunction point of a new cycle).

THE SEMI-SQUARE

An arc of 45° from the cycle's stationary point moving counterclockwise associates with the 15th degree of *Taurus*, and the 15th degree of *Aquarius* moving clockwise. The common denominator shared between Taurus and Aquarius is that they are both *fixed* signs of the *Eastern* Hemisphere. Signs belonging to this quality are determined, hard to change, strongly self-willed, and inflexible in their attitude. And in general, signs associated with this hemisphere are self-initiating. Both these factors give us a clue about the basic nature of the semi-square. This aspect may reveal willful attitudes that tend to keep us rut-bound, unadaptable, and uncompromisingly resistant to needed changes taking place in the environment. However, the undertone of the fixed quality might also suggest that semi-squares contain some degree of stamina, peristence, and purposefulness. When channeled constructively, they can supply us with the extra measure of strength and conviction needed to help us sustain our efforts in minor, not too obvious, ways. They give us a little drive and push and are suitably used when tackling small scale projects and lesser daily challenges. Astrologers have linked the semi-square with irritability, irksomeness, and mild frictional strain. It has been rightly called the "nuisance" aspect.

The *lower semi-square* correlates with the sign *Taurus*, operating thru the *Scorpio dwad* in the *Virgo decanate* of this sign. It is also connected with the *2nd house* and the planet *Venus*. Tension here is still in its rudimentary stage of formation within our consciousness. Yet it is *starting* to become inwardly discordant and uncomfortable for us. Our growing malcontent usually is projected outwardly in the environment, attracting incidental conflicts or indirect obstacles. Its influence usually leaves us feeling inconvenienced in some manner. Preceding the full lower sextile (which technically is the first aspect of consciously rational expression), the lower semi-square still operates in a blind, subjective manner. It serves as a psychological warning flag, indicating where we are becoming congested in our attitudes and unwisely stubborn concerning the need for a personal change. Our unconscious attachment to habit is being challenged here for the benefit of our own growth. This aspect is to teach us to value and appreciate the variability of life, seeing small changes as presenting us with personal advantages. It pressures us to adapt rather than stagnate.

With the exacting, analytical *Virgo decanate* involved the lower semi-square indicates a tendency to become irritable and critical of issues at hand. Here, we expect everything to function properly and smoothly the first time, and thus can become quite riled and provoked for the moment when things invariably don't. This results in a peevish pickiness about matters that are relatively irrelevant or unimportant in the long run, at least according to the evaluations of others. In short, this aspect represents our petty grievances, disclosing where we are apt to be perturbed by trivial malfunctions and minor mishaps. Nevertheless, as Virgo is innately correctional in its nature, we best utilize our lower semi-square by developing a willingness to make practical, minor adjustments. This allows us to turn this level of tension into a mobilizing force necessary for useful activity. The *Scorpio dwad* adds intensity to the reactions typical of this aspect, plus implies a tendency to force matters in a one-tracked manner rather than accept alternative measures. It accentuates temperamental response, in which we tend to be touchy, fault-finding, and judgemental (especially towards others). It inclines us towards hasty or premature evaluation. We need to become more moderate in our feelings here, more poised and calm, and more able to flow with conditions without resentment. The Scorpio undertone indicates a need to redirect such frictional energies thru controlling self-will, harnessing the passions, and mastering emotional expression.

The *upper semi-square* corresponds with the sign *Aquarius*, operating thru the *Leo dwad* in the *Gemini decanate* of this sign. It also associates with the *11th house* and the planet *Uranus*. While the lower semi-square ties in with earth-water elements (emphasizing its tendency to resist changing the status-quo of affairs), the upper semi-square combines the more self-expressive fire-air elements Because it is an aspect of the waning hemicycle, it deals more with the dispersal of energies into the community. Rather than being shaped and moulded to sensibly adapt to external conditions (lower semi-square theme), this aspect inclines us to attempt to mould the environment according to our own social vision of how things should ideally be. We thus become irked and agitated by the realization that our objectives have limited appeal or workability on the mass level. Due to the air correspondences involved, disturbances register more upon a mental level than visceral (suggesting that the individual may be more consciously aware of them). Friction is felt whenever we try to enforce our ideals and goals upon others in an uncompromising, often insensitive manner. And as we continually meet up with resistance, stubborness, or indifference from others we attempt to reform, we end up feeling exasperated and disillusioned. Since the upper semi-square precedes the upper semi-sextile, its subjective tension is likely due to an underlying sense that there is something more to be experienced even beyond ideal social cooperation. At this point in the cycle, we are beginning to psychologically withdraw back into ourselves in an (unconscious) effort to reconnect with our spiritual essence, and this demands an internal struggle to repolarize.

The *Gemini decanate* warns against over-rationalizing one's concepts, as there is a tendency to allow abstract, intangible principles to override the tangible human factor, resulting in a lack of empathy and compassion. The Gemini factor also is teaching us to remain mentally adaptable concerning our attitudes towards social consciousness. The *Leo dwad* brings in a degree of overbearingness and authoritarianism that will need to be kept in check if this aspect is to become an asset. Due to the Aquarius-Uranus influence, the upper semi-square can be sporatic and unsettling in its nature, presenting us with sudden turnabouts or unexpected minor obstacles often due to the unforeseen actions of others. We are also equally capable of inexplicable provocations and abrupt reactions when annoyed that usually reflect premature or hasty judgement on our part. For unenlightened individuals with no social aspirations, upper semi-squares can show an obnoxious tendency to defy, shock, and stun others thru the display of crank behavior, eccentricities, or exhibitionistic activity (misuse of Leo dwad influence) serving no sensible purpose. These aspects can define strange quirks in human nature, implying social maladjustment, that seem forever out-of-tune with standard conventions of society. We must make an attempt to use them in a manner that does not alienate us from others who could otherwise creatively cooperate with us.

THE SEXTILE

An arc of 60° from the cycle's starting point moving counterclockwise brings us to the cusp of *Gemini*, and the cusp of *Aquarius* moving clockwise. The sextile thus has an emphasized association with the air element, suggesting that it is a mentally energizing aspect. It represents a vital phase in the cycle where we can apply much intelligence and inventiveness in expressing the principles indicated. I view sextiles as being natural catalysts for efficient brain and nervous system activity. Their orientation is distinctly perceptual and is especially connected with the development of reasoning faculties. The sextile is an explorative aspect, eager for new learning experiences. Under its influence, we are encouraged to reach out towards the greater social environment in many directions whereby we can grasp external benefits. Sextiles urge us to obtain helpful information about life thru objective observation. They spark the desire for education, communication, and general exchange of energies with others on all levels. The sextile allows us to become curious about life and its unlimited variation. It represents *active* expression of creative forces seeking constructive synthesis.

Unlike the more tranquilizing trine, the sextile is stimulative and less content with a sense of sameness. While not weaker than a trine, it merely has less inclination to apply itself as passively or as consistently (due to the additional stimulus of two different but complementary elements combined, which tends to be felt as pleasurable). While trines indicate relatively more inner states of consciousness (since their innate attunement and harmony of forces easily support internal well-being), sextiles are necessarily more situational-oriented. They coax us (they don't push us like squares do) to self-express freely according to various options and alternatives provided by our environment. But opportunities close at hand will require a bit of personal exertion if they are to actualize.

The degree in which we are willing to participate in the activities indicated by our sextiles will determine the extent of our benefits. Otherwise, like the air element itself, the sextile can just as readily feel quite at home remaining uninvolved on an abstract, mental level (urging one to live exclusively in his head) and thus may not be motivated to apply its promise in a down-to-earth, tangible manner. Opportunities then slip away from us. Therefore, any appealing attribute indicated here will demand our personal attention and effort if it is to be incorporated into our character.

The *lower sextile* is associated with the sign *Gemini*, operating thru the *Gemini dwad* in the *Gemini decanate* of this sign. It also corresponds with the *3rd house* and the planet *Mercury*. This aspect represents the attraction of opportune experiences in the everyday environment that can help us gather factual knowledge about life which we can use for our personal advantage. Lower sextiles stimulate mentation, enabling us to make logical, concrete connections between the various components of any immediate experience. With the lower sextile, we are actually encouraged to keenly observe life activity on its surface level rather than plumb its depths. An abundance of these sextiles is commonly found in the charts of those who appear highly curious, alert, clear-headed, and vibrant in response. They are mentally agile, open, and eager to learn new things. The individual can be multi-faceted and versatile in his expression. However, an overload of mismanaged lower sextiles (especially in a chart already low in conjunctions or squares) can accentuate the typically Geminian tendency to scatter one's attention over too wide a range of short-lived interests, thereby minimizing the ability to make solid accomplishments or long-lasting achievements. Being too susceptible to mundane distractions, we have difficulty focussing and concentrating our energies and thus tend to restlessly hop around from one activity to another without taking the time or making the effort to adequately digest and assimilate what we have encountered. The result is superficial awareness. Without constant new diversions, we can become very bored with life. Or we could become the dilettante or "jack-of-all-trades" type who prefers to dabble and is less driven to specialize in any one area.

Yet when effectively channeled, lower sextiles instill a bouyant, enthusiastic attitude about self-expression. We become highly animated, filled with zest, and optimistic about our ability to learn more about the exciting world around us. We are also better able to connect all the diverse things we learn about into a more coordinated whole. Our adaptability becomes a positive asset, allowing us to undertake productive action successfully. Few or even no lower sextiles in the chart (especially one lacking the compensation of Gemini placements, 3rd house emphasis, or a prominent Mercury) denote less *motivation* (not necessarily capacity) to actively pursue educational outlets. The individual may be less inclined to initiate communication with others, or is less stimulated by feedback. He tends to be less open to the ideas of others and may be too subjective in his views on life. Adaptability to changes in the everyday environment is less evident. There may also be little inclination to be mobile and on the go, compared to one with many lower sextile aspects. But check the whole chart first.

The *upper sextile* corresponds with the sign *Aquarius*, operating thru the *Aquarius dwad* in the *Aquarius decanate* of this sign. It thus also links itself with the *11th house* and the planet *Uranus*. This sextile's scope of awareness is broadened and extended to a more social application of the principles involved. The upper sextile can offer us special opportunities to help reform ourselves and our environment thru progressive thought. Aspiration and insight (even intuition) rather than mere surface curiosity trigger self-expression at this phase. We are motivated to experiment with life's opportunities from a more impersonal, detached perspective. The upper sextile is indicative of some degree of brilliancy or the flashing spark of creative genius. It encourages innovative mental expression and allows us to perceive an overview of the many complex factors of any concept. However, much will depend upon the evolutionary status of the individual (a factor not easily ascertained by analysis of the natal blueprint alone) as to whether this aspect's highest potential will be evoked and used. For those who are still heavily ego-bound (or psychologically operating exclusively thru planetary urges represented within the orbital field of Saturn), the upper sextile could merely stimulate an interest in active participation in novel, exciting, thrill-oriented affairs normally centered around group involvement. Release of nervous energy here tends to be sporatic and unpredictable.

In general, upper sextiles (like all upper aspects) are more goal-oriented than lower ones. They tend to stimulate curiosity about the future development of present potentials. They also urge us to promote social ideals that can actualize thru projects aimed at improving community affairs (or general interpersonal activity). These energies are not easily self-disciplined and normally do not operate thru established methods and traditional procedures. Instead, they are more likely to uniquely express themselves. Many upper sextiles in the chart suggest an out-of-the-ordinary capacity for mental and social enlightenment. They could indicate precociousness, above average tolerance, inventive spirit, and often high-strungness (due to a quickened nervous system). The individual will likely need challenging, although uncommon, mental interests to keep him stimulated and satisfied. There may be a capacity for technological fields of study. Few or even no upper sextiles could lessen the drive to explore the unknown or untried. The individual may find active participation in broad social affairs less appealing. That which is unconventional, radical, or even controversial may be less provocative and even threatening to his mental status quo. Again, first check to see if the chart shows a compensation thru Aquarius placements, 11th house emphasis, or a prominent Uranus.

THE SQUARE

An arc of 90° from the cycle's stationary point moving counterclockwise brings us to the cusp of *Cancer*, and the cusp of *Capricorn* moving clockwise. The square thus correlates with the *earth-water* element and is naturally inclined to draw its energies inward. Therefore, the square aspect is internalizing in its stress. Its tensions are first and foremost rooted from within. As both the upper and lower square link with the midpoint of each hemicycle, they represent major tension points within the entire cycle. Like the conjunction (and opposition), the square corresponds with the cardinal quality exclusively, and thus it is to be viewed as a dynamic aspect providing us with much drive and impetus to initiate change. Its frictional nature is best relieved thru decisive action demanding direct struggle, aggressive effort, and greater energy expenditure. Squares in general are crisis-oriented, forcing us to act in an explicit manner that allows for purposeful turning-points in consciousness. Planets involved in square aspect interact from a somewhat defensive pose and do not easily synthesize. They seem to follow the line of most resistance. The planets tend to block and thwart each other's basic intentions. But while the urges of the two planets resist smooth, peaceful integration, they are also prone to challenge each other's right of expression. The friction that results gives this aspect a vital sense of push, manifesting as a heightened release of force. Usually, one planet rejects the values of the other. This is typically the slower-moving planet. The faster-moving planet often feels boxed in, inhibited, and resentful of the demands imposed upon by that slower-moving planet until it has struggled to reorient itself. And at this phase, it *must* reorient its direction. Squares are quite uncompromising.

While it is stress-producing (not just tensional), the square also provides us with the powerful thrust of concentrated energy needed to confront and overcome major obstacles that stifle our growth processes. Squares challenge us to act rather than continue to endure the pain and discomfort they generate, and they are prevalent in the natal charts of people whose lives are filled with crucial events. The acute sharpness of this 90° angle often tends to agitate the planets, pressuring them to suppress energies *or* express with forceful assertion. Thus, inhibition *and* over-drive are problematic here. I know of no sure-fire way of determining how a square aspect will manifest in this regard. The astrologer will have to find out first-hand from the client. Normally, the individual begins life inhibiting the potential shown by his square aspect and later, due to challenging crises, begins to exhibit over-drive until he learns to balance his expression here. But not always (since the reverse is also possible). The square is probably the most situational of all aspects in that it forces us to eventually confront conflicting circumstantial affairs that can only be satisfactorily resolved (or understood) thru head-on, no-nonsense encounter. These pertinent issues demand our full and complete attention. This is particularly so if the square occurs in fixed signs and/or involves planets in their fall placements.

Theoretically, the faster-moving planet has reached a point in its cyclic development (at least according to the specific theme outlined by the actual square aspect involved) in which it now must operate according to a new structure or foundation that can give it additional power to grow further. This is why squares have been referred to as stumbling blocks or *building* stones. Squares represent the *momentum* to develop further. Actually, the square teaches us how to become more selective with the way we express its principles, or else we pay the price for our ignorance. It enables us to deal with difficult situations without giving up, once we reorient ourselves to accepting challenging tasks at hand. By denying our ability to handle such challenges, we only evoke the frustrating, self-blocking aspects of the square. According to ace astrologer Sylvia Carroll, "The square does not feel unpleasant unless the energy backs up on you. Tension here can feel exhilarating as long as it is flowing in action and not dammed up. It is only frustrating when you have no outlets to apply the tension." She suggests a constructive way of dealing with natal or transiting squares is to *consciously* seek out activities that require demanding energy. In other words, become involved with personal efforts that can sensibly accommodate such intense, driving force. I've heard this referred to off-hand as "appeasing" the aspect. It makes sense to me.

The *lower square* corresponds with the sign *Cancer*, operating thru the *Cancer dwad* in the *Cancer decanate*. It also associates with the *IC/4th house* and the *Moon*. Stress shown by the lower square is often indicative of *subconscious* conflict that tends to threaten our personal sense of security. These squares theoretically should begin to operate in childhood, usually thru negative conditioning (mixed messages) within our early family environment and upbringing. We are normally quite subjectively wrapped up with our lower squares, even into adulthood. Our typical manner of confronting stress patterns here is thru the building of protective blockages, barriers, shells, and shields (all involving introspective focus) which, in themselves, only further jeopardize our attempts to establish lasting inner security. The lower square exposes our root vulnerabilities, disclosing where we tend to act or react irrationally and regressively. We are likely to be overly defensive here. These squares are harder to deal with than the upper ones, since the source of stress is more deeply pocketed within the recesses of our interior self. Here, we are challenged thru the pressure of internal and external life crises to confront those behavioral attitudes that, when left unresolved, continuously uproot our psychological foundation. Life will force us to break away from habitual responses developed in the past (even former incarnations) that no longer can nurture and emotionally support our ongoing development.

We now need to establish a new support system or vital base of operations for ourselves, suggesting the relinquishment of former security symbols. Many lower squares in the chart can denote the development of subconscious defense-mechanisms. We tend to be over-protective of ourselves due to root vulnerabilities that have taken hold of our consciousness. We often cling to our personal hang-ups (no matter how stressful) yet are easily threatened by challenging external conditions that force us to let go of our psychological crutches. Thus, an overload of mismanaged lower squares emphasizes the stress of insecurity and uncertainty. The individual bottles up his internal conflicts. He tends to be caught up with negative past experiences that he has difficulty putting into proper perspective. One essential purpose of the lower square, in my opinion, is the constructive digestion and assimilation of experience, and this calls for discrimination. Here, we are to learn (and often the hard way) what facets of past experience are worthy of psychological digestion and assimilation. That which is not supportive to our ongoing growth must be released from our consciousness if we are to continue developing. The individual with an abundance of lower squares is challenged to discover what attitudes promote or thwart his capacity for self-nurturance. Few or even no lower squares could denote one who has not been overly impressed or intimidated by past conditioning factors. Yet he may not have experienced the necessary developmental crises in his early years (such as parental rejection, neglect, or disapproval) that could eventually sensitize him towards recognizing the existence of psychic pain and distress. In later years, it may become harder for him to relate to the subjective stress of others. His approach towards delicate, poignant human issues may be more mental than gut-level. Lower squares help us develop a sense of depth. When lacking, we are less able to recognize the power of our subconscious. Plus we may remain unaware for some time of the subtle stress factors programming our surface behavior. Lower squares in the chart involving the Moon, Cancer placements or the 4th house take on greater significance.

The *upper square* corresponds to the sign *Capricorn*, operating thru the *Capricorn dwad* in the *Capricorn decanate* of this sign. It also associates with the *MC/10th house* and the planet *Saturn*. While subjective insecurity and the drive for personal safety characterize the lower square, stress patterns concerning the upper square result from the conscious pressure of social responsibility. The undertone of Capricorn and Saturn suggest that a sense of inadequacy, guilt, and a fear of consequences are more emphasized here, resulting normally in self-blocking. These squares generate suppression or inhibition due to our struggle with external control factors (symbolic authority figures in our life). The drive to manage and maintain one's own boundaries in the social environment is emphasized

here. Although internal pressures are more well-defined
with the more objective upper square, they may also be
more frustrating since the individual is consciously aware
that his personal drives are often antagonistic to what is
expected of him by his society. However, these squares
represent a greater measure of self-discipline and
purposeful direction. Thus, it may be easier to
constructively utilize these tensional forces thru the pursuit
of worldly ambitions. They goad us to achieve and
accomplish in the outer world. We are forced to recognize
our obligations here as strength-producing rather than
burdensome. With our upper squares, we are to learn to
endure and persevere rather than buckle under. Negatively
expressed, upper squares denote ruthless self-preservation. They appear to be more power-oriented than are the
more passive, internal lower squares.

Many upper squares in the chart emphasize an approach
towards life that is overly-cautious and mistrustful. Here
we tend to prevent ourselves from showing any surface
vulnerability, and often by calculatingly avoiding those
people and situations that trigger such feelings. Or else we
may attempt to conquer these threatening conditions with
undue forcefulness and aggression. Negative upper squares
can express as overdrive, cruelty, domination, and
lawlessness (reflect upon Hitler's Venus/Mars conjunction
in upper square aspect to his 10th house Saturn, or sadist
Marquis De Sade's Mars in upper square to his Saturn). On
the other hand, few or even no upper squares could suggest
one who is less prone to feel restricted or oppressed by the
authoritarian elements of his existing society. He tends to
accept the standards imposed by the general status quo
without undue resistance or frustration. However, as these
squares urge us to take on challenging ambitions and
objectives that influence our world, a deficiency of them
could reveal less internal impetus and incentive to
overcome external obstacles in life that are self-limiting.
We are thus less driven to exercise proper control,
discipline, and responsibility for the major affairs of our life.
Properly handled upper squares promote greater
self-reliance plus the capacity to build firm, well-structured
foundations in the greater world around us.

THE TRINE

An arc of 120° from the stationary point corresponds with the cusp of *Leo* moving counterclockwise, and the cusp of *Sagittarius* moving clockwise. As both signs represented here belong to the *fire* element, the trine emphasizes expression that is innately creative, warming, and positive in its orientation. The trine evokes a strong sense of self-contentment, internal confidence, and general well-being. Traditional astrology has associated the trine aspect with good luck, ease, comfort, prosperity, happiness, and favorable circumstantial outcomes. While all this may be true, it is important to realize that the trine in itself does not pressure us to struggle or exert ourselves to strive and achieve in the forceful, assertive manner of the square. Nor does it stimulate an eager response to act upon opportunities at hand in the more lively, energetic manner of the sextile. And unlike the more determined, self-motivated conjunction, the trine allows us to passively receive the beneficial conditions it presents to us without the intense focus of interest and attention characteristic of conjunctions. Primarily, the trine is an aspect of relaxation, peace, harmonious reception, and pleasurable response. It operates without friction and discomfort. But with such a lack of pressure, strain, and tension (it is a stress-reducer), the trine doesn't supply the impetus needed to push us into decisive action in a challenging manner that fosters dynamic change. Trines are preservers of the status quo of affairs. In this respect, they act like soothing sedatives, calmly smoothing out potential conflicts in a gentle, tranquil, non-abrasive manner. However, since the planets involved are not driven to confront crises head-on, they often follow the line of *least* resistance (unlike the square). Nevertheless, trines are highly creative. When used for optimum benefit, they are productively talented (due to their easy-flowingness of self-expression). Trines have a magnetic appeal about them.

What is seldom realized is that trines are equal in strength to squares. But because their energy is often turned inward, they *appear* to be less influential in external affairs.

Yet without such internal focus, we are seldom able to attract what we desire as easily. Magnetism involves receptivity, which in turn requires our interior focus. If we are too busy activating ourselves in the world, we are less able to draw things towards us since we are more wrapped up with having an impact upon our environment rather than allowing ourselves to be passively receptive to that environment. Thus, trines are more apt to represent inner states of consciousness manifesting as creative insight, visions of ideal expression, or a fuller awareness of factors that produce true harmony and artistic synthesis. We tend to feel inspired and elevated by our trines since they reveal to us a sense of perfect attunement of principles. Trines (even those formed by progression or transit) reflect subjective conditions that make us feel self-satisfied and secure. They don't have to project into the external world to make us become aware of their presence. This is probably why transiting trines do not always manifest as noteworthy events. Instead, they more likely describe our subjective attitudes during the time period indicated by the transit in question.

The *lower trine* correlates with the sign *Leo*, operating thru the *Leo dwad* in the *Leo decanate* of this sign. It then also relates to the *5th house* and the *Sun*. The lower trine tends to be creatively self-expressive, pleasure oriented, and somewhat exhibitionistic (of course, much depends upon the nature of the planets involved. Venus trine Jupiter is likely to be more joyous and free in its expression than Saturn trine Pluto, for example.) It is an aspect of whole-hearted and vibrant expression. Due to the fixed undertone, the lower trine can steadily pour out its creative potential with little deliberation. This aspect best energizes itself when there are elements of recreational activity present. One of the drawbacks of lower trines is that they seek the pampered, effortless way of doing things. They are not willing to endure struggle, toil, or sustain strenuous effort to obtain their desires. From a human point of view, these trines could foster a spoiled nature craving to be indulged and satisfied by the efforts of others. Yet positively expressed, the lower trine can be used to promote creative flair, dramatic self-display, active demonstration of talent, and a natural aptitude for showmanship (often expressed with much vitality and command of attention). Potential leadership ability can here manifest with little effort, since lower trines are powerfully magnetic and charismatic. One's ability to shine, radiate, attract recognition, and gain popular approval is promised a suitable outlet with these aspects. People with an abundance of lower trines often feel special, lucky, blessed, and generally untouched by the usual hardships of life. They are less prone to accept restriction and limitation as part of their world. An overdose of mismanaged lower trines can create a "royalty complex" in which the individual expects the world to revolve around his own exclusive, self-promoting desires. Instinctively shunning whatever requires hard work and self-discipline, this individual would rather coast thru life establishing no serious objectives outside of personal sensual fulfillment. In the chart of a weak character, an overload of lower trines may tempt one to be too self-contented to confront life's many challenges. The individual feels unduly privileged and usually lacks the initiative and willingness to inaugurate activity himself without first soliciting the effort of others he charms.

Personal dissipation and energy wastage can become problematic with this aspect phase, since it has none of the necessary safety brakes found with the lower square. With lower trines, laziness can result if self-satisfaction becomes too pronounced. This is apparently less the case if the chart is balanced by at least one T-Square (and especially one operating thru the aggressive, self-starting Cardinal mode). And particularly so if one of the planets in trine aspect is also a member of that T-Square. Few or even no lower trines can suggest a basic lack of creative know-how. This condition lessens one's self-confidence and self-esteem. One's capacity to attract pleasurable outlets for self-expression is minimized. Joyous spontaneity is less evident, as well as the willingness to display one's talents in front of others. Thus, the individual will have to make a more conscious effort to build these qualities into his ego-structure if so desired. In general, lower trines may disclose areas in our past evolutionary history where we

had to work at heightening the creative expression of the
planets involved thru exercising the will. Our present
benefits might have been the direct result of resolving
conflicts and challenges when these planets were in lower
square phase in the past. Great soul effort here could be
indicated when at least one of the planets is now in its
exaltation placement. Pay special attention to lower trines
involving the Sun, planets in Leo, and the 5th house.

The *upper trine* corresponds with the sign *Sagittarius*,
operating thru the *Sagittarius dwad* in the *Sagittarius
decanate* of this sign. It also ties in with the *9th house* and
the planet *Jupiter*. This trine seeks its creative release thru
more expansive avenues of collective expression. It tends to
be less egocentric than the lower trine, suggesting that
personal gratification can occur as a result of social
interaction. The upper trine urges us to benevolently share
our blessings with others. It is an aspect of generosity of
spirit. It is a source of personal uplift and inspiration,
enabling us to elevate our consciousness to lofty levels of
idealism, understanding, and wisdom. The upper trine is
more universal in its scope. If a Higher Octave planet is
involved in an upper trine, the effect is strongly conducive
to the unfoldment of psychic awareness and the
comprehension of highly abstract principles. Pleasure can
come from the exploration of theoretical concepts, which
tend to be impractical at times and hard to apply in the
everyday world. The ability to apply foresight, however, in
personal affairs is often excellent. We best utilize these
trines when we unselfishly participate in some social cause
(usually geared towards cultural betterment), since all
upper aspects need collective channels for their expression.
As upper aspects are more impersonal and easily worked
out within larger frameworks of experience, the upper trine
can be used for the enlightenment of others as well as for
self-illumination. Its basic nature is humane, tolerant,
philanthropic, and freedom-seeking. This is an aspect of
great expectation and hope for the best. Optimism becomes
an attracting force for growth. The areas of life (houses)
and behavioral attitudes (signs) linked with this trine
reveal where and how we can instill faith in ourselves and

have unquestioned trust in higher protection or inner guidance. We seldom doubt or underestimate our blessings here; in fact, we naively tend to overestimate the "luck" factor.

An overdose of mismanaged upper trines in the chart could foster undue optimism, blind faith, procrastination, and irresponsibility. We may be tempted to sidetrack personal commitments or unrealistically attempt to escape from directly dealing with the unpleasant features of our life, instead desiring to remain uninvolved. There is a dreaminess quality inherent in this trine that often makes us innocently unaware of the stress signals in our life (and very much so when these trines involve Jupiter or Neptune). At all times, upper trines warn us not to overdo a good thing or over-extend ourselves in activities, since they hardly recognize limits. Few or even no upper trines suggest that inspiration is rarely experienced, or that one's vision of greater horizons can be diminished due to a basic lack of faith, hope, and charity. We are not easily convinced of the power of belief. We are also less inclined to view life from a more broad-minded, philosophical perspective. Or we can be less open to accepting and sharing idealistic concepts with others.

Trines manifest as gifts or special skills we have struggled to develop in past lives. We once gave out these positive energies to others in our past, and now these benevolent forces return back home to us to ease and support *our* lives by enabling us to become more sensitive to the love and wisdom which abounds in us. Trines are here for our use at any time. If we choose not to express ourselves thru them, they become latent and inactive (since they are capable of full relaxation and rest). Check to see if a third planet is squaring one of the planets in trine aspect. If so, that planet can act as a catalyst providing the trine with enough dynamic tension to prevent it from becoming non-productive. Likewise, the trine itself can serve as a healing channel assisting us in resolving the stress indicated by that inter-connecting square. The planet that is thus tied in with both the trine and square indicates a highly vital, transformative principle in the individual's life that can effectively trigger dynamic growth once understood and valued.

THE SESQUI-SQUARE

An arc of 135° from the stationary point moving counter-clockwise associates with the 15th degree of *Leo*, and the 15th degree of *Scorpio* moving clockwise. The common denominator shared between Leo and Scorpio is that they are both *fixed* signs of the *Western* Hemisphere. The sesqui-square has been considered to be a minor aspect of agitation, but with tones more forceful and discordant than the semi-square. This is not surprising, since it corresponds with both the *water* and *fire* elements, which are more volatile and emotional than earth and air. The undertone of the fixed quality suggests that willfulness is still a problem here. Basically, I interpret the sesqui-square as dealing with the consequences (Western Hemisphere emphasis) of a lack of composure and self-restraint in interpersonal situations. The individual is pressured to apply more self-control and emotional poise if he is to effectively chan-nel this aspect, since here he tends to react irrationally or act immoderately at the expense of others. Due to the intensity of water and fire combinations, the sesqui-square tends towards extremism in behavior, leading towards inconsistencies in expression. This aspect also appears to involve a greater degree of sudden upset and unexpected disruption that temporarily stuns, shocks, or jolts our sensibilities and/or those of others we confront.

With this aspect, we are apt to react to minor conflicts in an overly forceful manner, which tends to throw situations off-balance or blow them out of proportion. Here we are easily ruffled, emotionally in flux, and often at odds with an unprecedented turn-about of events out of our control. Our ineffectiveness in controlling the situation evokes resentment and mild anger. Situations under this aspect tend to break down or fall apart at the last minute, which leaves us feeling momentarily scattered and disorganized. Like the semi-square, this aspect calls for more calmness, patience, and objectivity. Our outward expression of inner dissatisfaction regarding disturbances here only further inflames problems in most cases, since our reactions are usually out-of-place or inappropriate for the occasion represented. The tendency to over-dramatize issues here leads towards misjudgement.

The *lower sesqui-square* correlates with the sign *Leo*, operating thru the *Aquarius dwad* in the *Sagittarius decanate* of this sign. It also associates with the *5th house* and the *Sun*. As the lower sesqui-square falls midway between the self-indulgent lower trine and the self-corrective lower quincunx, it represents a tensional point in the cycle wherein the natural urges of the lower trine show signs of becoming troublesome in relationships. And this is often because we overstate them in an anxious effort to prove our personal significance. The power-seeking, authoritative side of Leo is more evoked here than is its joyous, creative side. Thus, this aspect represents a somewhat abrasive display of egoism. It is unduly attention-seeking in a childish way that alienates others. The misguided expression of will tends to produce minor obstacles that thwart our ability to cooperate. As our personal sense of pride and honor is often overblown, any level of criticism puts us on the defensive. The drive to feel self-important could make us behave in a dominating manner that others find obnoxious and unattractive. We tend to come on too strong here at the expense of others.

The *Sagittarius decanate* denotes an underlying urge to exaggerate or overdo self-expression. The tendency to ignore or indirectly defy restraints imposed by the environment is characteristic of this aspect. We demand complete freedom from the control of others, but often try to establish this in an awkward, immature manner. We are apt to have an unquestioned belief in the rightness of our attitudes. The *Aquarius dwad* further emphasizes rebelliousness, and introduces an element of unpredictable response in which we seem out-of-step with the rhythms of others. Our ability to grow thru interpersonal affairs, therefore, necessitates a willingness to adjust and reorient our desires based upon a greater recognition and respect of the needs of others (a concept which starts to take shape at the lower quincunx phase). Because it pressures us to realize the limits of our self-will, the lower sesqui-square instills a degree of personal discomfort and frustration whenever we attempt to enforce our uncompromising demands in relationships. Our autocratic approach towards matters here seldom produces the satisfying results we confidently anticipate, but almost always unexpectedly falls short of our expectations. Inner discord results when we come to realize that we cannot have our way in the world all the time, and yet such discord is imperative if we are eventually motivated to become more self-analytical and selective in our use of creative power.

The *upper sesqui-square* correlates with the sign *Scorpio*, operating thru the *Taurus dwad* in the *Pisces decanate* of this sign. It also ties in with the *8th house* and *Pluto*. In general, the upper sesqui-square is more indirect in expression than the lower sesqui-square. Minor interpersonal conflicts are less obvious on the surface. Since this is an aspect of the waning hemicycle, it suggests a deeper awareness of the self in relation to another. However, we are pressured to use our often penetrating insight to strengthen our unions rather than attempt to manipulate or coerce others to fulfill our own darker motivations. The Scorpio undertone is to teach us how to respect the rights of people rather than forcing our own subjective values upon them. Disruption occurs due to our inner compulsion to try to remake others in order to appease our fixed desires of how they should behave. Our efforts at remoulding people thru subtle power-plays is often met here with unexpected resistance on their part, arousing mutual antagonism and resentment. Likewise, their attempts to alter our patterns of behavior is interpreted as harassment and domination. Misunderstandings that result here lead to temporary breakdowns or break-ups. We create further stress for ourselves by remaining insistent and unreasonable in our demands.

The upper sesqui-square tests our ability to tolerate and genuinely accept people *as they are*. Since this aspect follows the purging upper quincunx, it represents a new surge of energy that has come about thru a rebirth of values. Yet our transformation in consciousness should not compel us to enforce others to reform according to our growing vision. If we are to humanely apply the higher inspirational urges represented by the upper trine phase which follows this aspect, we must still work at cleansing our personality of all residual negativities (emotional blind-spots) which will otherwise restrict our ability to expand consciousness safely and wisely. Although less outwardly volatile than the lower sesqui-square, the upper phase can be more relentless in satisfying its aims. The *Taurus dwad* emphasizes stubborn, unyielding attitudes which will need to be re-evaluated. The *Pisces decanate* implies a potential for distortion or misperception, thus self-deception, regarding our motivation for "rehabilitating" others. Any attempt to act in devious ways only tends to further confuse issues at hand. The in-depth perception linked with this aspect should not encourage us to domineer situations in a covert manner. Unrelieved thru proper social outlets, the build up of dissatisfaction here can often result in explosive release of emotional tension.

THE QUINCUNX

An arc of 150° connects with the cusp of *Virgo* moving counterclockwise, and the cusp of *Scorpio* moving clockwise. It thus corresponds with signs that naturally analyze and dissect, motivated by a need to make essential modifications that improve the capacity to function. Thus, the quincunx aspect suggests that the planets involved first must re-assemble their energies before they can be properly utilized in a manner that benefits the individual. It is an aspect of a highly correctional, therapeutic nature, urging us to undergo major and minor adjustments (usually thru the process of alteration or elimination) that help put the functions of the planets into clearer focus so that we can apply them in a more useful manner. The quincunx seems to require that we observe our usage of energies in a careful, methodical way so that we can learn how to become more selective, discriminating, organized, and efficient in the handling of activities represented by the planets. Until then, the quincunx pinpoints how and where we tend to drain forces in a haphazard, non-productive fashion for some time before we skillfully synthesize. However, in an attempt to bring our impulses into proper alignment, the quincunx is constantly (although indirectly) at work helping us regulate our expression of urges with greater self-control and discipline. Its basic role is that of breaking down and removing those non-effectual attitudes that interfere with our ongoing growth.

Normally, these self-depleting attitudes are not that obvious to us. Conflicts here do not, in other words, evoke a crisis situation as dramatically as the more emphatic, hard-driving square. Nor is the overall perspective of matters at hand as acute as found with the opposition. The quincunx can be viewed more aptly as a "nagging" problem, operating over an extended period of time. It lacks the intensity and strength of impact required to bring its tension to our surface consciousness until, almost in a fateful manner, circumstances develop forcing us to give it our utmost attention. Usually, at this point, a whole crop of irritating but interrelated problems manifest, forcing us to take purposeful action resolving matters once and for all. And although these dilemmas appear to suddenly plague our life, they have actually been in operation long beforehand. This phenomena seems to especially apply to the double-quincunx pattern called the Yod, which will be discussed in detail in a later chapter. Note that the quincunx connects signs whose elements are incompatible according to traditional astrology (fire-earth, earth-air, air-water, water-fire); plus it also involves signs of dissimilar qualities (cardinal-mutable, mutable-fixed, fix-ed-cardinal). The only other aspect similar in make-up to this is the semi-sextile. The difference here, however, is that the quincunx is related more to the opposition rather than the conjunction and thus must contend with a greater polarization of forces. This implies to me that disorganization can be quite a problem with this aspect, although on another level, such marked dissimilarity could represent a special capacity for handling a diversity of factors. Perhaps we are less disturbed by things of a disorderly, uncoordinated nature and can function with such an irregular arrangement effectively. But I tend to think this ability is at least rare. Since the quincunx is an internalizing aspect (earth-water emphasis), disturbances turn inward, interfering with the well-being of both body and soul (quincunxes are noted for their proclivity for somatic and mental health problems of a draining, devitalizing nature).

The *lower quincunx* correlates with the sign *Virgo*, operating thru the *Virgo dwad* in the *Virgo decanate* of this sign. It also relates to the *6th house* and the planet *Mercury*. This quincunx has often been referred to as the "health quincunx," implying its tendency to disorganize energy patterns upon the physical level. Its presence in the natal chart should alert us to the possibility of somatic malfunctions, and especially if the planets involved relate in any way to the 1st and/or 6th houses (or their rulers). We normally experience the lower quincunx thru frustrations in our routine activities (particularly in the working sphere) until we learn to make those necessary adjustments that result in greater competency, efficiency, orderliness, and perfection of technique or skill. Until we sensibly analyze what is exactly required of us here, we are out-of-focus and somewhat on-the-fence concerning the correction of minor flaws of operation that keep problematic areas unresolved. Until then, we tend to feel ill at ease with ourselves. Because the lower quincunx has the undertone of Mercury fused into its nature (and because it links up with the mutable quality), it indicates how and where a needed *mental* adjustment must occur before loose ends here are to be consciously recognized and more clearly ironed out. We are to discern how to pull our forces together so that they eventually function in a more practical, workable manner. Our awareness of attitudes needing alteration is apt to be more objectified thru our day-to-day circumstances, and especially thru those testing out our capacity to render service and useful assistance to others. The lower quincunx is to teach us that the creative power fully realized at the lower trine phase must be properly controlled thru discrimination if it is to reach a state of greater perfection.

The *upper quincunx* corresponds with the sign *Scorpio*, operating thru the *Scorpio dwad* in the *Scorpio decanate* of this sign. It thus also connects with the *8th house* and *Pluto*.

The upper quincunx has often been called the "death quincunx." But unless the regenerative side of this aspect is recognized, much of its true significance may unfortunately be overlooked. Its correctional focus is more psychological and permanent in its operation, since it associates with the water element and the fixed mode. This quincunx compels us to probe deeply within ourselves in an attempt to strengthen the awareness gained thru the preceding opposition phase, suggesting that we must test out the profound implications of our interpersonal perspective. This allows us to transmute our awareness to even higher levels of consciousness. However, the Scorpio-Pluto undertone indicates that self-mastery (turning power inward) must now be sought out if this aspect is to benefit our inner growth. The upper quincunx is an aspect centered around the use or abuse of intense desire and willful emotionality. We are to eventually make long-lasting adjustments on the *feeling* level. The planets involved need to undergo mutual transformation if they are to provide inner resources that we can draw upon during crucial times of need. We are seldom aware of these psychological adjustments until we are confronted with crises creating emotional upheavals (and this is usually thru some separation or forceable removal beyond our control). Otherwise, there is a tendency for disorganized psychological attitudes to remain embedded in our subconscious, making adjustments harder to clarify and resolve. Yet there eventually comes a time for significant self-assessment whereby we can release pent-up forces that can renew us as well as rejuvenate others we contact. As this quincunx refers more to the health pattern of the psyche rather than just the welfare of the body, positive reorganization can lead to a deeper integration of self. Once we learn to inwardly alter whatever is no longer of value for our inner growth, we find ourselves more capable of undergoing a rebirth upon the level of relationship, in which we more creatively learn to share and exchange energies with others. Life will force us to inspect those personal attitudes that are best outgrown rather than retained.

THE OPPOSITION

An arc of 180° from the starting point corresponds with *Libra*, operating thru the *Libra dwad* in the *Libra decanate* of this sign. It also correlates with the *7th house* and the planet *Venus*.

Like the conjunction, the opposition does not technically fall into the category of either a standard waxing *or* waning aspect. It, too, is partly shared by both hemicycles. However, it actually initiates the waning hemicycle and will behave more like a waning aspect when *separating*. On the other hand, an *applying* opposition may operate more like a waxing aspect.

Applying oppositions may imply a more difficult time sharing the energies represented in an actual relationship, due to a measure of self-interest. Separating oppositions may reflect a greater amount of awareness concerning the functions of both planets involved and how to utilize these energies in a relationship with a greater sense of give-and-take. The exact opposition point is apt to indicate a degree of enlightenment that allows the individual to observe the planetary energies from a more meaningful vantage point. They no longer operate instinctually from this point onward. And so, perhaps, separating oppositions might represent planetary principles that are to be made conscious and highly objectified thru the dynamics of relating.

I find the opposition to be very intriguing in terms of its dynamics. Although normally less self-blocking than the square, the opposition still manifests much tension in its attempt to balance the polarized urges represented by the planets and signs involved. It is an aspect allowing for a fuller "face-to-face" awareness of the functions of both planets. Depending upon the individual's ability to skillfully coordinate, the opposition can result in a satisfactory compromise in which needs are mutually satisfied thru complementary exchange. When well integrated, the planets enhance each other's functions, pulling together for the benefit of the greater whole. Normally for this to occur, the individual must have a healthy, open attitude about the nature of *both* planets; valuing their strengths and virtues, and learning to act them out in his life with greater equality. This is basically due to the fact that standard oppositions also connect signs that are natural polar opposites which need each other's energies to effectively perform. However, it is when one planet becomes too closely identified with at the expense of the other (the neglected, undervalued one) that the fine balance required for constructive activity becomes difficult to achieve. And the results are a lack of stability, poor coordination, bad timing, mutual discord, and separative action.

But the characteristic trait of the opposition I find so interesting is its capacity for psychological projection, in which the undervalued planet's expression is projected onto another individual who then must play out that planet's role. This is why oppositions often involve stress in relationships (in contrast with the square, which is more apt to struggle within itself). The more we tend to block or deny the activity of that undervalued planet within our own consciousness, the more we attract it (often thru its negative expression) in somebody else who tends to apply it in a manner that literally opposes the urges of the planet we do personally relate to. If resistance towards integration persists, then we can expect both planets to behave antagonistically, constantly pulling apart or battling each other. Objectivity is thus lost, and relationships are then marked by conflicts, stalemates, and impasses. With such strong Libra undertones, the opposition could represent indecision resulting in an inability to take any type of action. In other words, the opposition could inhibit effective action in some cases, and thus can remain chronically problematic. While the planets can never blend together in the manner of the conjunction (nor are they meant to since this would take away the broadened perspective oppositions offer us), they can reinforce each other's needs in a mutually agreeable manner. They seem to function in their most balanced way when we allow ourselves to alternately project both planets from time to time, so that we can objectively witness how they operate outside of our own consciousness. In this fashion, we can learn more about them thru the expression of others (who offer us new insights into how the planetary urges can be developed). We normally tend to project the slower-moving planet of the opposition (especially if it is a Higher Octave planet), unless it is conjunct the ASC, in the 1st house, or is the ruler of the 1st. The opposition is perhaps the aspect most prone towards externalizing stress thru relationship in its attempt to promote greater awareness of ourselves in reference to others.

If oppositions are the dominant aspect in the chart, the individual may continuously feel pulled in two opposite directions and may thus have difficulty taking decisive personal action in life. He may not easily commit himself to any singular interest in the determined, concentrated manner of the conjunction-dominated person. He tends to be more readily influenced by his relationships or the environment at large. Yet poorly integrated oppositions indicate a lack of self-determinism. The individual usually does not encourage himself to be self-starting but may psychologically lean upon others to help motivate him into action. He is more likely to compromise with others according to their terms in order to prevent conflicts in his associations, although they nevertheless remain imbalanced. However, the greater purpose of oppositions is learning how to share ourselves with others in a sensible manner allowing for an adequate measure of fair-play, justice, and give-and-take. We are not benefited by constantly giving in to people and challenging situations simply to avoid tensional confrontations. In some cases (i.e., oppositions involving Mars or Uranus in the 1st house), *we* are the ones who must learn how to integrate ourselves with others and cultivate rapport rather than antagonize or pull away and remain separative. Many oppositions suggest that objectivity could be well-developed. If so, we can use our widened perspective of life to help us become more aware of the needs of others. Partnerships will be very important for our growth, since oppositions assist us in understanding more about ourselves thru the contrasts most unions present to us. Our internal tug-of-wars are better brought out and more clearly objectified thru involvement with others. By allowing ourselves to freely associate, we can become highly self-illumined. Although an abundance of oppositions describes a life of many ups and downs (since oppositions tend to vacillate and alternate), they enable us to develop depth of perception.

Few or even no oppositions in the chart, on the other hand, could denote the need to become more conscious and considerate of others, as well as more willing to involve oneself with the social environment. The lesson of sharing will be emphasized in the individual's unions. Normally, even if appearing reasonably sociable, this type of person is likely to feel somewhat cut off from the influence of others (due to his own unconscious self-containment). Or he may feel less able to effectively deal with conflicts in his relationships in a mutually satisfying manner, since he has been less conditioned to cooperate and reach a happy medium. A lack of oppositions could suggest the individual is not as likely to evaluate or deliberate before acting upon situations. Due to his own subjectivity or poor observation ability (oppositions tend to observe life from a distance, which affords greater perspective, rather than actively participating in any experience), he may not easily tune into the motivations prompting the actions or reactions of others he has to deal with. Or he may be less inclined to confront people face-to-face concerning difficult adjustments, and thus often meets problems indirectly. Since oppositions enable us to see the many sides of any issue, the individual here may not be as open to viewpoints and temperaments contrary to his own. He will need to better view himself in all relationships and become more aware of how his own self-absorbed nature can create imbalance. While normally left alone to independently pursue his personal interests without hindrance from others, his tendency to become too wrapped up in himself stifles his growth potential. By making a more conscious effort to get outside of himself, cultivate constructive alliances, and become more willing to support the development of others, greater harmony and inner balance manifest.* Again, compensation factors off-setting this potential for exclusive self-interest and narrow perspective of others are indicated by a stellium in Libra, a strong 7th house, and/or a prominent Venus.

*Note that in all delineations of this chapter referring to a *lack* of any aspect, we are capable of more consciously developing the qualities associated with that aspect in a positive manner. Because we normally sense a void here, we tend to desire to bring more of what that aspect signifies to our awareness in an attempt to feel whole and complete. But this always requires conscious effort and consistent application. And because we try to become more consciously directed here, we tend to have greater control over our expression (since remaining unconscious and unaware implies little control or free will operating). Therefore, such delineations should not suggest absolute, static conditions. They more accurately describe our initial behavior while growing up and learning how to integrate ourselves. So don't be surprised to find a person lacking conjunctions and Aries emphasis who in actuality insists on managing his own life, is productively self-involved, and is very careful not to let himself lean or depend upon others. He may even seem to be too self-reliant. What this is saying is that such an individual has made during the course of his life experience a more concentrated effort to evoke such characteristics due to a conscious desire for expanded, more well-rounded personal growth. This phenomena can also easily be seen to apply to one who lacks emphasis of a certain element or quality in the natal chart.

2
Uncommon Aspects

Centuries ago, the master philosopher Pythagoras taught that numbers could unlock the secrets of the geometry of the Universe. He proposed that each number was in itself a living principle having a meaningful soul quality revealing a fundamental law of existence. And it was upon understanding the relationship of numbers to each other in their natural sequence that mankind could comprehend its own special relationship within the divine order of things. Pythagoras' early teachings paved the way for the development of modern day numerology. It now appears that one way for astrologers to tap into the intrinsic meaning of any aspect is by analyzing the numerological symbolism of that number by which the aspect in concern divides the circle. For example, division of the circle by *three* results in the *trine* aspect. The *square* divides the circle by *four*. Just as the number 3 might offer insight into the principle of the trine, the number 4 could express the archetypal nature of the square aspect. Continuing along this line of thought, division of the circle by *one* represents the *conjunction*. The *opposition* divides the circle by *two*. *Six* would thus correlate with the *sextile*. *Eight* associates with the *semi-square* and its multiple, the *sesquisquare*. And *twelve* would correspond with the *semi-sextile* and its multiple, the *quincunx*. Note that the aspects reviewed in Chapter One thus represent the circle divided by 1, 2, 3, 4, 6, 8, and 12. These are the aspects most commonly considered by astrologers. But what about those aspects that divide the circle by 5, 7, 9, 10, and 11? And what about numerical divisions beyond 12?

As pioneered in the mid-1950's by its foremost living exponent, John Addey, harmonics analysis indicates that the circle can be divided by any number or its multiple and still offer relevant meaning. Therefore, all integral divisions of the circle may be valid. The harmonics theory is much more complex than this, but it does at least lend itself to Pythagorean concepts. I highly recommend reading

Addey's *Harmonics in Astrology* (published by Cambridge
Circle, Ltd., U.S.A., 1976) for a more complete reference.
The focal aspect plus its multiples are all members of one
"family" or "series." The multiples draw their primary
meaning from the main division number that produced
them, and thus all share a common theme. It is interesting
that in this oncoming Aquarian Age of astrology, we are
now starting to view aspects in a collective sense. Such
aspect groupings may provide astrologers with many
missing links in aspect analysis.

Division of the circle by *five* gives us the *quintile* aspect of
72°. Division by *seven* represents the *septile* aspect of
approximately 51½°. Dividing the circle by *nine* produces
the *novile* (nonagon) aspect of 40°. Division by *ten*
establishes the *semi-quintile* (decile) aspect of 36°, while
division by *eleven* represents the rarely-mentioned
undecagon aspect of approximately 33°. Information about
these uncommon aspects is scant in astrological literature.
Yet they all may have a distinct association with the subtle
facets of our spiritual development. In this chapter, I will
review the *quintile*, the *septile*, and the *novile* in more
detail. As very little is known about these aspect dynamics,
their numerological correspondences might help shed some
light concerning their functions in the chart. There are
several books available on the market dealing with
numerology. Ones that have been helpful to me in this
context are *The Secrets of Numbers* by Vera Scott Johnson
& Thomas Wommack (Berkely Medallion Books, NYC,
1974, paperback), *Numerology For a New Age* by Lynn M.
Buess (DeVorss & Co., Calif., 1978, softbound), and *Sacred
Science of Numbers* by Corinne Heline (New Age Press,
Inc. Calif., 1971, softbound). Heline's book is a must for the
esoteric-oriented astrologer, as she draws from many
branches of the wisdom-teachings throughout the ages (the
Kaballah, the Tarot, the Bible, the Vedas, Theosophy,
Rosicrucianism, Freemasonry, etc.) and ties them all
together, presenting the reader with a fascinating overview
of each number's deeper significance. For those interested
in finding out more about how the Pythagorean teachings
directly apply to the meaning of aspects, read Michael
Meyer's *A Handbook For the Humanistic Astrologer*

(Anchor Books, NY, 1974, softbound). Especially read Part
Two, Chapter 7. Once you feel you have a basic grasp of the
principles of each number, you may want to go back and
reconsider the aspects presented in Chapter One from a
numerological perspective to see what correspondences you
can perceive.

THE QUINTILE

While our standard aspects were devised long ago by
Ptolemy in the second century A.D., the quintile was
introduced later in the 17th century by astronomer-astrol-
oger Johann Kepler (who also gave astrology the
semi-square, the *sesqui-square*, and the *septile*). Being a
Neo-Platonist and very much intrigued by the Pythagorean
concept of the "harmony of the spheres," Kepler was one of
the "modern" intellects to further advance the harmonic
basis of aspects. The quintile represents the *5th Harmonic*.
The quintile family includes multiples such as the
semi-quintile (36°), the *sesqui-quintile* (108°), and the
bi-quintile (144°) plus other subdivisions. John Addey
associates the entire "quintile series" with the use or abuse
of power and authority. He also found it to be linked with a
pronounced tendency to be very one-pointed and intensely
driven in a specialized field of activity. In its destructive
expression, the quintile group was discovered to be
prominent in the charts of both criminals and the victims
of violence, social revolutionaries (Robespierre, Danton),
and dictators (Hitler), according to Addey's research. In
its positive expression, the quintile series has also been
prominent in the charts of writers, inspired artists
(Mozart), and scientists (Einstein).

Esoteric schools of astrology have claimed that quintiles
were known and given special attention by the Initiates of
the ancient mystery schools, and have been associated
with hermetic magic. Unfortunately, like most occult
traditions, this is impossible to substantiate since early
esoteric teachings were supposedly never committed to
writing but were transmitted orally from century to
century. Nevertheless, in this regard, the quintile was
considered to symbolize an aspirant's creative soul

alignment with the Will of the Cosmos, suggesting that quintiles have occult, transcendental undertones. If this is so, then it should be obvious that the Will of the awesome, inscrutable Cosmos is not easily channeled thru the normally fragmented consciousness of the average individual still bound by the limited confines of his personality-centered will. Perhaps this should tell us that quintiles in the natal chart only fulfill their lofty, universal potential once we have struggled to become more self-realized. Otherwise, in an individual still unawakened to the reality of his spiritual identity, the quintile could either remain dormant and inoperative, or else could be uncontrollably activated in a compulsive and abusive manner (as Addey's research tends to indicate).

The number five has been symbolized by the pentagram, or the five-pointed star. The upward pointed pentacle is said to represent the creative spiritual forces filtered thru the mind, while the downward pointed pentacle denotes destructive, involutionary forces working against the evolutionary process. This could explain why the quintile may indicate the power of the mind to both create *and* destroy. Numerology associates the number five with the will to experience the (five) senses. It is said to be the number of man. The manner in which it is normally described in numerological literature sounds to me like a composite of *Jupiter* and *Uranus* principles (with *Mars* undertones.) Uranus in this context does not appear to represent its higher humanitarian expression, but instead seems to indicate its more willful, untamed, lawless, and inconsistent side. Basic themes of number five deal with freedom, exploration, adventure, restlessness, experimentation, change variety, the lack of routine or system, and general indulgence of the senses. Numerology claims five as the number of sexual magnetism and erotic activity. Interestingly enough, Addey has also suggested that the 5th harmonic has "relevance in assessing sexual proclivities and aberrations."[1] Esoteric numerology sees five as portraying the internal struggle we must undergo to harness the five senses in an attempt to rise above their domination.[2]

The general opinion concerning quintiles is that they are indicative of uncommon facets of human capacity expressing a notable degree of creative genius, rare insight, and mental artistry. As Dane Rudhyar has stated in *The Astrology of Personality*, the quintile "shows the creative freedom of the individual in moulding materials into form that are true to the idea they are meant to express."3 In other words, the quintile enables one to construct (mental) form in an ideal manner that most perfectly reflects the archetypal purpose of that form. In an occult sense, this becomes an exercise in mental transmutation, implying a phase of evolutionary development where the mind can literally be used in an alchemical manner. Quintiles seem to describe the potential of abilities normally considered exceptional or gifted, and abilities that are not necessarily developed or conditioned by experiences in the external environment. Instead, they are apt to originate from a deeper resource within. To bring the promise of the quintile into productive use could suggest that the individual first understand and accept that mind and matter are essentially one and the same.

Dealing with more than just the initial desire to create, quintiles might provide an extended mental perception or knowingness of those particular elements within an abstract concept or physical object that are of prime creative value. They thus allow us to grasp a holistic overview, plus grant the power and single-mindedness required to bring such a rare perspective into sharper focus, integrating all intricacies involved into a more unified whole. Quintiles may require that we refine technique and skill to a masterful degree before they can be satisfactorily applied. Astrologers should therefore be somewhat conservative in their assessment of the import of natal quintiles, since their focus may be more cosmic than worldly. It wouldn't be surprising if, for most of us, quintiles are only active during dream activity, deep meditation, and other altered mental states of consciousness.

In reference to the quintile's general theme of extended perception, Addey has also indicated that the quintile series might be very much "connected with the mind, and with the gnostic faculties. That is, they are concerned with the faculties by which we *know*, and the means by which we receive and communicate knowledge and information."[4] Addey is of the opinion that strong connections involving Saturn and Uranus in the 5th Harmonic Chart indicates the "born astrologer." I was naturally pleased to find this out, since I have an exact lower quintile between these planets in my natal chart! Addey has also linked the 5th harmonic with *impairment* to those powers and faculties related to the transmission of knowledge, resulting in brain damage, nervous disorders, and all the defects of the senses (i.e., blindness) or organs of speech and communication.[5]

For those who wish to experiment with the symbolic system used in Chapter One, the quintile establishes its lower phase at the *12th* degree of *Gemini* moving counterclockwise, as well as the *18th* degree of *Capricorn* moving clockwise. Note that these degree correspondences are irregular, unlike the consistently symmetrical correspondences of previously analyzed aspects. This fact may emphasize the quintile's uniqueness. The *lower quintile* would thus correlate with the sign *Gemini*, operating thru the *Libra dwad* in the *Libra decanate* of this sign. It would then also relate to the *3rd house* and the planet *Venus*. The *upper quintile* would correlate with the sign *Capricorn*, operating thru the *Leo dwad* in the *Taurus decanate* of this sign. It thus links with the *10th house* and the planet *Saturn*. A common denominator that may prove significant here is that both decanates are Venus-ruled.

References:

(1) John Addey, *Harmonics in Astrology*, Cambridge Circle Ltd., U.S.A., 1976, p. 111.
(2) Corinne Heline, *Sacred Science of Numbers*, New Age Press Inc., Ca., 1971, p. 36
(3) Dane Rudhyar, *The Astrology of Personality*, Doubleday, N.Y., 1970, p. 322.
(4) John Addey, "Harmonics, Genetics, and Disease," *Astrology Now*, Vol. 1, No. 7 (Oct. 1975), p. 30.
(5) *Ibid*, p. 30.

THE SEPTILE

The septile aspect corresponds with the number *seven* and thus the *7th Harmonic*. Throughout the ages, the number seven has been associated with sacred, holy matters as any student well-versed in religious symbolism knows. Numerology interprets seven as a very occult number. It seems to deal with self-knowledge, interior analysis, the search for ultimate meaning or wisdom, and involvement with introspective or research-oriented studies. It is a number that urges us to ponderously investigate the deeper essences of reality. Seven is the number of meditation, contemplation, solitude, and isolation. It suggests a sabbatical from the surface concerns of the material world, in which inner assimilation can take place (the Bible states that God rested from His labors on the *seventh* day of Creation). Seven tends to be remote, aloof, and other-worldly. Not being a very sociable number, it seems to work best in privacy and seclusion. For the most part, number seven seems to suggest to me a composite of the principles of *Saturn* and *Neptune* (with *Pluto* undertones), at least according to how it is normally depicted in numerological literature. It has been referred to as the number of rest and completion. But as Heline notes, "rest does not refer to a cessation of activity but to the emergence from Chaos into a higher and more perfect Order."[1]

According to John Addey's research, the 7th harmonic or "septile series" discloses one's capacity to receive inspiration. He states that the septile may denote "the ability to sense the mysterious whole behind the parts of a subject..."[2] plus "the capacity to embrace intellectually the formative idea or principle behind a thing and so participate in the dynamic energy which that idea imparts."[3] Addey found the 7th harmonic very prominent in the charts of clergymen, or those who exercise the "priestly function"[4] in society. Considering the numerological profile of number seven, Addey's findings would seem quite appropriate. The septile's mystical undertone is likely due to its urge to understand wholeness and completion. Like the "quintile series," the septile family is very notable in the charts of creative artists. In his excellent article titled "The Seventh Harmonic and Creative Artists," Charles M. Graham supports Addey's research when stating that "seven refers to creativity as the fusion of form and matter through the workings of (divine) inspiration."5 Graham points out that the 7th harmonic (or septile grouping) is significant in the charts of visual artists such as Picasso, Raphael, Leonardo da Vinci, Cezanne, Rodin, Matisse, and Modigliani. It is prominent in the charts of musicians such as Mozart, Schubert, Chopin, Berlioz, Wagner, and Tchaikovsky. The 7th harmonic is also emphasized in the charts of George Bernard Shaw, Yeats, Lewis Carroll, and Robert Louis Stevenson. Graham's research indicates that the 7th harmonic is particularly notable in charts of romantic poets such as Blake, Shelley, and Lord Byron. Other creative and inspired thinkers indicative of the creativity of this harmonic are Immanual Kant and Albert Einstein.

Similar to the quintile series, John Addey has found a link between the septile and its multiples with sexual activity (erotic inspiration), stating that they "provide a horoscopic key to certain factors in the psychology of sex."6 I would imagine that the septile family would tie in with the more repressive, self-denying, turmoil-producing aspects of sexuality (Saturn-Neptune-Pluto undertones) or celibate inclinations, which both pressure the sublimation of the sex-force...unlike the more self-expressive, experimenta-tional, willful quintile series. Such redirection of the libidinal drive has long been regarded as a prerequisite for artistic inspiration and creative drive.

Dane Rudhyar in *Person-Centered Astrology* connects the septile with the "anti-social" quality implied in number seven, stating that this aspect represents actions that "are not acceptable according to the definite norm of social-cultural behavior in the person's environment or class."7 He also feels that the septile "can be interpreted in a super-personal sense as acts compelled by a collective need, an occult power or fate; and these may lead to 'sacrifice' and a symbolic life."8 Doris Thompson expressed the septile as revealing "a fated inevitability with a compulsion to certain actions; an unrecognized force with hidden activation."9 Delphine Jay suggests that the septile "carries with it a fatalistic tinge that springs from situations that appear to be beyond ordinary meaning. This tinge creates a consciousness-expanding struggle within, forcing the native to search beyond the obvious."10 She considers the septile series as having "a natural predisposition to the occult, psychic, or mystical. They seem preoccupied with the idea of intellectual or relentless divine faith."11 Michael Meyer sees the septile as introducing "the unpredictable, irrational elements of experience, symbolizing the ability to respond to the call of one's destiny and to use unfit or left-over...materials for the purpose of fulfilling a definite goal of a karmic nature."12

The septile establishes its lower phase at approximately the 21½° of *Taurus* moving counterclockwise, as well as the 8½° of *Aquarius* moving clockwise. The *lower septile* would theoretically correspond with the sign *Taurus*, operating thru the *Capricorn dwad* in the *Capricorn decanate* of this sign, associating it also with the *2nd house* and *Venus*. The *upper septile* would then correspond with the sign *Aquarius*, operating thru the *Taurus dwad* in the *Aquarius decanate* of this sign. It thus could link with the *11th house* and the planet *Uranus*. Fixed signs are involved in both phases, with strong Venus-Saturn-Uranus undertones. Again, degree correspondences are highly irregular.

While there is no official symbol yet accepted for the septile aspect, I'd use the suggested ⓢ when noting it in the natal aspect column. Besides obviously indicating an "S" for "septile," this symbol also reminds me of a serpent enclosed within the circle of infinity. Serpents themselves have been eternal symbols of wisdom and regeneration ("be ye therefore wise as serpents...")13 It is probably then *wise* to observe septiles in natal charts as *potential* capacity. There is still much more to know about them before we enthusiastically broadcast their import upon clients (or ourselves). I can't see the value of informing an individual that his septile to Saturn or Pluto, for example, represents where he will "compulsively" encounter an "inevitable fate" or "irrevocable destiny" seemingly beyond his control. Do you?

References:

(1) Corinne Heline, *Sacred Science of Numbers*, New Age Press Inc., Ca., 1971, p. 55.
(2) John Addey, *Harmonics in Astrology*, Cambridge Circle Ltd., U.S.A., 1976, p. 121.
(3) *Ibid*, p. 121.
(4) *Ibid*, p. 62.
(5) Charles M. Graham, The Seventh Harmonic and Creative Artists," *Astrology Now*, Vol. 2, No. 13 (June 1976), p. 87.
(6) John Addey, *Harmonics in Astrology*, Cambridge Circle Ltd., U.S.A., 1976, p. 120
(7) Dane Rudhyar, *Person-Centered Astrology*, CSA Press, Ga., 1972, p. 167.
(8) *Ibid*, p. 167.
(9) Doris Thompson, "The Septile - Aspect of Fate," AFA Bulletin, 1975, Vol. 37, No. 1, p. 17.
(10) Delpine Jay, "Teaching Harmonic Charting," *Astrology Now*, Vol.1, No.11, (March 1976), p.7.
(11) *Ibid*, p. 7.
(12) Michael Meyer, Nancy Kleban, "Numerical Approaches to Phase Interpretation," *Astrology Now*, Vol. 1, No. 7 (Oct. 1975), p. 38.
(13) *Holy Bible - King James Version*, St. Matthew, Chapter 10, verse 16.

THE NOVILE

The novile aspect represents the number *nine* and the 9*th harmonic*. Numerology associates nine with principles that seem very Neptunian. It is the number of selflessness and breadth of universal understanding. It expresses itself thru compassion, tolerance, forgiveness, benevolence, and a willingness for personal sacrifice for the upliftment and healing of humanity. Like number seven, nine is a number of (spiritual) completion and fulfillment. It is all-encompassing. Its orientation seems unquestionably emotional, being an expression of the power of the Universal Heart. Nine is typically associated with unfinished business (since it is the last phase of a life cycle, according to numerology) and it thus suggests either a sense of loss or the willingness to relinquish personal desires for the sake of universal betterment. It operates behind the scenes in an undercurrent fashion in preparation for a new cycle of beginning. Esoterically, number nine has a special evolutionary influence. To quote Heline, "the strange phenomena of nine in its power (suggests that) no matter by what number it is multiplied...it eternally reproduces itself."1 She views it as "the major vibratory power governing human evolution."2 Nine becomes "the special numerical power by which man comes into contact with his inner self, unfolds his latent divinity, and attains to that state of interior illumination which is known by the name of Initiation."3 Both exoteric and esoteric numerology view nine as being able to experience the widest gamut of life's dramatic experiences, both the lowliest and the most divine and inspired. No wonder it is a number associated with rare understanding of life.

Rudhyar sees the novile as representing a "process of gestation by means of which the idea or the beautiful form is brought to a condition of organic viability."4 In The *Astrology of Personality*, Rudhyar also speaks of the novile as an aspect that "*may* indicate spiritual rebirth or initiation in the realm to which the planets refer. It signifies 'birth out of captivity.' "5 David Cochrane in *New Foundations for Astrology* connects the 9th harmonic aspects (novile series) with nurturing energies striving to reach fruition, and suggests its keywords are "devotion" and "careful preparation."6 John Addey points out that the 9th harmonic is equivalent to the Hindu "Navasma Chart," which primarily is drawn up to describe the potential marriage partner. But besides the marriage partner, Addey suggests that this chart also can describe an individual's inner "ideal."7 He analogizes that like fruit to a tree, the novile represents culmination. Meyers states that the novile aspect "has been said to represent the identification of self with a purpose and function related to a global or universal scheme. The novile can also be seen as the symbol of initiation, the emergence into a totally new realm."8

Frankly speaking, the above novile interpretations are still too Neptunian for me to establish a clear-cut definition of its function in the natal chart. Perhaps Neptunian-oriented principles are what they are because they defy clear-cut definitions. The themes that seem to be emphasized here, however, appear to concern subjective growth thru sacrifice, selflessness, and deep assimilation of spiritual insight. Perhaps the "captivity theme" of Rudhyar is in reference to the pull of material inertia suggested by the experiences of past cycles that now must be inwardly reviewed thru the natural processes of nine, implying the need to refine such experiences to almost an ultimate degree and to thoroughly merge our ego with the end-results of such refinement (which may be what the gestation period requires of us before it can bring forth a sense of spiritual birth or rebirth). In a stimulating lecture given at the 1979 NASO Convention in Atlanta, Leyla Rael-Rudhyar stated that the novile implies the "ability to see meaning in everything...thus it is an aspect of rebirth based upon *meaning*..."9 In general, other astrologers have felt that the novile has at least subtle, mystical influence. As an aspect testing the depths of our abilities, it operates from an unconscious level and often concerns something from the past (past lives) that may tend to hold our potential in limbo until we strive to give of ourselves altruistically from the heart and not just from the mental level. The novile may assist us in our attempt to unify energies, resulting in a more encompassing sense of oneness.

The novile corresponds with the 10*th* degree of *Taurus* moving counterclockwise, and the 20*th* degree of *Aquarius* moving clockwise. The *lower novile* thus associates with the sign *Taurus*, operating thru the *Virgo dwad* in the *Virgo decanate* of this sign (which might imply emotional adjustments enabling a higher sense of personal value). It would then also correlate with the 2*nd house and the planet* Venus (with both idealistically operating at their highest potential). The *upper novile* relates with the sign *Aquarius*, operating thru the *Libra dwad* in the *Libra decanate* of this sign. It also thus links with the 11*th house* and the planet *Uranus* (with both likely functioning upon a humanitarian, socially-reformative level). Common denominators of both novile phases are the representation of *fixed* signs belonging to the *Eastern* Hemisphere, plus emphasized Venus undertones.

References:

(1) Corinne Heline, *Sacred Science of Numbers*, New Age Press Inc., Ca., 1971, p. 74.
(2) *Ibid*, p. 75.
(3) *Ibid*, p. 75.
(4) *Ibid*, p. 75.
(5) Dane Rudhyar, *The Astrology of Personality*, Doubleday, N.Y., 1970, p. 322.
(6) David Cochrane, *New Foundations For Astrology*, Astrological Counseling & Research, Fla., 1977, p. 35.
(7) John Addey, *Harmonics in Astrology*, Cambridge Circle Ltd., U.S.A., 1976, p. 96.
(8) Michael Meyer, Nancy Kleban, "Numerical Approaches to Phase Interpretation," *Astrology Now*, Vol. 1, No. 7 (Oct. 1975), p. 38.
(9) Leyla Rael-Rudhyar, *1979 NASO Conference*, Atlanta, Ga., August 31, 1979.

3
Dissociate Aspects

The Moon at 1° Aquarius is clearly in opposition aspect to the Sun at 1° Leo. Yet if this same Moon at 1° Aquarius was aspecting a 29° Sun in Cancer, the aspect would still be considered a valid opposition, with an orb within minutes from exactitude. However, this type of opposition is called an "out-of-sign" or dissociate aspect. Is a dissociate aspect in any way different in its influence than a standard aspect? It should be, for it represents a definite variation from the inherent *sign* relationship of the standard aspect. Ideally, the opposition aspect occurs when two planets are exactly 180° apart, which means they are in signs of the same quality and of compatible elements. Also, these two signs are natural polar opposites. However, in a dissociate opposition (as in the above example), the change in sign position of the Sun alters the natural sign relationship of this aspect since *Aquarius* and *Cancer* establish a *quincunx* pattern. Aquarius is a fixed sign while Cancer is of the cardinal mode. Here an air sign is in opposition with a water sign instead of fire. And obviously, Aquarius and Cancer are not polar opposites. All variations found in such a dissociate aspect are thus determined according to the sign placements of the aspecting planets.

Dissociate trines occur from signs that either square or quincunx each other. Dissociate squares involve signs that either trine or sextile one another. Out-of-sign oppositions involve signs that naturally quincunx each others, while out-of-sign sextiles can occur from signs that either square or semi-sextile one another. How should we interpret these out-of-sign aspects? First of all, a dissociate aspect will still express itself according to the nature of the *angle* formed between the planets. A dissociate square will attract the same situational challenges as a standard square. Yet on a *psychological* level, a dissociate aspect is apt to react quite differently, since the variation of the aspect's sign relationship modifies attitude and motivation. Thus, out-of-sign aspects will have a greater impact upon the level of character rather than the level of circumstance.

DISSOCIATE CONJUNCTION

The out-of-sign conjunction involves signs that naturally *semi-sextile* each other. While standard conjunctions imply a single-minded concentration and focus of energies, dissociate conjunctions are less unified and one-tracked on the psychological level. Since there are now two different signs involved that have dissimilar motivations, the urges shown by the planets do not blend or merge together as easily (and especially if the planets themselves have contrasting temperaments). Thus, dissociate conjunctions may express with less coordinatioh or strength of purpose. The individual may not feel as motivated to assert himself in the direct, spontaneous, head-strong manner of the standard conjunction. He tends to act with less intensity, or else he may feel awkward and uneasy about expressing himself here, even though he will still be driven to act. Being less determined about how he will act out his impulses (since the underlying semi-sextile influence tends to make him evaluate), the individual tends to hesitate before thrusting himself into activity. Nevertheless, the semi-sextile undertone could suggest the individual may be able to draw from inner resources of a less apparent nature (imagination, physical magnetism, strong survival instincts, psychic sensitivity) that he can use to further his advantage when initiating personal action. In this regard, the out-of-sign conjunction may actually be more resourceful than the standard one, and may be less limited in the manner in which it utilizes the urges of the planets involved. But typically, one tends to become confused as to how to best synthesize the different behavioral traits of the signs, resulting in mild frustration. The individual will have to become involved in activities in which the needs of both signs can be satisfied.

DISSOCIATE SEMI-SEXTILE

The out-of-sign semi-sextile involves the underlying influence of the *conjunction* or the *sextile*. When the two planets of the dissociate semi-sextile are both in the same sign, there could be a psychological reluctance to venture out further from one's subjective world towards those nurturing experiences which could foster the growth of a personal resource. The influence of the semi-sextile (being a subtle aspect to begin with) is perhaps even less noticeable when in dissociate aspect. Potentials here may be even more latent. The conjunction undertone could suggest that the individual is not yet ripe and ready to work with his inner or outer resources until he is able to establish a better sense of identity or self-image. Positively, this type of dissociate semi-sextile could supply more drive and push towards the manifestation of potential assets as one learns to become more self-related and unified in direction. When the dissociate semi-sextile involves signs that sextile, the individual may be more psychologically curious about how potential resources can be applied. He may have aspirations concerning the future, idealistic application of present benefits in the making. To some extent, he might be able to find an intelligent or inventive way of attracting such resources. The stimulation of the underlying sextile keeps the dissociate semi-sextile from being inertia-prone due to the fact that the individual is more psychologically restless and desires to do something with the potentials shown. His awareness of the value of his resources is better-developed than one with the standard semi-sextile.

DISSOCIATE SEXTILE

The out-of-sign sextile involves signs that naturally *semi-sextile* or *square* each other. In both instances, these underlying influences suggest a lack of easy facility typical of the standard sextile. The dissociate sextile involving signs that semi-sextile one another is the less bothersome of the two. Although the individual has no trouble attracting constructive opportunities, he may feel less stimulated by them and thus may pass them up. The passivity of the semi-sextile undertone psychologically discourages open self-expression. There tends to be a slight inner resistance towards learning new things, and therefore the individual will have to make a more conscious effort to become more flexible and adaptable in attitude if he is to fully benefit himself from experiences he attracts. However, personal opportunities shown here could be obtained easier since this type of dissociate sextile is less prone towards distraction and the scattering of interests. It is less restless than the standard sextile. Stronger concentrative ability is suggested here, although versatility is somewhat diminished (limiting one's range of expression). There may be more gut-level, instinctive know-how concerning the positive use of urges presented here plus a capacity to more carefully nurture the development of such urges. Benefits may manifest more slowly in the individual's life, but tend to be more valued and appreciated. When the dissociate sextile involves signs that square each other, psychological tension is greater. The experiences the individual attracts do not often satisfy his inner need for challenge and confrontation, and again prove less stimulating or appealing in the long run. Or else he may be prone towards applying more drive and push in situations that don't really require this of him. The individual could create obstacles here that are unnecessary and inappropriate for the nature of situations he attracts. In short, he usually tries too hard to accomplish what is normally best obtained with less effort (over-drive), or else he may block himself from opening up to beneficial new experiences due to an inner sense of insecurity or inadequacy (inhibition). He will need to develop greater objectivity about himself here. However, the underlying influence of the square could pressure the individual to better control and discipline the restless energies of this aspect (since all sextiles require some amount of personal exertion if they are to be productive influences in our life). The key lies in knowing how much effort is needed for best results.

DISSOCIATE SQUARE

The out-of-sign square involves signs that either *trine* or *sextile* each other. Although the individual attracts challenging situations that tend to force him to confront matters head-on, he may psychologically lack the stamina and determination to deal with such demanding circumstances (since both trines and sextiles seek easy, effortless solutions and are not inclined to endure stress very well). The inner drive required to work thru problematic outer obstacles is normally inadequate. And thus both types of dissociate squares are less prone towards accomplishment thru struggle and effort. Standard squares are much more potent due to the fact that the signs involved here sharply challenge each other's expression, resulting in a level of friction that helps develop a vital sense of push and force. In dissociate squares, the signs involved do not agitate each other, resulting in less impetus to take decisive action resolving predicaments the aspect normally attracts. When well-managed, the dissociate square involving signs that sextile each other could prove to be a most stimulating type of tension, since the underlying sextile influence may enable the individual to objectively recognize the reason for his inner conflicts rather than continue to unconsciously act them out in a habitual manner. Perhaps it indicates he has an inner need to learn about why his urges work at cross-purposes. He may be more open to ideas concerning how he can better handle his energies here (unlike the more defensive standard square). In my opinion, any sextile aspect or sub-influence can act as the best antidote for any square aspect. It encourages the breaking up of rigid patterns in a manner that is more appealing than threatening. Thus, instead of having here what has often been called a "weaker" square, we may have one that has the potential to become more enlightened once the individual realizes that he can intelligently tackle his problems. The underlying sextile influence can give extra self-encouragement and optimism.

Well-managed dissociate squares involving signs that trine one another suggest that the individual's personal sense of harmony and well-being allows him to accept challenges with greater faith and confidence. No matter how difficult situations tend to get, this individual inwardly believes that things will work out for the best due to his persistent efforts. Negatively, the individual may attempt to sidetrack committment to responsibilities or obligations presented by the square that essentially should not be avoided or ignored. Problems here will not improve or go away unless he deals "squarely" and realistically with such challenges. Instead of inwardly expecting to stumble upon instant, magical solutions, this individual should allow the trine influence to provide him the creative insight and vision to help him resolve his conflicts. He will need to cultivate more self-discipline and control plus resist the temptation to procrastinate.

DISSOCIATE TRINE

The out-of-sign trine involves signs that either *quincunx* or *square* one another. Similar to dissociate sextiles, dissociate trines involve underlying influences that tend to trigger psychological discord and uneasiness, although the external affairs naturally attracted by the trine are themselves not stressful or discomforting. The individual usually feels more ill-at-ease than would be reasonably expected, since outer conditions associated with the trine are normally easy-flowing and pleasurable. When the dissociate trine occurs in signs that quincunx each other, the individual does not easily adjust psychologically to the benefits he nevertheless readily attracts. He is out-of-focus on some inner level of himself, resulting in a subtle dissatisfaction which tends to interfere with his ability to relax and enjoy whatever is indicated by the trine. As quincunxes pressure us to carefully analyze and make needed corrections thru reorganizing our energies, the individual here may become too unnecessarily caught up with making minor adjustments in areas that really don't require them, since the trine is suggesting that things are already in a state of harmony. The individual simply doesn't interpret matters this way even if it seems obvious to others. Although trines encourage whole-hearted, creative expression, this type of dissociate trine denotes a lack of inner poise and self-confidence. The individual feels less self-assured about any talent shown here, and even feels slightly irritated about how he expresses his abilities (being unduly perfectionistic). Perhaps he may be too inwardly disorganized and at loose ends with himself to effectively utilize his personal assets, good fortune, or leisure time (quincunxes encourage non-productivity when mismanaged). On the other hand, a well-managed dissociate trine urges the individual to improve his skills in small ways. He seldom takes them for granted, but tends to be more consciously aware of their development (unlike the standard trine). When the dissociate trine occurs in signs that square each other, outer situations operate too smoothly to satisfy the inner drives of the individual. He may psychologically expect or demand some element of challenge or struggle, but instead experiences a sense of internal conflict when he realizes that conditions he attracts here simply cannot accommodate his intense needs. This leaves him unfulfilled, to the point that he may willfully create obstacles just to generate the level of tension he likes to feel, thus introducing disharmonious factors into otherwise peaceful situations. Because of the defensive nature of the square, this dissociate aspect could denote talents and skills that can be abused or aggressively utilized. All these above manifestations are representative of the over-drive side of the square. But since squares can also be self-blocking, the individual may also harbor repressive attitudes that thwart his ability to feel self-satisfied by activities indicated here. Although he may reveal ease of expression on the surface, inwardly he may feel friction and a subtle sense of anxiety or stress. Inhibition and insecurity may prevent him from displaying his creative gifts confidently. Positively, the square undertone could supply the normally leisurely, indulgent trine with enough added drive and impetus to dynamically focus upon purposeful creative activity.

DISSOCIATE QUINCUNX

The out-of-sign quincunx can occur in signs that either *trine* or *oppose* each other. The orb must be kept small (3° or less). When the dissociate quincunx operates thru trining signs, the individual inwardly may have a positive or optimistic attitude in approaching the needed adjustments indicated. He may show a more vital interest in reorganizing those parts of himself that keep him from functioning at his optimum potential (since he can sense or visualize the ideal of what he can further develop into, and this can inspire him). Thus, there may be a psychological willingness to improve oneself in small but meaningful ways, and sometimes in a manner that can even be enjoyable or appealing to this individual. Perhaps he is inclined to seek out creative channels for his self-corrective urges. Less of the nagging irritability of this aspect may be felt due to the easy, tensionless nature of the trine undertone. And yet, this quality can also be detrimental to some extent in that it could encourage an adjustment to the ongoing problem itself (trines can promote laziness and procrastination) rather than adjusting by working diligently at finding a suitable solution (here again, the trine confidently expects everything to work itself out without having to make any personal effort). This aspect may suggest a greater measure of self-assurance in coping with the subtle challenges of the quincunx dilemma plus enough idealism to eagerly desire to improve conditions here.

When the dissociate quincunx operates thru signs that oppose one another, there may be a greater and potentially clearer perspective of issues presented here than is typical of standard quincunxes. The individual innately feels the need to establish inner balance thru the outer adjustments he makes. However, he may feel less motivated to make these needed adjustments without the psychological support and backing of others. Perhaps one of his most important personal adjustments is to learn to be less dependent upon others and more willing to test out his ability to be self-reliant. Somehow, his attitudes about relationships need to undergo reassessment. The opposition undertone seems to reinforce the quincunx's tendency to separate or forcibly remove whatever impedes growth (since oppositions can suggest urges that pull apart). Thus, psychological equilibrium may be very important here if the individual is to constructively work on improving himself without losing the awareness of the purpose of such an effort. Perhaps adjustments can be made easier once the individual is more willing to cooperate with others and show greater consideration for their needs. Negatively, he may lose a sense of balance and find himself battling oppositional forces inside himself that keep him torn apart and psychologically fragmented, which could manifest outwardly as serious mental or physical health disturbances. He will need to objectively confront those inner attitudes that tend to stifle his developmental ability, keeping him from living an organized, productive life.

DISSOCIATE OPPOSITION

The out-of-sign opposition involves signs that naturally *quincunx* each other. This suggests the necessity of making important corrections or adjustments in one's perspective concerning relationships. Usually an opposition allows a broader view of both sides of a situation, in which we clearly either learn to reconcile differences or embroil ourselves in continued conflict and antagonistic exchange. But one with a dissociate opposition may not readily observe situations as clearly or as accurately (remember that quincunxes can be out-of-focus, and this could create minor distortions or an inability to perceive the finer details of a condition). Thus, contrasting factors operating in relationships are not readily perceived by the individual. His eventual realization of this blind-spot tends to irritate him. This aspect tends to generate more uncertainty and anxiety in the handling of relationship challenges since the signs involved lack the coordination power typical of polar opposite signs. Because of this, the dissociate aspect attracts but cannot sustain the magnetism to hold the attraction in the manner of the standard opposition, and this proves to be psychologically disturbing for the individual. While external conflict may be less apparent in his actual unions, inner conflict is apt to be more acute. This implies the need for a subtle mental or emotional reorganization of one's process of awareness concerning others. The individual must work harder to more accurately receive messages from people if he is to resolve inner distress.

4

The Grand Trine

Ideally, when at least three planets at different points of the chart all trine each other in the same element, the aspect configuration thus formed is called a *Grand Trine*. The prototype for the Grand Trine in the natural Zodiac involves the three fire signs, since the first 120° angle from the 0° Aries starting point in the aspect cycle falls at 0° Leo moving counterclockwise, and 0° Sagittarius moving clockwise. The Grand Trine therefore visually creates a large triangular pattern across the chart. It is a specialized configuration designed to promote high idealism, insight, and vision as well as creative self-expression and well-being. The Grand Trine can potentially indicate confidence and self-assurance, optimistic expectation, a sense of pleasure, easy-flowingness, inspiration, expansion of creative power, and a general sense of protection due to inner faith and hope. No wonder traditional astrology has viewed the Grand Trine as a highly benevolent influence. However, modern astrology is now becoming aware of the potential drawbacks of a mismanaged Grand Trine.

Remember that a Grand Trine is first and foremost composed of three separate trines. As stated before, the trine aspect is ease-oriented, reducing pressure, tension, and strain. Being concerned with leisure and self-gratification, it does not motivate us to struggle and further grow thru the acceptance of greater challenges. It even appears static and inoperative at times when unable to find pleasurable outlets for expression. Not motivated to cope with frustration or restriction, the trine desires to freely enjoy itself in a state of internal relaxation and harmony, unhampered by outer interferences. In this respect, the trine focusses somewhat unrealistically upon personal satisfaction at the expense of developing strength of character (which usually is attained thru stress and conflict). Too many trines in the chart can reflect a self-indulgent temperament that repeatedly avoids self-discipline or attempts to ignore major responsibilities in his life. The effect can soften an individual, reducing much of his potential drive and willingness to act upon life in a dynamic manner. Trines poorly handled instill a sense of false security, resulting in a non-productive form of passivity that keeps one from ever being motivated to surpass any existing talents or skills. He is simply content with what he is receiving freely from life and sees no purpose in altering this pattern.

This state of affairs can be even more amplified with the Grand Trine. Such a configuration can actually become a source of even greater inertia and stagnation if the individual doesn't have a proper sense of balance in his consciousness (symbolized by a sufficient number of squares and oppositions in the chart - and especially if some of these are also aspecting any or all of the planets forming the Grand Trine). This multiple aspect could present an abundance of "luck" working throughout life for some. And it depends upon the overall character profile shown by the entire chart whether such "luck" actually benefits and strengthens or retards and weakens one's inner development. According to Barbara Watters in *The Astrologer Looks At Murder*, many criminals (even murderers)[1] have been found to have the Grand Trine in their natal charts, along with people who are easily defeated by the rigors of life and who instead turn to addictions or anti-social lifestyles. In the chart of the criminal, the Grand Trine may serve to minimize any incentive to struggle with limiting environmental conditions in the realistic manner that best allows one to successfully overcome such limitations maturely. Criminology has observed that chronic criminals do have an unrealistic, childish view of the world in which they expect or demand that the environment give in and submit to their personal needs or else be punished. They are usually motivated by an illusionary, unquestioned feeling that they can overpower and gain ultimate control over any social condition (if they so will to), and thus do not have to submit to laws their "weaker" victims adhere to. Watters states that for some criminals she researched, the presence of the Grand Trine only served to make the individual's selfish or ruthless activities turn out even more successful (literally getting away with murder for some) for a longer time

period than would be expected. Of course, all this
represents a very distorted, low-level use of the Grand
Trine and therefore will only apply to a very small
percentage of individuals.

Much depends upon how many planets are involved in the
Grand Trine formation when it comes to interpretation,
plus the basic nature of these planets. The more planets
tied in, the greater the danger of imbalance and character
weakness. Undue self-indulgence, personal excesses, and
passivity tends to be further emphasized, for example,
when the Moon, Venus, Jupiter, or Neptune are
involved...or when signs like Taurus, Cancer, Leo, Scorpio,
or Pisces are strongly represented in the overall chart.
Note that these particular signs share sensuality as their
common denominator. On the other hand, planets such as
Mars, Saturn, and Uranus (sometimes Pluto) are too
innately active and driving by themselves to ever allow for
complacency or stagnation. Similarly, signs like Virgo,
Capricorn, and Aries need to be constantly busy and active
to function normally.

An individual with a Grand Trine may find many of his
personal needs are provided for by people or general
situations early in his life. He is apt to feel insulated from
the harsher realities of living, at least in certain situational
areas. Grand Triners can grow up unconsciously expecting
special treatment, unique privileges, and understanding
support from the environment, but seldom feel driven to
work for these benefits. Here, we run the risk of adopting a
"something-for-nothing" approach to life, regardless of
whether we have earned or merited what we want. Our
hopeful anticipation that life will always supply our needs
simply because we wish this to be so is often actually
reinforced by the positive, pleasant outcome of many of our
experiences. One may truly *have* a charmed life with the
Grand Trine. Yet, a subtle drawback with this pattern is
that the individual may fail to develop and exercise the
psychological muscles required to meet and effectively
resolve major life crises head-on. Even though the tide
normally flows in his favored direction, he inevitably will
meet up with outer resistance at some time if, in actuality,

he is stagnating rather than growing. And when this happens, he may not be able to adequately deal with problems he must directly confront. Especially in those house areas where the planets of the Grand Trine are found.

At this critical point, *any* major difficulty could overwhelm or paralyze him, leaving him feeling too powerless or helpless to dynamically alter these uncomfortable conditions. Due to previous conditioning, the individual may once again resort to becoming overly dependent upon the active effort of someone or something else to provide him with instant relief from the stress he is going thru. This could encourage escapist behavior (especially in Grand Water Trines), in which he acts according to the line of least resistance in an attempt to protectively buffer himself from the external conflict that is seemingly threatening the comforting structures in his (inner) world. And if this cannot be secured, then the individual may withdraw into himself and do absolutely nothing about the predicament; this, of course, is an extreme reaction suggesting pathological undertones, and thus one that is not going to be taken by most individuals. It is only suggested to show the incredible power of the Grand Trine to shield or protect the human psyche from what is seen as dangerous or harmful.

Multiple Grand Trines (although rare) can be even more debilitating since at least twice the amount of planets are not involved. But much depends upon the aspects one Grand Trine makes to the other(s). For example, if a *Fire Grand Trine* interconnects with an *Air Grand Trine*, what results is actually a potential *Grand Sextile*, which can be dynamic due to the fact that there are three *oppositions* and six *sextiles* thus formed. This can be very stimulating. But if these two Grand Trines do not connect because the orbs are much too wide to even consider, the individual has an extremely difficult time integrating the various parts of himself. This out-of-the-ordinary condition could indicate one who drifts or merely flounders in life and seldom has enough drive or impetus (thus suffers bad timing) to accomplish anything relevant. Although talents and skills may be present, they are prone to be wasted due to a lack of motivation or practicality. What makes it worse is that this type of individual may seldom even care if he is not living up to his greatest potential, due to the illusionary sense of inner harmony and well-being the miltitude of trines here produces. More information concerning the Grand Sextile will be given in the next chapter.

In general, the greater the amount of stressful aspect contacts coming from other planets in the chart to planets composing the Grand Trine, the greater the capacity for modification of its influence and expression. This is usually the situation to be found in most charts having this configuration. An isolated Grand Trine (or one that makes no outer contacts involving major aspects---specifically squares and oppositions) is able to keep its identity in tact, for better or worse. It is not easily affected by other parts of the nature and tends to operate autonomously, similar to an unaspected planet. It is able to express according to its pure form. Again, this type of Grand Trine is almost non-existent. And even if you should find one, realize that transiting planets are continuously forming challenging outer contacts. Nothing in the chart is allowed to remain absolutely static and self-contained unlimitedly. And so, if supplemented by a T-Square or a Grand Square in the chart (especially one that interconnects), the Grand Trine can provide just the necessary amount of positive rein-forcement needed to aid an individual in resolving dynamic stress patterns, while it in return can be supplied with added energy and drive to turn it into a highly productive and invigorating source of creative or spiritual power.

In the hundreds of charts studied for the presence of Grand Trines, I found relatively fewer well-known personalities with such a major configuration. It is obvious that those few who did have them in their horoscopes were able to put them to work and did not allow their benefits to be wasted. Most prominent individuals seem to have had to struggle, persist, and overcome great odds before being allowed to climb to the successful positions they are known and remembered for. Perhaps this explains the lack of Grand Trines in their charts.

FIRE GRAND TRINE

With the *Fire Grand Trine*, the creative, inspirational power of the trine is more evident since the element of fire is in itself vital, self-expressive, and spontaneous in action. It seeks to experience itself thru the direct exhibition of its potential. Although vision may be emphasized with this Grand Trine, so may be the sense of personal significance or power, manifesting as egotism or heightened self-pride. The individual may appear very fortunate in that he is able to wholeheartedly engage himself in exciting and somewhat daring activities with little fear, insecurity, or frustration. He tends to be an action person, constantly in motion, with little inclination to remain still for any length of time. Usually, a natural adventurous streak is found plus an appealing sense of innocence, which allows this individual to take risks and gambles without much forethought. He is not normally the calculating type but prefers to act out impulses on the spot. He tends to take his right to freely do as he pleases when he pleases for granted, since what he wants to do normally only concerns himself, suggesting he believes he has individual privilege. Striving to remain independent and autonomous, he expects to be able to express himself without interference from others. He only demands that the environment be ready to fulfill his immediate needs at any moment without delay or resistance. His faith in himself as well as his sense of personal protection from harm is often so ingrained that he may be willing and eager to attempt anything, disregarding impossible odds, in order to fulfill his own goals and objectives. Humility is not one of his common virtues. However, with the dynamics of the Grand Trine involved, the individual's strong and unshakeable belief in himself does allow him to succeed in his endeavors more often than not. Once committed to a personal objective, he can easily display much courage, inner strength, confidence, and enthusiasm.

He may, however, unconsciously be very demanding of attention, loyalty, and even service from others (fire is the royalty element) while remaining emotionally unaffected by or even oblivious to their personal needs, especially if these needs are subtle or indirectly expressed. This is not to suggest that one with the Fire Grand Trine is cold and unfeeling, since fire is a warm and generous element (especially Leo). It simply suggests that you first must get this person's *attention* away from his self-absorbed interests for the *moment*, and then he *may* be willing to put a lot of energy into contributing to your personal welfare. It just won't come instinctively, since that's more water's domain. Of course if this type of individual personally responses to your needs, you must remember to *openly* demonstrate your *sincere* appreciation of his efforts! He thrives on it. Seriously, the Grand Trine operating thru this energetic element normally gives vitality-plus (which may manifest more as physical stamina or high resistance to germs rather than peppiness, since trines do not always overtly express). The individual tends to be lucky with his momentary impulses but will still need to apply the brakes upon his boundless drive to enjoy life to the fullest. Without proper rest, he is prone to burn himself out too early in life, plus wear others down. I have personally noticed that strong fire emphasis sometimes manifests as total self-involvement, giving some people an aloof or reserved nature in social situations instead of the bouyant, vivacious nature one would expect. Rather than be content to live a life of exclusive self-absorption, it is more advisable for one with this Grand Trine to actively seek out leadership roles in life or ones that demand a high degree of physical or creative output. Challenges that allow for dynamic interaction help keep this type of Grand Trine productive rather than stagnant. (*Thomas Jefferson - Mohandas Gandhi - Winston Churchill - Fidel Castro - Albert Schweitzer - Herman Melville - Gustave Flaubert*).

EARTH GRAND TRINE

With the *Earth Grand Trine*, the calming, comforting, attracting power of the trine is emphasized. Earth, like the trine, seeks to preserve the status quo of existing conditions it feels securely supported by. Both element and aspect do not respond well to drastic, critical changes in life affairs. The individual with this type of Grand Trine is bound to feel a deep sense of inner security and stability in the physical world. Due to the powerful magnetism of this configuration, he is readily able to be sustained upon the material level due to an abundance of opportunities to receive tangible support and worldly position if so desired. In this respect, the Earth Grand Trine can become the most physically comforting of them all. The capacity to attract, accumulate, and skillfully manage resources is usually powerfully developed. Yet the drive to venture out into the world and make an aggressive effort to obtain such resources is often lacking. In the chart of a less ambitious individual, this Grand Trine is apt to express as a very self-indulgent, materialistic influence or one that keeps the individual firmly rooted and centered in the limited world of matter (which may not be desirable for inner growth in the long run). One of the constructive features of a well-handled Earth Grand Trine is that it has remarkable endurance and persistence, allowing the individual to steadily concentrate his attention upon concrete objectives without being distracted or thrown off course. Once committed to a goal, he is able to work long and hard towards valued accomplishment. He succeeds because he can skillfully consolidate his vast energy reserves and *contently* plod on until he achieves the solid results he desires. However, unlike mere earth emphasis alone, the dynamics of the Grand Trine suggests an extra measure of inspiration, insight, and vision. The individual may possess tremendous organizational ability and practical know-how, since earth trines enable one to visualize perfect or ideal structure and form. There can be an uncommon amount of common sense shown. Creative resourcefulness is one of this Grand Trine's special assets.

Earth Grand Triners can be the phenomenal builders of life who sense their own power and creative strength best when they witness it thru lasting material achievements or worldly attainment. Since the security need and sense of value is so ingrained in their consciousness, they are rarely inclined to take risky chances and almost never gamble with life in the bold, cocksure manner of those with the Fire Grand Trine. Instead, they tend to deliberate and shrewdly evaluate conditions before making any important moves. Usually, their timing in such matters is excellent.

Nevertheless, all this strong earth reinforcement tends to produce a conventional, conservative temperament that often lacks the sparkle of imagination and flair. Although the individual's inner strength and determination to succeed is awesome to others, he tends to lack charisma. Negatively, the individual is so innately attuned to routine and system that he is prone to resist making dynamic changes in life, and sometimes can get stuck in ruts that support his weakness for comfort but keep him living on the mundane surface of life. The pursuit of gratifying the physical appetites could over-shadow the quest for deeper self-awareness. Work and productivity are often over--valued at the expense of inner development, even though these people usually gravitate towards positions of organizational management in which they delegate work roles for others to perform (since Triners are not apt to exert themselves in a strenuous manner). It is advisable for one with this Grand Trine to actively seek out material ambitions that allow for creative utilization of practical resources to help keep energies here from congesting and becoming inertia-prone. (*Joseph Stalin - Napoleon - Aristotle Onassis - Robert E. Lee - John L. Lewis - Mohammed Ali - John Lennon*).

AIR GRAND TRINE

With the *Air Grand Trine*, the idealistic, expansive, wisdom-gaining aspects of the trine are emphasized. The element air, like the trine can feel satisfied living in its head without having to express itself overtly in the external world. Both element and aspect share as a common denominator the natural inclination to conceptualize and create on an abstract level. Thus, the impractical side of the trine can be more evident with this configuration if the individual is unable to ground his idealistic insights. This individual is likely to be very socially curious, broad-minded, and tolerant (trines are benevolent and easy-going). But he may not necessarily find himself deeply or passionately involved with others on a more one-to-one basis. The natural inclination here is to remain detached, observant, non-commital, and basically free to explore whatever attracts the attention of the mind. Great inner satisfaction occurs when he is able to have a variety of relationships that put few demands upon him. This suggests that one with an Air Grand Trine may find it quite a challenge to remain emotionally constant with another without interpreting this as a stifling entanglement. Nevertheless, this Grand Trine confers above-average educational ability, an eager intellect, and an ability to have a wide perspective of life. He can take pleasure in learning new information about the world he lives in, and thus tends to be the "eternal student" type. Yet, as his rational faculties are normally well-developed, he is apt to objectively consider all sides of any issue (sometimes endlessly) before being able to *comfortably* arrive at any lasting conclusions. However, life seldom presses him to make any final decisions, since it instead promotes his capacity for new mental insights. Because it is easy for him to detach and function upon an impersonal level, he may readily generalize his outlook upon life.

One with an Air Grand Trine can exude much social appeal, enhancing his popularity. He has charisma on the one-to-many level. He can easily attract friendly cooperation from others, due to both his casual easygoingness and his ability to become all things to all people. For the most part, this configuration denotes one with natural charm, congeniality, appealing openness, and an innate facility for expressive communication. Yet in a weak character, the Air Grand Trine describes one who attemps to use his above-average powers of persuasion or cleverness (the con-artist type) to coax others to act on his behalf or for his personal immediate advantage. In addition, there may be a tendency to view life from a superficial level, in which the individual perceives human conditions only from the quality of surface appearances. And with the natural sense of well-being the Grand Trine instills, he may view his shallow evaluations as intellectually superior to that which others observe. Although creative thought is one of this Grand Trine's special assets, the individual may not make the effort it takes to anchor his ideas, ideals, or abstract insights in a manner that makes them easily comprehended and thus workable in the external world. The reality of his mind may not touch base with the reality of his social environment. It is advisable for one with the

Air Grand Trine to express himself in communication fields or ones that offer a stimulating range of broad social contact so that he can dynamically circulate and express himself rather than remain isolated in a self-contained mental ivory tower. (*Lord Byron - George Orwell - Dwight D. Eisenhower - Marlene Dietrich - Tommy Dorsey - Farrah Fawcett - Janis Joplin*).

WATER GRAND TRINE

With the *Water Grand Trine*, the passive, receptive, and protective power of the trine is emphasized. Water, like the trine, seeks tranquility and a soothing sense of peaceful exchange. Both element and aspect share the enjoyment of sensual satisfaction and responsiveness to inner states of consciousness as common denominators. The individual with a natal Water Grand Trine appreciates enrichment on an emotional level, just as one with an Earth Grand Trine values prosperity on the material level. This individual responds to subtle undercurrents in life easily. His powers of detection are above-average, suggesting some degree of psychic sensitivity. However, his impressionability can be transformed into a creative, productive asset once he is able to harness his delicate emotionality. The flowing expression of his feeling nature permits him to withdraw easily into his inner, private world where he often experiences contentment on deeply subjective levels. He may feel personal gratification when exploring the vivid world of his imagination or reflecting upon the past. He at least feels inwardly nourished and secure during his cherished periods of seclusion, privacy, stillness, and rest. Yet unless there are adequate dynamic principles operating in the chart (*i.e.*, fire planets in angular houses, cardinal squares or oppositions, or even a Fixed T-Square for added stability and determination), this particular Grand Trine can foster an escapist temperament too vulnerable to effectively channel its emotional overload in a constructive manner.

There tends to be shown here an exaggerated need for dependency, general mothering, safety from threat or harm, and psychological insulation from the harsher facets of reality. And the more subtle these needs express themselves, the more potentially insidious. In my opinion, this is the only Grand Trine that readily can become problematic, since the emotional self-containment it represents makes this individual hard to get to know intimately. Negatively, he may feel he is disconnected with the outer world (since water is a unifying element which, when blocked, can feel out-of-tune with its surroundings). He then may lose touch with his conscious awareness of himself and may passively allow unconscious forces to take over. Yet on the other hand, the ability to connect with unconscious impressions can make this a very fertile Grand Trine when used to plow the inner human terrain. Since one of the prominent features of the Water Grand Trine is its uncanny ability to sense the underground energies of people, its presence in the chart can indicate (inner) success in fields of social service. Due to the individual's well-developed sense of empathy and sympathy, he can be very supportive and nurturing of others in a manner that is healing and therapeutic. A Water Grand Trine could represent the evolutionary blooming of the ability to attune to the needs of the mass consciousness with much compassion. Here, one can become the hidden comforter or healer of the sick, the weak in spirit, the troubled, or the socially rejected. Thus, this type of configuration is an asset for psychiatric work, medical fields, or psychic counseling. However, due to the absorbing nature of this Trine, the individual will have to learn how to detach his feelings if he is to function constructively, since he tends to be deeply affected by the woes of the world. In a weak character, this could make one feel easily defeated, dejected, insecure, lonely, and flat unable to cope with stress. In general, the Water Grand Trine denotes the gentle dreamer who retires or withdraws into a self-made world of fantasy, illusion, and imagination. If he can positively channel his urges, he can do exceptionally well in fields involving specialized creativity, beauty, glamour, or the fine arts. He also can find success in areas allowing him to probe into the hidden mysteries of life, in which a fine awareness of subtlety is required. (*Robert Schumann - Jules Verne - Madame Curie - Jean Paul Sartre - Israel Regardie - Jean Harlow - Marilyn*

Monroe).

DISSOCIATE GRAND TRINE

Not all Grand Trines are formed from planets in three signs of the same element. When one is formed from two signs of the same element but one of another, there is an underlying *square* and *quincunx* influence created by the sign placement of that one planet in the other element. This condition thus represents the *Dissociate Grand Trine*. I advise going back to Chapter Three and reviewing what was said about the Dissociate Trine, which should help you delineate this type of configuration. In general, the Dissociate Grand Trine has a bit more drive and activation in its make-up than does the standard Grand Trine. A Dissociate Grand Trine, however, may decrease some of the protective power normally associated with this configuration. But although it may seem less easy-flowing for the individual, the underlying influences here could give it enough subtle tension to prevent it from otherwise operating too passively. Although this type of Grand Trine may sometimes function as if it is short-circuited, its complexity often makes it more challenging for the individual psychologically. The Dissociate Grand Trine is named according to the element that dominates. *Hans Christian Anderson* had a Dissociate *Water* Grand Trine, which obviously helped stimulate his sense of fantasy and creative imagination. Novelist *Sinclair Lewis* had a Dissociate *Air* Grand Trine and wrote books centered around the social abuses of his times. Time will tell how *Prince Charles* manifests his natal Dissociate *Earth* Grand Trine. In my limited study of this configuration, I was not able to find an example for the Dissociate *Fire* Grand Trine. Hopefully, your research will find some examples.

THE KITE

This seldom discussed configuration is actually a modified Grand Trine. Here, a planet is found at a fourth point in opposition to one of the planets in the Grand Trine. At the same time, it sextiles the remaining two planets. In addition to the dynamics of the Grand Trine itself, the Kite also receives the added stimulus of the sextile and the opposition aspect. It thus is a composite of three trines, two sextiles, and one opposition. I interpret it as a more dynamic indicator of success in life. The planet that is sextile to the two points of the Grand Trine represents a stimulating (often mental) outlet for the creative outpour of this configuration. Any special benefits indicated by the Grand Trine usually channel themselves into the natural activities indicated by the drives of this focal planet, often filtering thru its natal house position. The Kite may actually be more versatile in its creative application, since the sextile influence encourages eagerness of self-expression plus provides ample outer opportunities for such expression. The natal area where the planet of the Grand Trine opposing this pivotal fourth planet is found can indicate where special talents and skills are prone to direct themselves; the planet will suggest the nature of the drive to be expressed, but the fourth planet will act as the catalyst. The stimulation derived from the presence of these other supplementary aspects serve to heighten the individual's awareness of the Grand Trine's vast creative or spiritual potential, encouraging a fuller activation of its promise within a wider range of circumstancial experience. With the inclusion of the opposition aspect, there is heightened awareness of how this Grand Trine can be applied to the social environment. This type of configuration becomes thus less self-contained.

MINOR GRAND TRINE

This common configuration occurs when one planet sextiles two planets in trine aspect in the chart. The planet that sextiles the other two should ideally be at the *midpoint* degree. This midpoint planet helps further facilitate the naturally flowing exchange of the trine, enabling it to attract upon a more *conscious* level opportunities for the expression of talents in the environment. The individual here is more alerted to the potential alternatives of that trine's creative expression. He may even be more inventive or versatile in the manner in which he releases his abilities here. The Minor Grand Trine is less static and passive than the more contained Grand Trine, and therefore it is even more inclined to put its constructive energies to active use. In general, the Minor Grand Trine gives an extra measure of intelligence and objectivity, assisting the individual in presenting his natural aptitudes to others with greater adaptability. He may be more able to skillfully communicate its energy better, and with some degree of intuition.

References:

(1) Barbara H. Watters, *The Astrologer Looks At Murder*, Valhalla Paperbacks Ltd., Wash. D.C., 1969, p. 31.

5
The Grand Sextile

This configuration is not a common one to come across in natal charts. It must involve at least *six* planets found at six different points in the chart. All of them must first and foremost sextile each other, which tends to create a chain-effect reaction. The *Grand Sextile* thus creates a large *hexagram* pattern across the chart. Within this configuration are actually *two* Grand Trines and *three* oppositions. Considering the presence of multiple Grand Trines, the saving grace of the Grand Sextile is its three oppositions. They stimulate an awareness that we need to give back out to the environment what we readily develop here within us if we are to use such a plentitude of opportunities in a balanced, constructive manner. Because of the grandness of this configuration, we best use it when supporting the growth of a social cause that drives us to make use of the full range of our talents and skills. It can denote an above-average degree of versatility. Aid and assistance come from many varied areas in our environment as long as we remain open, cooperative, and able to complement the needs of others. These oppositions also remind us to consciously coordinate our activities and direct them towards external objectives, rather than contain them for our self-centered advantage. We are stimulated to creatively mobilize our forces here and reach out towards the world.

With two Grand Trines involved here, the creative resources are abundant and need to be actively tapped. Here exists an enormous overload of capacity which demands to be actively exploited. If diffusion or stagnation is allowed to develop (prompted by the passivity of multiple Grand Trines), this condition is very much like the spoilage of ripened fruit. Talents that are in their peak of expression then begin to diminish due to their lack of activation. The temptation to procrastinate, become lazy or indifferent to the powers of this configuration should be avoided at all cost. This individual normally exudes a special magnetism that could have a beneficial, charismatic influence over others. He seems to do more favorably when allowing

himself to spread out in a variety of experiences in life (due
to the branching effect of the six sextiles).

However, with at least six of the ten normally used planets
tied into this configuration, the chart as a whole is likely to
have few squares. Therefore, the Grand Sextile may
require that we make a special, conscious effort to work
harder at developing inner discipline, greater endurance,
patience, and the ambitious drive it takes to insure a fuller
utilization of our special gifts here. Otherwise, lacking the
drive and impetus of squares, we might merely become
privileged, gifted dilletantes who are nevertheless too
restless and over-stimulated to ever master any of our
skills. The Grand Sextile at least implies a "jack-of-all-
trades" influence, although with greater social access than
one with mere natal sextiles.

THE FIRE-AIR GRAND SEXTILE

With these energizing, out-going elements represented
here, the tendency to instigate stimulating activities with
burning enthusiasm, optimism, and vibrant self-expression
is quite strong. However, the staying power and
persistence to follow thru with impulses is weakened.
Talents depicted here are usually evoked and activated
during periods of spurt activity, and usually when
inspiration and impulse runs high. Otherwise, this
individual is not as inclined to be methodical, systematic, or
long-planning in his efforts. Instead, he is spontaneous in
his self-expression and thrives on the momentum of the
here-and-now, which he knows how to creatively take
advantage of. Practical concerns (especially minor details)
are seldom considered when initiating new and exciting
activities. As he is apt to ignore or low-key his own
limitations, he may energize himself to do the impossible at
times. However, the special assets provided here can be
used with flair, color, style, and vibrancy. The individual
can be quite innovative with these energies.

As this person is usually very extroverted, animated, and
mentally stimulating, he tends to attract more social
attention of a positive nature than most. People are likely to
feel enlivened in his presence, although also slightly

overwhelmed by his ready on-goingness. If he can learn to tone down his inclination to jump around buoyantly from one activity to another and instead more carefully attend to matters, he will find this configuration to be of great personal value. This type of Grand Sextile could get more accomplished instead of spinning off in a multitude of diverse directions if Mars, Jupiter, and Uranus are not involved in it, since these planets increase restlessness and impatience with whatever produces slower results than anticipated.

THE EARTH-WATER GRAND SEXTILE

With all the receptive, indrawing signs represented here, the normal tendency is to approach all areas of creative potential with more conservatism, greater industriousness, and a sense of careful organization. Staying power is stronger, giving this type of Grand Sextile a highly productive power than can realistically benefit many areas of the individual's life. Talents and opportunities indicated are pursued with a desire for practical application as well as emotional gratification and material security. With this configuration, the individual is motivated to retain the fruits of his efforts, unlike the fire-air Grand Sextile which rarely seems to possess what it creates or initiates. The stability and purposefulness of the sensible earth signs minimizes the danger of this Grand Sextile swinging off into too many scattered directions at once. Social activities emphasized here usually coordinate better with each other.

The three oppositions will require that the individual interact with the social environment with more flexibility. In general, earth and water signs adapt more poorly to changes and alterations in the outer world than do the fire and air signs. They are geared toward preserving and securing rather than expending and releasing. Thus, one with this configuration is often less willing to innovate, experiment, or follow thru with sudden impulses. He is also likely to actively pursue less interests and therefore does not tend to spread himself too thin. The expression of nervous energy here is less sporatic, temperamental, and unevenly modulated. Because of the presence of both a

Grand Earth Trine and a Grand Water Trine, the sensual nature is apt to be very well-developed and able to be channeled in highly imaginative ways. Whatever routines are necessary for the thorough development of creative enterprises are more easily accepted and undertaken by this individual. But due to the somewhat unenergetic nature of these elements, Mars, Jupiter, and Uranus involved in this type of Grand Trine benefits its expression and keeps it vital.

DISSOCIATE GRAND SEXTILE

With the *Dissociate Grand Sextile*, the underlying influence of the *semi-sextile*, the *square* and the *quincunx* operates when only one planet out of the six is out-of-sign. If more than one planet is dissociate (which to me automatically suggests a Grand Sextile that is not going to be easily integrated), these underlying influences are even more emphasized. On a psychological level, this condition could be beneficial due to the presence of the square sign relationships, even though the undertone of the quincunx may imply that the individual's attitudes here tend to vacillate, adjust slowly, or are counter-productive. I imagine that this version of the Grand Sextile is more common to see in practice. While on some level a Dissociate Grand Sextile could be more troublesome and less easy-flowing, it may also bring to the individual's attention an awareness of the beneficial effects of tension, viewing it as an agent for successful achievement. He may even feel a slight degree of anxiety and inner stress when not putting the Grand Sextile's capacity for rare self-expression to use. How an individual chooses to respond to this composite of energies cannot be reliably pinpointed by the chart itself.

6
The Grand Square &
The Mystic Rectangle

The *Grand Square* is technically formed when two oppositions square one another, creating a large square configuration across the chart. Ideally, all four planets are in the same quality. It is not a typical pattern to run across in charts, although not as rare as the Grand Sextile. It is often felt as a difficult configuration to be born with and can be especially restrictive and self-limiting for the individual who shows little capacity for self-discipline and moderation in life. He is to struggle under somewhat frustrating conditions, all of his own making, that could force him to learn to properly direct vital energies or else run the risk of becoming scattered and drained (particularly with the Mutable Grand Square). As he begins to concentrate upon how he can better utilize this powerful energy field, the individual may discover a reservoir of inner strength.

If we handle this pattern poorly, our life may seem fraught with inner disharmonies and tensions that trigger stressful, burdensome situations in our outer environment. Since a Grand Square is composed of four square aspects, it induces an internal sense of friction, strain, and pressure. Yet the dynamic convergence of forces generated here can supply just the necessary amount of extra psychological fuel required to become thoroughly engrossed in an outstandingly purposeful lifestyle. Since the Grand Square is also made up of two oppositions, it allows one to develop a sharper sense of social awareness. These oppositions offer the perspective, balance, and poise needed to make this configuration conducive of inner harmony. Or they can pose relationship conflicts that evoke antagonism and discord, drawing more negative energies to us thru the actions of others. Much will depend upon the free will of the individual as well as the effectiveness with which he will use this complex dilemma. The Grand Square will always have a very noticeable effect upon him one way or another. It is suggestive of complicated, crucial karmic lessons that must be resolved according to the nature of the quality which composes it, and thru the circumstantial affairs of the houses occupied by the planets involved.

CARDINAL GRAND SQUARE

This configuration seems to operate easiest when the individual engages in activities of an energetic, vigorous, on-the-go nature. The agitation of the four squares increases the already impatient, assertive temperament of this quality. They are likely to stir the individual into taking quick but sometimes poorly planned action. Tensions felt here keep him active and on-the-move, but he is often too charged up with excess energy to complete whatever he has impulsively initiated. While he may appear to start personal projects with an above-average degree of drive and thrust, he lacks the staying power to follow thru with his plans to their desired conclusion. The two oppositions denote others will present him with the challenge of learning to be more self-controlled, reliable, and consistent. Although he may choose to openly resist all pressures to be more disciplined in favor of doing his own thing, he seldom has a well-defined, workable idea of what that actually is.

The oppositions functioning thru the cardinal mode warns that cooperation and consideration of others are critical determinants of ultimate success in fulfilling personal objectives. He has to first learn to willingly share himself in the activities of others and cultivate sociability before he can expect to have others assist him with his immediate goals. By learning to harness his tremendous energy reserves and by applying more commonsense in his actions, the individual can avoid the usual pitfalls of this Grand Square (which are impetuosity, reckless moves, bad timing, over-assertion, and head-on confrontations with others. Accident-proneness may also be indicated due to thoughtless impulsiveness...especially if Mars and/or Uranus compose part of the configuration). In general, there can be exhibited an overdose of push, drive, momentum and aggression. Ambition to succeed is very strong along with the competitive streak that insures success in those areas where he single-mindedly applies himself. Natural impulses that are not acted out with prior deliberation or forethought can easily create disorder and excitable conditions. This is bound to be an eventful incarnation of many situational crises and ever-changing relationships calling for quick, decisive action on this individual's part. Yet this often tends to be taxing on the physical level.

Although often feeling frustrated by obstacles that block direct action towards the expression of conscious needs, the individual may eventually learn to apply his enterprising, head-strong temperament with greater persistence towards tackling one major objective at a time. This will demand that he curb his basic hyperactive nature and learn to slow down his frenetic tempo. Important lessons denoted by the Cardinal Grand Square are developing patience, inner composure, endurance, steadfastness, and learning to better organize time and energy. Without these qualities, this person tends to rush off into new areas of activity before projects at hand have been allowed to bloom to their fullest potential. Through the lack of keen planning, he often denies himself any rewarding accomplishment. When acting too prematurely or with an unnecessary sense of urgency, his actions fail to bear satisfying results. He does have much energy to burn, but without establishing centeredness, he is likely to create short-lived sparks that can quickly die out. (*Douglas Fairbanks, Jr. - Mickey Mantle*).

FIXED GRAND SQUARE

This configuration could be considered as a most trying and testing cross to bear, as it represents attitudes in one's consciousness that have been repeated troublespots for the individual for several incarnations. It now may manifest thru deep-seated, hard to eradicate problems in this life that demand one's full concentration. The Fixed Grand Square tends to work its powerful energies out on the will and desire level, creating inner frustrations often leading to emotional crises. The four squares intensify the willfulness and unyielding fixity of this quality. Here the tendency is to compress feelings and fortify the will to such an extent that pressures internalize upon the deeper levels of the psyche, resulting in enduring blockages or inhibitions. The individual can become very crystallized in his feelings. Emotional flexibility is needed to keep him from becoming rut-bound.

The two oppositions reflect conflict centered around his possessiveness and firm resistance towards compromising or sharing with others. This individual will have to learn the hard way how to become less bull-headed and absolute in his demands if relationship interests are to work out in a mutually satisfying way. Although the Fixed Grand Square suggests powerful inner fortitude, awesome determination, and masterful planning ability, it also implies rigidity and a temperament too habitual to allow for needed adjustments. The individual will thus be challenged to become more willing to make changes, adapt to others, and actively seek out new alternatives in self-expression. Unlike the Cardinal Grand Square, which has difficulty being motivated to finish up whatever projects it readily initiates, the Fixed Grand Square conglomerates activities yet over-strains itself by trying to master too much at any time. Its phenomenal endurance and dogged persistence can be abused here. This person does not want to lose control of his personal interests and will rarely allow others to take over matters indicated. If Mars, Uranus, or Pluto composes part of this configuration, then intolerance, dictatorial behavior, and obsession with power are usually emphasized (especially in the house affairs shown).

As this is the Grand Square of extremism, the energy it generates can draw out the most purposeful, dedicated expression as well as the most debased and cruel. The individual is constantly pressured to cleanse his potent feeling nature in this incarnation and clear out all lingering resentments, hostilities, jealousies, and festering hatred. The emotional inner disharmonies he battles with can easily turn their congested energies back into the physical body, manifesting as psychosomatic health problems involving deep build-up of toxins not readily removed. Usually the body parts corresponding to the four fixed signs are most vulnerable. Illnesses stemming from the tensions of the Grand Square are more likely to be of a chronic or incurable nature, as stress factors here are very much ingrained and harder to alter. Problematic symptoms then can become more settled in the mind and body. Life will inevitably teach this person how to soften his will and open up his heart to a more universal level of love. Once he earnestly devotes himself to uplifting, spiritual service with a more *conscious* sense of selflessness, he can much better break up the destructive crystallization of this configuration. By accepting life on *its* own terms with a sense of compassion and understanding rather than forcing it to satisfying his own uncompromising demands, he can become a stabilizing anchor for many. (*Mao Tse-Tung - Albert Schweitzer*).

MUTABLE GRAND SQUARE

This restless configuration seems to operate best in all fields of mental expression. However, the stress created by the four squares often manifest as agitated nervousness and extreme restlessness, although they also heighten the individual's altertness and mental vigor. The main problem of this Grand Square is its inclination to spread interests over too wide a range to be successfully contained and controlled by the individual. Although quite stimulating and knowledgeable, he is likely to be very inconsistent and unmethodical in the execution of his plans of action. The Mutable Grand Square poses frustrations due to undue changeability, poor concentration ability, indecision, negative suggestibility, and a tendency to give in to external pressures rather than resist or challenge. This person is prone to over-adapt, adjusting to situations that are not to his personal advantage. And although he may search in life for intelligent meaning and purpose, he seldom disciplines himself enough to apply the knowledge he gathers at random.

The two oppositions denote that the individual needs to more deeply integrate his sense of logical analysis and conscious reasoning ability (concrete mind) with his faith-potential and theoretical concepts or beliefs (abstract mind) in order to successfully communicate his potential. His tendency is to waver, vacilliate, and remain uncertain about his needs in partnerships. This can eventually create added instability or unreliability in his unions, which then create conflicts. The Mutable Grand Square shows no direct, driving urge to activate energies in the straightforward, dynamic manner of the Cardinal Grand Square. Nor does it display the steadfast, consolidating approach towards power and control like the organized Fixed Grand Square. However, it can sensitize the individual to responding to a more refined degree of awareness, although often in a manner that renders him too worried or apprehensive about every facet of conflicts he cannot mentally resolve. This can produce a disturbing degree of nervous strain that can exhaust and deplete the vitality of this person (particularly with Mercury, Mars, Saturn, and all the Higher Octave planets occupying the signs Gemini and Pisces, since air and water signs do not stabilize and center themselves easily).

Tensions here can at least impair the individual's use of his intellectual faculties until he actively and consciously makes an effort to steady and deepen his mentality. This will involve applying greater discrimination and judgement in matters relating to the planets involved. To avoid running in circles mentally or becoming aimless in direction, the individual may have to learn to control the over-expression of the mind. Since peace of mind is hard to achieve, he may benefit thru meditation, contemplation, and reflective self-analysis. To me, this Grand Square is like a windmill in a windstorm. Although varied and highly talented (sometimes even overloaded with mental abilities and skills), this person seldom focusses intensely enough upon any one interest to the point in which he can master techniques or develop a definite personal style of expression. Perhaps the greatest drawback of this type of Grand Square is that it lacks the spirited strength of conviction and the assertive self-thrust to overcome limiting outer conditions. Instead, it tends to blend into any current situation regardless of how unproductive or non-challenging. Illnesses here can work themselves into expression thru the respiratory system (which is intimately linked up with the thought process), the nervous system, and the mind. The symptoms tend to come-and-go, unlike the chronic, lingering symptoms of the Fixed Grand Square, or the acute, crises-like symptoms of the Cardinal

Grand Square. This Grand Square most effectively works out its tension thru creative effort in all educational fields or communication outlets. (*Nathaniel West - Evelyn Waugh*).

DISSOCIATE GRAND SQUARE

If at least one planet of the Grand Square falls in a sign of a different quality, the configuration that results is actually a Dissociate Grand Square. With this condition, note that the sign placements of all four planets are not representing natural square relationships, nor is one of the oppositions involving natural polar opposites. Thus, an opposition will indicate an underlying *quincunx* relationship. The out-of-sign planet also creates a *trine* pattern to one of the planets plus a *sextile* aspect to the remaining other. The trine and sextile sub-influences may either ease off the level of frustrating tension (psychologically, not circumstantially) by prompting a more flexible, creative attitude concerning the expression of stress factors indicated, or it may further diffuse consciousness in a manner that keeps the individual from directly confronting the dilemma represented in the forceful manner that squares require. The out-of-focus quincunx may even further prevent tensions from clearly defining themselves until the typical pressure of the Grand Square lacks the intensity needed to develop the fuller awareness of how to confront and resolve matters here.

Yet considering the adjustable nature of the quincunx, the easy-flowing and inspirational nature of the trine, and the flexible nature of the sextile, a *Dissociate Fixed Grand Square* could help minimize rigidity and resistance to change. It thus may resolve itself easier than the standard Fixed Grand Square. On the other hand, these influences operating thru a *Dissociate Mutable Grand Square* could work towards the individual's disadvantage for obvious reasons.

Like the Grand Trine, the Grand Square should also be considered as a closed configuration, suggesting a greater capacity for self-containment. In this case, self-containment can accentuate the general discomfort of this pattern (whereas self-containment with the Grand Trine tends to feel more comforting and protective). Therefore, any outside planet that is trine, sextile, or even quintile any of the four planets in the Grand Square can become a beneficial source of relief, assisting the individual in constructively channeling these energies. If several planets have such relief aspects, then note the nature of the one that is the most exact in orb (and especially if it also rules an angle in the chart and/or aspects more than one of the planets of the Grand Square). For dedicated humanitarian Albert Schweitzer, the relief planet that helped him transmute the stress of his *Fixed Grand Square* was *Venus* (representing love, social awareness, values) in *Sagittarius* (sign of faith, missionary spirit, inspiration, benevolence, international appeal) which ruled his humane, socially concerned *Libra ASC* (suggesting personal action and self-generated effort made for the behalf of others).

GRAND SQUARE INVOLVING ANGLES

When the Grand Square is formed by three planets at different points in the chart *plus* the ASC, it can suggest an individual who may experience above-average difficulties involving the emergence of personal identity out into the greater environment. Major crises shown here may heavily pressure him to confront and alter his concept of self-image. The major difference between this version of the Grand Square and the standard one is that an angle, and not a planet, is involved. Although the ASC and MC can be as important in influence as any planet, they do not represent dynamic *urges* that drive us to express. Instead, thru the coloring of the sign they fall in, these angles more aptly describe our attitude towards external conditions we personally confront. In other words, angles do not actually give out energy, but are more receptive to forces generated outside of our field of consciousness. In this case, the urges of the three planets interact with a great level of tension and filter themselves out *thru* the ASC point, according to the behavioral expression of the ascending sign. The same goes for the MC when involved with the Grand Square. Thus, this type of Grand Square tends to give a certain amount of focus and direction the standard version completely lacks. Thus, due to such an externalizing focus, tensions triggered by such a configuration may more easily *ground* themselves thru circumstantial activities, often in the characteristic manner of the ASC sign. This does not imply that they are any better handled, however, but just that they are less prone towards *internal* self-containment. The powerful energies of the Grand Square denote that this individual's presence is strongly felt by others he directly confronts, for better or worse. This type of Grand Square could provide one a more objective focus of attention (since the ASC is actually part of the ASC-DESC axis or opposition, suggesting external awareness) than one formed solely by planets.

When the MC is one of the four vital points of the Grand Square, it can typify an individual with powerful potential in the realm of professional involvement, social status, public ambitions, and worldly control or managerial positions. It may enable him to work dynamically towards his accomplishments in a manner that sometimes appears too aggressive and head-strong (Cardinal Grand Square), power-seeking, manipulative, or dominating (Fixed Grand Square), or erratic, inconsistent, and ineffectual (Mutable Grand Square). Nevertheless, the MC as a focal point of the Grand Square gives the individual the capacity to channel his pressing drives towards societal challenges. Positively expressed, this configuration could indicate the potential for notable achievement once the individual has been able to overcome great odds. In general, both these modified types of Grand Squares suggest an emphasized ability to exteriorize the acute tensions represented in a manner that is less scattering and diffusive. It seems to me that *any* Grand aspect configuration needs to become engrossed in a larger-than-life goal or objective (any social project that enables the individual to get completely outside of himself) if one is to beneficially handle its enormous overload of energy. These configurations need appropriate activities to bring out their grandness.

THE MYSTIC RECTANGLE

While this interesting configuration is not related to the Grand Square, it nevertheless represents another potentially tensional, closed aspect pattern. The Mystic Rectangle ideally involves two sets of *oppositions* whose ends both *trine* and *sextile* each other. It thus visually forms a large rectangular pattern across the chart. This configuration, perhaps first brought to astrology's attention by Dane Rudyhar in *The Astrology of Personality*, may be representative of "practical mysticism,"1 since it involves two potentially awareness-revealing, illuminating oppositions that can creatively reach ideal or inspired fruition (trine influence) thru intelligent, innovative utilization of energies (sextile influence). However, much depends upon the level at which the oppositions are experienced by the individual (since the opposition aspect can also express itself as disharmony, imbalance, separative forces, and irreconcilable tension). Normally, the challenges of the two oppositions are more effectively encountered than would be otherwise expected, due to the integrative influences of the linking trines and sextiles. Conflict and discord determined here now have a stimulating, encouraging impetus for satisfying resolution, suggesting that such oppositions are less prone towards being paralyzed by impasses and stalemates. Any perspective gained can here be more self-expressively utilized in a growth-producing manner. Attempts towards productive activity in relationships are better able to be more objectively evaluated and balanced in their execution thru *insight* and *intuition* when this configuration is positively expressed.

THE HARD RECTANGLE

This configuration involves two sets of *oppositions* whose ends are both *semi-square* and *sesqui-square* each other. Charles Jayne is to be given credit for naming this multiple aspect pattern.2 Unlike the aforementioned Mystic Rectangle, the Hard Rectangle suggests that the oppositions are more pressured to activate reconciliation due to subtle, indirect tensions. Here there is implied a greater application of will to accomplish harmony and balance. Yet considering what was said about the nature of semi-squares and sesqui-squares in Chapter One, these influences could also spark further antagonism and a lack of needed compromise with others, making this a very hard rectangle indeed to control. But normally, the stimulation of minor conflicts triggers these oppositions to act with a bit more drive than is typical of standard oppositions. The additional factor of tension here could give this configuration an extra dose of strength and purpose when well-managed.

Naturally, both these rectangle configurations can be presented in a chart in their dissociate form. In my own chart, I have a Dissociate Mystical Rectangle (in addition to a Dissociate Grand Trine and a Dissociate T-Square). And frankly, my inner life has demanded that I make many subtle adjustments in consciousness (all nevertheless intense) that few outside individuals realize. I seem to be constantly working on myself in one way or another and, if anything, need to completely relax and assimilate the fruits of my efforts in a pleasurable manner without feeling an anxious need to further correct myself. And while there are still further factors in my chart to reinforce such an orientation, I would imagine all dissociate aspect configurations suggest the necessity of some degree of not-too-obvious attitude adjustment, regardless of outer circumstances. For those interested, I suggest setting up examples of both the Dissociate Mystical Rectangle and the Dissociate Hard Rectangle to see what underlying influences might come into play, at least upon the psychological level of awareness. Then interpret accordingly. While these dissociate configurations may actually be too subtle to practically consider, attempting to delineate them may at least be a good mental exercise strengthening your understanding of principles.

References:

(1) Dane Rudhyar, *The Astrology of Personality*, Doubleday, N.Y., 1970, p. 332.

(2) Charles Jayne, *Horoscope Interpretation Outlined*, AB Publication, N.Y., 1970, p. 13.

7
The T-Square

When two planets oppose one another while both are
squared by a third planet, the configuration thus formed is
called a *T-Square* (also referred to as a T-Cross). This
aspect pattern appears to visually form a large T formation
across the chart. Tracy Marks, in her most informative,
thorough book titled *How To Handle Your T-Square*, has
suggested that the T-Square can be found in at least 40% of
all natal charts.1 It thus should not be considered as an
uncommon configuration to come across in actual practice.
In fact, according to my studies of hundreds of natal charts,
it is *the* prominent configuration found in the majority of
charts of well-known individuals who have made an
above-average impact upon the world. The planet that
squares the opposition is often called the focal or "apex"
planet. It basically gives the astrologer an important clue
about a very dynamic principle that the individual normally
has trouble integrating into the awareness-process of the
opposition without at least causing internal disharmony,
inner imbalance, or tensional self-blockage. And this is
eventually expressed thru the individual's relationships.
Such a potent tensional pattern is discomforting for the
individual due to the tendency of the apex planet to
continually challenge the balance, harmony, and poise the
opposition ideally seeks to attain. This pivotal third planet
is apt to excite the opposing planets into expressing
themselves in a separative, conflicting manner rather than
in complementary exchange. The sign and house position of
this apex planet pinpoints where this tension is most
acutely felt. The sign and house position of the point in the
chart *opposite* the apex planet (referred to often as the
"empty leg" of the T-Square) seems to play a very central
role in directing the individual as to how to best work out
the dilemma indicated by the T-Square. The attitudes
typical of the sign plus the situational experiences denoted
by the house placement of the empty leg will offer more
insight into the ideal resolution of this complex pattern.
And the manner in which one is best able to do this is
suggested by the basic urges and drives of the apex planet.

The T-Square is decidedly more energizing and self-motivating than the Grand Square. This is due to the added friction of uncertainty created by the empty leg, thus implying that it is an open configuration and thus not easily self-contained. At least the Grand Square is a symmetrical structure that is able to support itself more solidly, while the T-Square lacks full inter-connection of the quality represented, and is therefore more unstable and easily upset. However, due to the closed nature of the Grand Square, it often becomes an unbroken and continuous stress pattern lacking direction, in which the individual becomes caught up within the tensional boundaries indicated without being readily impelled to challenge and overcome their limiting influence. On the other hand, the T-Square is simply too agitating, frictional, and compelling to accept without a psychological struggle.

The opposition involved here suggests the need to develop greater objectivity and considerate awareness of the rights and needs of others. The apex planet that squares this opposition can intensify such matters and often indicates the nature of frustrations, blockages, habitual insecurities, and defensive reactions originating within the individual himself that instigates such relationship awareness. If he seemingly cannot cope with the pressing challenges of this configuration, he may then upset others and attract discordant situations due to his own (often unrecognized) antagonistic, self-centered actions. If the apex planet is mismanaged, then the opposing planets tend to project upon each other in a most negative manner. Nevertheless, conflict between these opposing planets is seldom allowed to reach the stalemate condition that standard opposition sometimes can, since the apex planet keeps them continually activated in a manner that overtly manifests their potential conflict. This is one reason why the T-Square is so characteristically dynamic in its operation. No urge here is allowed to remain latent or indirect. Of course, this same squaring planet can become a source of further agitation, sometimes putting unnecessary stress upon the opposing planets than would not normally be required of them to resolve their conflict. In other words, the planet squaring the opposition planets can really keep these planets in a state of imbalance in which they feel quite separative and out of tune. But at the same time, this squaring planet can also help play a needed mediating role, when properly handled, that prevents the opposing planets from becoming unresolved in their action. Constructively applied, all excess energy evoked by the powerful T-Square often becomes highly provocative, pushing and driving the individual onward with a well-defined sense of aim and direction, while forcing him to confront and overcome obstacles in his path. This is most likely due to the fact that the apex planet gives the individual a definite external outlet for the forward momentum of these tensional energies that is not found in the Grand Trine, the Grand Sextile, or the Grand Square.

CARDINAL T-SQUARE

An individual with this dynamic configuration has many growth-accelerating lessons to learn in the areas of his life concerning personal energy expenditure, enterprising self-generating activity, and the concentrated direction of attention applied towards major here-and-now objectives. This T-Square can give one much vitality, drive, and assertive impulse. But it can also keep the individual in a constant rush or frenzy on the action level, in which he may attempt to over-do in his desire to accomplish too much too soon. This may also be seen when any T-Square falls in angular houses (and most so when Mars and/or Jupiter is involved). A Cardinal T-Square is normally the most invigorating and extroverted of them all. It propels one to enterprise exciting situational activities that require much aggression, courage, straightforwardness, and active personal effort. Life for those with this driving configuration may seem like one circumstantial crisis after another. Yet while he is often eager and ready to have an obvious impact upon his environment, this individual may tend to buck the established way of doing things. He personally will need to develop greater self-discipline, inner timing, outer patience, and a general sense of thoroughness and organization if he is to succeed in his ventures. Since he is usually vulnerable towards poor planning, he will have to consciously analyze the practical facets of his own impulses to see if they actually will help him move *ahead* towards the realistic attainment of his goals. There will be significant direct confrontations in his life that he will be pressured to meet head-on. Yet by teaching himself to look before leaping into new activities, he will be less prone to exert his vital energies in a thoughtless manner. It is especially important if Mars, Jupiter, or Uranus is involved in this T-Square (and even more so if one of these planets is at the apex point) that the individual learn as early in his life as possible to observe restraint and see the value of respecting his personal limitations. Since physical activity is often emphasized here, he will need to live a lifestyle that allows him to be on-the-move and ready to make quick changes. Yet the more self-aware he allows himself to become, the more purposeful these changes become. (*Oliver Cromwell - Francisco Goya - Marie Antoinette - Bonnie Parker*).

FIXED T-SQUARE

The individual with this configuration is likely to meet up with many intensive lessons in areas that test his expression of fixed desire, willful emotion, and attachment to what he personally values. The urge to retain whatever is possessed is very powerful. Acceptance of and respect for other people's values and possessions may be a prominent karmic theme. This individual can be almost obsessively persistent in matters that deeply attract him. Yet he often runs into rigid stalemate situations due to the impact his stubborn streak has upon others he otherwise easily draws to himself. His own demanding, fixated needs tend to completely block those of others. His natural ability to hold tight to himself and not give into pressure makes him seem almost immune to outside influences. It wouldn't surprise me if people with Fixed T-Squares prove to be highly resistant to virus and bacteria (especially those strains that are associated with acute, short-lived symptoms). While this T-Square is seldom as energetically active as the Cardinal T-Square, its enormous power reserves and emotional stamina help the individual to endure all sorts of setbacks and obstacles without buckling under, giving up, or losing his purposeful sense of direction. The individual is driven to build something solid, secure, and long-lasting for himself in this life. Internal pressures here help consolidate his will, urging him to be intensely determined to succeed in his efforts at all cost. Highly goal-oriented, his consistent, single-minded approach towards objectives can almost be ruthless at times. The apex planet will often act like an unexpected (and thus emotionally upsetting) catalyst, helping him dislodge stagnant feelings and desires in a manner that forces him to change. It is primarily in the life area shown by the house placement of the apex planet that adaptability to outer change is very poor, and where adjustments are made unwillingly. The individual's deeply-rooted drive to manage other people can create a battle-of-the-wills situation with others he attempts to power-play with. You can see how especially difficult this type of T-Square could be in this regard if control-oriented planets like Saturn or Pluto were to operate at the apex point. One of the dangers concerning a mismanaged Fixed T-Square is that it can bottle up and compress negative feelings until they reach the ultimate pressure point, where they then release thru eruptive, violent activity. At this point, the individual may behave irrationally in a way that is either threatening to others or self-destructive, or both. Suitable outlets for the pent-up emotional nature (especially those that allow him to express far beyond the average, mundane level of feeling) are necessary for this person to constructively vent himself. In general, life will teach him by force to develop greater detachment and objectivity concerning his wants and desires. (*Napoleon - Leo Trotsky - Mussolini - Queen Elizabeth II - Kaiser William II - Dylan Thomas*).

MUTABLE T-SQUARE

An individual with this stimulating, mentally-challenging configuration can best work out tension thru active involvement in dynamic areas of thinking, education, communication fields, and even travel (due to the mental-mobile orientation of this mode). Typically, the stress generated by the Mutable T-Square can be taxing to the nervous system (often due to over-stimulation) as well as disruptive to thought processes. The individual must conscously resolve his constant restlessness and boredom with most life situations if he is to ever accomplish anything of lasting significance. He is prone to be driven to live moment-to-moment, does not like to plan far ahead, and thus normally is not goal-oriented. This type of T-Square can attract relationships whose conflicts center around contrasting ideas and opposing concepts about life. However, this tends to be energizing for the individual, since the mutable signs tend to be knowledge-gathering and eager to redistribute knowledge gained to others. Thus, this T-Square is often forced to work out its overload of nervous tension thru intellectual pursuits that require intensive study. The individual can feel driven to enlighten his society thru all forms of teaching. But normally, he lives in a continuous state of mental flux, resulting in vacillation and indecision about his direction. This quality keeps him on uncertain, non-committal terms with others until he learns to discipline and structure himself. He needs to define the purpose of his relationships if they are ever to stabilize. There is a tendency to spread oneself too thin by having too many intermittent interests to ever master any particular one. Even though marked versatility is indicated, there is also shown a lack of consistent or practical application of energy and effort. He is seldom stimulated long enough with any objective to insure its ultimate success. Like the Mutable Grand Square, flexibility tends to be a problem, encouraging him to adapt too readily to changing external conditions rather than holding firm and stabilizing. Life will teach him to face challenges head-on with more determination (since he tends to sidetrack matters he finds uncomfortable). At all times, mental challenges in life are essential for this T-Square to become a productive source of strength. (*Queen Elizabeth I - Francis Bacon - Friedrich Nietzche - Hermann Hesse - Erich Fromm - Manly P. Hall*).

DISSOCIATE T-SQUARE

When one of the planets of the T-Square falls in a different quality than the other two, the configuration becomes a Dissociate T-Square. Although any planet can be out-of-sign here, it is most significant when the apex planet is dissociate. With this condition, the underlying influences of

the *sextile* and *trine* are brought into play psychologically
for the individual, although this type of T-Square will
nevertheless function like the standard T-Square on the
situational level. Although the sextile and trine undertone
could represent the easing of internal pressures, allowing
the individual a bit more leeway as to how he can inwardly
respond to challenges he must meet, it also could suggest
that his psychological make-up has trouble relating to the
intense level of outer expression required of the T-Square.
He thus may feel less motivated to expend the necessary
amount of energy needed to overcome obstacles at hand.
Much depends upon the nature of the planets involved, and
especially the apex planet. Apex Saturn, for example, is
driven to work hard at surmounting obstacles with great
strength of effort and enduring patience, whereas Apex
Neptune is not. Therefore, even a Dissociate T-Square
pattern wouldn't weaken the drive of this Saturn very
much, while it could encourage Neptune to hope for
external forms of instant relief from stressful challenges.
Although the Dissociate T-Square requires needed
adjustments to be made in integrating inner attitudes with
outer realities, astrologers should not necessarily assume it
will manifest as a "weaker" T-Square (the same goes for all
dissociate configurations).

T-SQUARE INVOLVING ANGLES

When the T-Square is formed by two planets at different
points in the chart *plus* the ASC, I consider the
configuration to still be a valid T-Square. This can manifest
according to two patterns: two planets in opposition aspect
are squared by the ASC, or one planet opposes the ASC,
and both are squared by a second planet. I tend to feel that
the pattern having the ASC at the apex point is the more
dynamic of the two, since the two *planets* are in opposition
aspect to themselves (representing inner *urges* seeking
balanced awareness). A planet opposing the ASC is not
representative of the dynamic *exchange* of two urges, since,
the ASC technically does not describe an inner drive, but a
receptive point of intake. The ASC tends to be conditioned
by other factors in the chart, since it is actually part of a
house structure, whereas the basic drive or impulse of a

planet will always remain the same under any natal condition. Planets, being abstract life principles creating the framework of existence, *use* signs and houses to manifest themselves thru, but are not used by them. Signs describe only how a planet's drive might express thru attitudes and behavior, while houses only determine where this drive is likely to operate within an external field of experience. But signs and houses in no way alter that basic drive. Thus, while a planet (or sign) may condition the ASC, the ASC is not able to directly influence the planet. The same goes for the MC. This is at least how I view the situation.

Therefore, these two types of ASC-related T-Squares may operate "weaker" since they both lack the additional drive and force of a third planet. Both patterns direct whatever tension is generated towards the receptive ASC and relates it to the personal identity or self-image. Due to the stress indicated by the aspects made from the two planets, the physical condition of the individual may also be affected. Normally, *any* square to the ASC can sharply modify appearance or the body's general constitution according to the nature of the planet making the aspect, as well as coloring the individual's apparent temperament. Oppositions to the ASC do not seem to directly alter appearance or constitution, but instead tend to depict how the individual's overall personal presence is viewed by others, since oppositions deal more with *reflected* image. In general, T-Squares having the ASC at one point of their structure could be indicative of an "identity crisis." When the ASC is at the apex point, it receives *two* squares from the planets involved in opposition pattern. Any identity crisis here seems more acute and demanding of resolution. The individual will be forced to resolve internal conflicts (usually blockages) according to his own initiative. He learns to rebuild a new foundation of personal identity thru intensive self-confrontation. As he is normally very subjectively involved with the conflicts he experiences here, he is often unaware that they are self-generated for the most part. But once he is better able to transmute the inner tension indicated by these two squaring planets (suggesting that he also learns how to skillfully coordinate their opposition challenge), he may find himself less insecure, uncertain, or defensive about how others perceive him. Since the empty leg of this type of T-Square is at the DESC, the individual is to use the strengths gained thru self-awareness to help him relate to others more effectively. When the ASC functions as one end of the opposition, it receives only *one* square (from the apex planet) plus an opposition from the remaining planet. The individual still must first resolve the tension of the internalizing square before he can objectively integrate the opposing planet. With this type of T-Square, an identity crisis may be resolved quicker, since the drive indicated by that opposing planet urges him to focus outside of himself and interrelate (and usually, this opposing planet will be in the 7th house or at least conjunct the DESC, emphasizing relationship awareness). In addition, the empty leg is normally close to the MC, suggesting that the individual will need to direct his expression towards social involvement in the world.

When the T-Square is formed by the two planets at different points in the chart *plus* the MC, the individual may go thru a crisis involving his sense of "social identity." In this case, two planets in opposition aspect are both squared by the MC, or one planet opposing the MC and both are squared by the second planet. The dynamics involved are similar to what was said previously about the ASC-related T-Square. In general, the individual here is challenged to find his true place in the world in which he can contribute something meaningful to society. He is normally driven to accomplish and achieve in the eyes of others, who then will judge the quality of his effort. Due to the presence of the opposition aspect plus the MC, this type of T-Square suggests greater external awareness and objectivity concerning issues that need to be met (unless the apex planet also conjuncts the ASC). When the apex planet conjuncts the DESC, the theme of social identity is highly accentuated. In *How To Handle Your T-Square*, Tracy Marks details many factors of consideration that may be applied towards these types of T-Squares as well as standard ones. Please refer to her book for more information in this regard.

THE APEX PLANET

Because the apex planet determines how the individual is to essentially direct the energies of the T-Square, it gains added importance in the chart. It sometimes can indicate the general tone of the horoscope. The apex planet describes the manner in which the T-Square is to express its tension and eventually resolve its dilemma. This potent planet indicates the nature of thrust behind the T-Square's dynamics. When a Higher Octave planet is found at the apex point, it may represent a special karmic purpose. Individuals born under such a configuration are urged to express drives that challenge the existing structures of society, although sometimes in a way that becomes too reformative (thus disruptive) for the Establishment to understand and accept. This is particularly so if this T-Square falls solely in angular houses, giving the individual more strength of impact upon his environment for better or worse. An individual with a Higher Octave apex planet can make notable contributions to the world promoting its welfare and needed progress, while still remaining personally distant, unattached, or alienated from mundane activities in the mainstream of daily life. Those who evoke the lower manifestations of these experimental T-Squares, however, could become poorly integrated in society or generally unbalanced in their relationships. They may be unable to align themselves with others easily and could be viewed as social misfits. In all cases, the more self-aware the individual is, the more safely and humanely are these special T-Square configurations likely to be expressed.

It is often worthy to note if another's natal or progressed planets conjuncts either the apex planet or the empty leg degree, which could then trigger this configuration into active expression in the relationship. That other individual may establish a very stimulating, although challenging, union with the individual, helping him confront and work out many karmic lessons. Yet if not kept upon a constructive level, this relationship could also instigate greater conflicts that could sow the seeds for difficult karmic patterns in future incarnations (theoretically at least). Mismanagement of energies can at least be detrimental for both parties involved in this lifetime. It may also prove helpful to note how one's own progressed planets or transits crossing over the apex planet or empty leg degree affect the T-Square. For example, when a transiting planet moves over the apex planet (and I would only concern myself with Jupiter onward here), it first translates its message to that planet, often thru some inner disturbance. This internal conflict may then register thru a situational challenge described by the planets involved in the opposition in life areas shown by their house positions. If it is one of the base planets that is instead triggered first, the contact relays its signals back to the apex planet where the tension is then first felt. The apex planet will thus set off the entire T-Square. There may be a sort of delay process observed here in this case before the full opposition is activated, particularly with transits involving Saturn, the Higher Octaves, or planets in retrograde phase. My theoretical assumption here is that regardless of what point of the T-Square is receiving transit contact, energies must first work thru the apex planet before the entire configuration can be set into motion. This is why we should do our best to value the most positive expression of that planet as soon as we are able to in our lives, so that when our T-Square is triggered off, it is energized to act in a productive, stimulating manner rather than in a chaotic, disorganized way.

When a transiting planet conjuncts the empty leg degree or one of the two midpoints of the base planets, the T-Square can also be catalyzed into expression. A planet that fills up the empty leg space forms a temporary Grand Square which is, again, stimulated into action according to the nature of the apex planet and thru the motivation of that transiting (or progressed) planet. As even a temporary Grand Square has no particular strength of focus (unlike the T-Square which will always point us towards certain directives, compelling activity in a designated area of life), this period may seem for the individual to be an epidemic of problematic life encounters that appear almost unresponsive to any lasting resolution. This person at this critical time in life may be forced to develop detachment, spiritual poise, and greater objective awareness. This is a testing phase. The stimuli of the two oppositions, once constructively activated, can draw in experiences that can allow the individual to have extended awareness, deeper perception, fuller perspective, and mature insight into life matters he now must deal with. The individual will likely witness the cumulative effect of his internal disharmony to the degree that he has failed to instill the positive values of that apex planet into his consciousness. The following delineations concern the influence of each natal planet when operating at the apex point of the T-Square, unmodified by that planet's sign and house placement, or by the remaining two opposing planets:

APEX SUN

The Apex Sun denotes much willpower, an ingrained sense of authority, and a wholehearted urge to accomplish big things in an independent, self-displaying manner. Pride and ego are often problematic facets of the individual's make-up. Since the Sun represents one's essential purpose for being or the main theme of one's life, the individual's prime objectives are seldom easy for him to fulfill in a self-satisfying way until he learns to become less demanding and self-centered. This type of T-Square could be the hallmark of significant leadership ability, powerful creative direction, emphasized individualism, and recognized achievement when productively channeled. This incarnation is likely to be highly important for the individual in terms of soul growth thru the development of strength of character and integrity. Stress here is best worked out thru the proper exercise of will and ego assertion. The individual's desire for recognition and honor urges him to boldly demonstrate his capacity for accomplishment, but often in a manner that can be too self-seeking and overpowering to others. His confidence in himself needs to be kept in check with a measure of humility. Otherwise, it is seen as arrogance and self-glorification. Although he can be intensely self-reliant, he will be forced to allow others to assist him in the manner of *their* own choosing. His willfulness reinforces difficulties represented here and attracts power struggles with others. The more uncentered he is with himself, the more attention-grabbing he tends to become. Although he is able to command the attention of others due to his larger-than-life personality, he may seldom command their respect and love. (*Galileo - Yogananda - Bette Davis - Marlon Brando - Vanessa Redgrave - Dylan Thomas*).

If in a *Cardinal T-Square*, the apex Sun indicates head-strong impulses, willful self-assertion, undue self-confidence, and bossiness. The individual's upfront "me first" is very evident to others, since it is typically shown thru his direct actions. His natural urge is to take over immediate affairs with much self-assurance concerning his ability to direct such matters on his own. However, he wants to be allowed to have full charge and thus does not pay attention to the suggestions or demands of others. His uncooperative streak tends to put him in situations involving face-to-face, open conflict with people who are incensed by his air of authority. Thus, this position could indicate spirited aggression on the individual's part that antagonizes others he confronts. There is usually much vitality shown here plus the capacity to be wholeheartedly driven to accomplish in those areas that the individual personally finds appealing. However, this person may sometimes intimidate or exhaust others with his ceaseless energy, non-stop activity, and strength of enterprise.

If in a *Fixed T-Square*, the apex Sun suggests an individual who can be highly obstinant and willfully resistant to most outside influences. In attempting to fulfill his major, long-planned objectives in life, he is capable of mowing down all obstacles in his path by never accepting defeat or submitting to the demands of others. He is powerfully determined to succeed in his fixed goals, but tends to attract enduring power struggles in relationships due to his unyieldingness. He is apt to express his inner sense of authority and command with much force and steadiness, but will have to learn the value of adaptability in his personal unions if he is to benefit from any resources they can provide him. Self-sufficiency is usually emphasized here, enabling the individual to independently plod on until his objectives have reached the level of fruition desired. He is less likely to actively challenge outside authority in the manner of the Cardinal apex Sun, since he is generally less demonstrative with his expression of will and power. Yet he is more likely to carefully plan, organize his strengths, and slowly but surely undermine such authority if it becomes an obstacle to the fulfillment of his committed goals.

If in a *Mutable T-Square*, the apex Sun indicates an individual driven to receive significance, recognition, and praise from his social environment for his mental achievements. He wants to feel proud of his abilities here, but can run the risk of nervous over-strain and physical exhaustion if he wills himself to push too hard to know as much as possible. Mutable signs usually need periodic rest, due to their low level of stamina. The individual is less prone to follow a consistent course in life and thus may find his main objectives undergoing constant changes and modifications. However, since the Sun represents the centering urge and inner drives that are purposeful, the apex Sun here is less prone towards the aimless scattering of abilities typical of the Mutable T-Square (compared to Mercury, for example). This person can be very ego-involved with his thought processes and thus may be less objective about their true worth. He may overrate the powers of his mind, and attempt to demonstrate ideas and theories in a proud,conceited, or know-it-all manner (Galileo had a Mutable apex Sun, and his adherence to his astronomical beliefs in spite of the threat from opposing authorities cost him his life). This apex Sun can at least be intellectually head-strong and determined, regardless of whether one's concepts are irrational or logical. The individual feels strong about this thoughts, but needs to become a better listener.

When the tension of the apex Sun is resolved, the individual can stand out as being someone truly special. He may be highly admired and well-regarded by others, and often because he has used his strength and willpower to present something relevant to his community, society, or the world-at-large. He now has established a better sense of his own inner center and doesn't have to over-exert himself to make his presence known to others. He is best able to operate in any authoritative position, directing important affairs with more wisdom, creative power, inner dignity, and organizational skill. One who positively expresses an apex Sun can usually become a tower of strength and support for many. He learns how to apply, never impose, his will in a manner that enlivens, energizes, and encourages others to optimistically respond to his objectives. His vitality becomes a source of warmth and encouragement for those he intimately relates with. Undue self-pride becomes transformed into wholesome self-esteem. This apex position indicates a high potential for fame, acclaim, and honors from the world.

APEX MOON

The Apex Moon denotes a sensitive individual with a highly-charged, easily triggered emotional nature. Instincts are acutely alive and active, but due to the stress of this configuration, they tend to operate from a defensive pose. Security is very important for this self-protective person, who may tend to feel easily threatened. He normally is prone to overreact to external stress factors, in which he either puts up barriers that keep him at a safe distance, or else withdraws deeply into himself in an attempt to tune out tensions. The feeling nature is bound to be in a state of constant conflict or instability until this person makes a conscious attempt to objectively reprogram negative subconscious conditioning, often the result of vivid, misunderstood impressions from the past. Although he craves lasting psychological comfort and support in his intimate relationships, his needs tend to fluctuate too rapidly due to his hard to control mood swings. In general, he will be challenged to become less subjectively attached to others, less vulnerable, and less touchy about himself if internal friction here is to be reduced. The apex Moon normally does represent the potential for an unusually high degree of receptivity, which generally urges the individual to actively work in the public eye on some level where he can feel needed. His nurturing, caring ability is often very powerful although his need for self-nourishment may be equally intense. This configuration could denote high-strung relationships with the mother or mother principle, the family in general, or the basic female archetype. Interestingly enough, two of the examples I was able to find were very popular Hollywood "sex" symbols (representing the glamorization of the feminine principle). (*Greta Garbo - Jean Harlow - Gandhi - Martin Luther King - Oscar Wilde - Walt Disney*).

If in a *Cardinal T-Square*, the apex Moon suggests hair-trigger emotionality whose overt expression often can quickly change the immediate atmosphere of the individual's relationships. This person can easily take offense due to hypersensitivity and can readily change his own mood (especially if the Apex Moon operates in Aries or Cancer). He often subconsciously instigates the very changes in unions that he consciously tries to avoid or protect himself from. He feels driven to direct his vibrant emotions out towards his environment in a dynamic, unrestrained manner. This apex Moon tends to be the most spontaneous and impulsive in expression. Although highly responsive and sensitively tuned in to the here-and-now, this person will need to exert greater self-discipline or control in the manner in which he vents his feelings. This can be better accomplished once he allows himself to feel what he feels more deeply, to reflect upon the reason behind his reactions, and to deliberate before he outwardly responds to these feelings, since he often lives on the raw surface of his emotions and is too eager to push uncomfortable impressions away from himself, back out into the external environment. Thus, his feelings are usually poorly-assimilated.

If in a *Fixed T-Square*, the apex Moon indicates one with inflexible emotional needs that can create great intensity on the subconscious level. Instinctive habits are deep-rooted in the individual's nature and are seldom open to change or modification. Inner defenses here may operate contrary to his consciously expressed feelings due to hard to objectify blockages (the "why do I overeat when I'm depressed" type of inner conflict). Emotional tensions are held onto tightly or are rigidly expressed, creating further disturbance. Possessiveness in general can be a problem, since the individual tends to psychologically attach himself to whatever becomes a valued security symbol. He may even be inclined to tenaciously cling to negative impressions and store them inside for long periods of time before life forces him to release these security-thwarting attitudes. The Fixed Apex Moon is suggestive of emotional stamina, but the individual will need to evaluate the purpose of enduring or persisting with reactions that are stifling or congestive towards the fulfillment of inner comfort. He lacks detachment and adaptability and thus tends to get stuck in the past, vividly reenergizing conditions that no longer exist in the present. Life will force him to undergo periodic emotional house-cleanings so that he can become free from burdensome psychological attachments. The tendency to over-control the outward expression of emotional discomfort creates pent-up forces on the subconscious level that eventually vent in an explosive manner that is apt to destroy outer securities.

If in a *Mutable T-Square*, the apex Moon denotes a high degree of emotional changeability, creating restless moods plus a craving for new and varied stimuli to appease feelings for the moment. The individual may find it easy and desirable to rationalize emotions or simply over-analyze them from surface point of view. He is normally at least driven to remove himself temporarily from his feelings and observe them as something separate from himself. While normally such detachment is beneficial for one's emotional growth and maturity, it here is more representative of a self-protective attempt to escape from directly dealing with the real impact of emotional conflict. This person can vacillate, waver, contradict himself, and often remain on-the-fence when it comes to establishing emotional commitments. Plus he may try too hard to intellectually interpret his basis for feeling rather than merely accept the fact that he is feeling something valid, even if it appears to make no sense at the time. A major problem with the Mutable apex Moon is that it often lacks depth of sensitivity to pick up upon subtle undercurrents in relationships and this is prone towards superficial response (this is less so when the Moon falls in Pisces, but very much so when it is placed in Gemini). The individual will be pressured according to the overall dynamics of the T-Square to learn how to comfortably absorb, retain, and assimilate the feelings of others rather than discount their significance. By doing so, he may be even better able to understand the meaning of his own responses with greater clarity.

When the tension of the apex Moon is resolved, the individual is able to feel more creative with his emotionality. This may render him extremely well-suited to sensitively deal with the public or the masses in general, resulting in much popularity and success in his chosen direction. Because he now can establish a more open, easy-flowing connection with his own inner feelings, he can have a marked outer effect on the emotional nature of others. He thus may have a gift for being able to nurture, care, soothe, and support the welfare of the weaker or the downtrodden. His influence here is calming, gentle, and protective, suggesting that he could excel in all branches of the healing arts, the social services, or work that involves intimate rapport with those who need help and assistance. He can also encourage others to tap into their own security needs, helping them become more receptive to their inner support systems. This individual can influence the masses to nourish its collective sensibilities in a manner that can help establish a greater foundation of kinship.

APEX MERCURY

The Apex Mercury depicts one with an ongoing drive to learn a dynamic skill, technique, or intelligent body of knowledge that enables him to expressively communicate to others in life. This individual is apt to focus much attention in educational or scholarly matters where he can energetically expend much mental or verbal energy. Usually, his mentality is highly stimulative and curious, but is seldom at rest. This person is normally continuously preoccupied with his thoughts in an analytical, discerning manner and actively seeks out mental challenges that are thought-provoking or even controversial. It is his critical

attitude that is often a main source of his relationship
problems, along with an ability to rationalize his behavior in
close unions to the point that he fails to comprehend his own
subtler motivations. He needs to stay in touch with his
feeling nature, his gut-level instincts, and his intuitive
hunches if he is to understand life from a greater level of
depth and perception. While his evaluations of the surface
conditions of current affairs may be highly intelligent,
clever, and keenly observant, he tends to lack the warmth,
sympathy, and depth of understanding needed to unify his
concepts in a manner that allows him to feel one with the
world. He tends to feel apart from that which he is
compelled to scrutinize. In addition, he often has difficulty
comprehending other-worldly intangibles that operate
beyond the normal level of reason. And if he does accept
abstract reality, he still feels driven to reduce it to limited
concrete terms that only he is able to express. (*Aldous
Huxley - Herman Melville - W. H. Auden - Richard Wagner -
Wilhelm Reich - Billy Graham*).

If in a *Cardinal T-Square*, apex Mercury accelerates the
mental processes, heightening the individual's ability to
quickly comprehend data. It is sign of a fast, energetic
learner. However, the individual has strong impulses to
immediately apply what he learns without much
deliberation or forethought. His tendency to make snap
decisions or jump to mental conclusions before studying all
necessary details encourages him to take actions that are
poorly planned and often premature in their execution.
Cardinal Apex Mercury is prone to have direct
communication problems with others that are openly
confronted, and usually because of its assertive, impatient
approach toward matters. The nervous temperament of
Mercury is here at its most acute, agitated state. The
individual himself is apt to be too easily activated and
aroused by his own thoughts to give his full attention to
those of others for any length of time. His mind is too busy
racing ahead of itself to allow for careful reflection and
thorough analysis.

This person needs to slow down and organize himself before
he speaks, since relationship friction here is often due to his

thoughtless, outspoken manner. This is especially so if Mercury falls in Aries or Cancer (both fire and water are volatile due to emotional undertones) but less so in controlled Capricorn or diplomatic Libra. In general, the individual tends to thrust his ideas out towards the world and needs outlets enabling him to vigorously communicate as well as use his mind to decide on issues needing quick resolution. This Mercury could represent the executive mind able to work under hectic, fast-paced conditions requiring last-minute changes of plans.

If in a *Fixed T-Square*, apex Mercury denotes one who does not like to have his thoughts challenged or modified by others. This individual is hard to impress or influence mentally, due to the strong resistance ability of the fixed mode. He tends to over-value his own thoughts and can be very one-tracked in how he applies them. He needs to be careful not to allow his resourceful mind to fall into rigid, rut-bound patterns since Fixed Apex Mercury can readily become narrow-minded, dogmatic, and too absolute in its thought processes. Life will teach him that his mind has the power to deeply affect others, but it can also shut him off from expanding his conscious understanding of matters due to his stubborn adherence to his opinionated attitudes.

His mental endurance can be phenomenal along with his concentration ability, and is better applied when tackling complex studies, detailed work, or projects requiring long-range planning and organization. Obstacles in these areas that appear to thwart or block his progress are likely to occur due to his inflexible, unadaptable approach. He may become too single-minded to recognize options and alternatives that could benefit the actualization of his mental objectives. Being willful on the mental level, he can attempt to enforce his ideas upon others while remaining unaffected by their feedback. This typically creates barriers in communication, with others normally resenting his overbearing manner and apparent disregard for their viewpoints.

If in a *Mutable T-Square*, apex Mercury emphasizes mental changeability, leading to nervousness and a lack of concentration. The individual can easily scatter his attention by becoming too mentally caught up in minor matters that distract him from his more important objectives. He feels driven to know a little bit about everything that momentarily stimulates his interest and can be highly inquisitive, but lacks the discrimination required to know what is actually relevant and what is inconsequential. Life will teach him how to use his mind more selectively, so that he does not fritter away his energies in a useless, nonproductive manner. Although normally very alert, observant, and able to learn a wide gamut of subjects, he finds it hard to discipline his mental faculties whereby he can effectively stick to one topic of interest until he attains a thorough, in-depth understanding. Thus, his comprehension of things can be shallow, since he merely skims the surface.

His lack of focus and centering could make him fidgety, irritable, disorganized, and even disoriented from time to time. This may be less so when Apex Mercury falls in Virgo, being a more stabilizing earth sign. However, it can prove quite problematic in diffusive Pisces. Change and variety are very stimulating for this person, but he can be very flighty in his unions and may cleverly avoid long-term commitments. Conflicts in relationships may be due to his lack of common sense, consistency, or depth. This Apex Mercury best directs its mental skills in areas where versatility and diversity are required. Talents are only wasted or not brought to their full potential when the individual refuses to apply his mind with more steadiness and patience. In general, he tends to worry, fret, remain indecisive, and talk more than act.

When the tensions of this T-Square have been resolved, the individual is better able to harness his above-average mental powers and wisely apply them in areas that involve dynamic communication, teaching, training, or the distribution of specialized information. Verbal fluency and/or manual dexterity can become important to his success, as well as his ability to efficiently handle relevant details. The individual may feel driven to impart knowledge to others he relates to and can be very stimulating in his relationships. He becomes a more willing student of life and has a constructive interest in sharing what he has learned. And what he has learned is normally of redeeming social value. His mind becomes a more flexible tool for promoting a fuller understanding of his world, and can analyze matters with true objectivity, logic, clarity, and intelligent perspective. And best of all, he is able to establish peace of mind now that he knows how to center his creative mental energies.

APEX VENUS

The Apex Venus describes an individual with a strong social drive and an active need to become more aware of people. Yet this person may feel basically unloved, unappreciated, or even unfairly treated in his intimate one-to-one relationships. Usually, he has values that are not compatible with those he attracts, creating emotional tensions and a feeling of inequality. Marriage is apt to pose challenging problems and normally centers around themes of give-and-take, free sharing, and reciprocal action. The individual usually wants to become involved in an ideal partnership free of conflict, tension, and challenging open confrontation. He craves peace and harmony in his unions, but often tries to secure this by blocking any potential for dynamic interaction. The result is that his relationships tend to have a static, unstimulating quality that often proves frustrating to his partners.

Apex Venus desires constant satisfaction and expects things to come the easy way without effort or struggle. If not careful, the individual can become lazy, passive, and too complacent to initiate the critical changes in his life that need to be undertaken. He has trouble being self-starting and leans upon others too heavily during difficult times. Frustration here can evoke an indulgent streak, in which the individual attempts to saturate himself in pleasure pursuits in a futile effort to relieve the pain and pressure of his inner stress. Sometimes, financial problems can occur due to his poor evaluative ability or impractical tastes. (*Toulouse-Lautrec - Claude Monet - George Sand - Irving*

Berlin - Anais Nin - Margaret Mead).

If in a *Cardinal T-Square*, apex Venus denotes an individual
who pushes too hard to attract others, gain their immediate
approval or acceptance, and generally solicit their aid or
support in the instigation of his current interests. He needs
to learn how to share with others and patiently cooperate
with their needs in a manner that is mutually agreeable.
Otherwise, he is apt to come on like an opportunist. New
developments are always occurring in his associations
which are normally exciting, dynamic, but openly
challenging in nature. There is a great temptation to jump
into unions impulsively and quickly expend affectional
interest in a short period of time because of head-on
emotional clashes, aggressive behavior, or arguments
stemming from inconsiderate actions. This is especially true
when Venus is in Aries and/or Mars or Uranus is one of the
base planets. This drive to leap before looking into
partnerships has to be kept in check.

The individual will have to learn to carefully evaluate the
pros and cons in a more practical manner before making
quick commitments he may later regret. He can show a
marked ability to deal with the public in a vibrant,
energetic manner that sparks their interest and
involvement. This can be an excellent configuration for one
who has to direct and coordinate the activities of others.

If in a *Fixed T-Square*, apex Venus indicates an individual
whose set, inflexible values stifle partnerships. He is
determined to have his way in his unions and sometimes
forces issues that only stir up conflict and resentment from
others due to his lack of compromise. Relationships often
end up in rut-patterns, going nowhere or progressing too
slowly to be of mutual value. But this person's willful
persistence urges him to emotionally hang on to a
relationship even if it proves intensely frustrating, rather
than allow it to undergo radical change or dissolve
altogether. There is often a detrimental possessive streak
shown here, plus a not-too-obvious fear of initiating new
encounters (perhaps because of their unknown factors).

Fixed Apex Venus is the least sociable and easy-going of them all, and is seldom motivated to be accommodating. The individual can enforce too tight a grip upon those he concentrates his steady attention upon in a manner that can make them feel trapped. Yet, paradoxically, he will struggle to retain his own independence, autonomy, and freedom of expression in his relationships. If Pluto is one of the base planets (plus if Venus falls in Scorpio), obsessive concern with the partner is emphasized along with deep-rooted jealousy or manipulation. Fixed Apex Venus can feel inhibited and self-blocked, and does not warm up to people until much time has passed and others have been sufficiently tested.

If in a *Mutable T-Square*, apex Venus pinpoints an individual who can be fickle in love and not too certain of what he values in relationships. He can be especially restless in one-to-one involvements that do not allow for periodic separations and space to emotionally breathe. The ability to come and go without restraint or complaint from others is important to this individual. Yet this often becomes a prime source of nagging agitation and constant criticism from his partners. Mutable Apex Venus describes the social butterfly who appears pleasant, congenial, and comfortable with all he relates with on a general basis. But he cannot readily attach himself to any particular partner and sustain his attraction for long without feeling claustrophobic.

Although the quest for an ideal love that fulfills one's mental values can be strong, this person seldom shows any enduring interest in the real love partners in his life, unless Saturn is one of the base planets. With Saturn involved, the individual works a bit harder at resolving conflicts before giving up. But even mutable Saturn tied in here suggests that the individual doesn't easily settle down in any union without at least putting it thru innumerable tests (especially on the communication level). Of course, this is typical of Venus square Saturn anyway. This individual appreciates relationships filled with sparkle, enthusiasm, variety, and intellectual stimulation. Yet he will still need to develop greater emotional depth and sensitive understanding.

When the tension of this T-Square has been resolved, it enables the individual to make significant contributions in all areas involving interpersonal affairs. He may find himself satisfying his need for ideal self-expression in the fine arts, cultural interests, general esthetic fields, social affairs, public relations work, or even legal, judicial channels (since he now is more in balance with himself and can better view life with greater impartiality and perspective). His awareness of people is enhanced and elevated, along with his ability to positively value, appraise, and love himself and others. He then interacts with people more diplomatically and with a greater sense of fair-play. In return, others are more encouraged to cooperate with him and assist with his valued personal objectives.

APEX MARS

The Apex Mars depicts a strong-willed individual with an intensified drive to act independently on his own behalf, always dynamically being in immediate control of his personal affairs at all times. This person often has head-strong urges and is capable of meeting up with direct interpersonal challenges without giving up or weakening his stance. Yet his normally assertive, aggressive temperament can become a major source of antagonism and conflict in his close partnerships due to his self-centered actions. He tends to energize and activate others to the degree that they either feel impelled to carry out his desires, or actively fight back.

This individual can become a subject of heated controversy. He is impatient with standard ways of doing things and often bucks all established authorities in favor of doing his own thing. He can be highly physical in his expression, full of vim and vigor. He is capable of exhibiting a dare-devil, bold approach to life, initiating objectives with energetic thrust. However, life will force him to re-evaluate the martial manner in which he tackles his exclusive, self-absorbed interests. The individual does best when assuming leadership roles, initiating pioneering projects, working strictly for himself, or directing activities requiring will-in-action for the sake of enterprising new and dynamically eventful activities. (*J. S. Bach - Thomas Jefferson - Ernest Hemingway - Muhammed Ali - Indhira Gandhi - G. A. Nasser*).

In a *Cardinal T-Square*, apex Mars reacts to opposition in a highly acute manner, often openly attacking whatever it confronts. The individual can act out his immediate desires in an impulsive but disruptive manner. He is apt to see himself as having enough courage, strength, and spirited drive for ten people (especially ten Grand Triners!) and normally has no trouble asserting himself. But luckily, Apex Mars operating thru this mode is more concerned with doing things rather than stubbornly resisting people, since cardinality means action and movement. It also emphasizes a will-to-dare obstacles in the environment, and therefore has a tendency to energize itself when operating under dangerous but challenging conditions (less physically but more psychologically so when Mars is in Cancer or Libra).

However, there is bound to be stormy, head-on collisions with others until this individual can better redirect his unbridled tensions into constructive effort-oriented endeavors. Normally, he has little staying power and thus does more favorably when plunging into active work that does not require long periods of attention. Or else he works in spurts. Physical, athletic movement is almost a must for this person to effectively release the high level of (sexual) tension he experiences. He needs to attract demanding activity allowing him to vent his aggressive energies in a healthy manner.

In a *Fixed T-Square*, apex Mars denotes a head-strong individual who can conserve his vital energy resources, enabling him to endure all hardships, setbacks, and outer obstacles with much determination while still plodding on until he finally secures his personal objectives. He is rarely prone to accept modification of his plans of action due to any external pressure. Instead, he can show a dogged, single-minded persistence in acting out his calculated urges, regardless of how challenging opposing forces present themselves. This can be the bull-dozer type who slowly but surely pushes anyone or anything out of his path that prevents or blocks him from moving closer toward his goals. The sheer one-tracked force of his self-driven actions can overwhelm or exhaust all opposing sides.

His strength of conviction tends to intimidate those who attempt to stand in his way. He can consolidate his will and refuse to give in and compromise, which thus becomes problematic in relationships. Life will teach him the value of becoming more yielding and adaptable. This person needs to realize that he has a hard time sharing his power and ability to control with others, and therefore should make a special, *conscious* attempt to acquiesce whenever he inwardly feels intensely resistant. Nevertheless, there is a marked ability for executive power (especially with Mars in Scorpio), giving the individual a talent for building mighty structures and directing complex organizations with self-assurance and confidence.

In a *Mutable T-Square*, apex Mars indicates an individual who tends to restlessly scatter or diffuse his *dynamic* nervous energy, yet often in a disorganized manner that accomplishes little of lasting worth due to the inconsistency of his efforts. Focus will be needed here if he is to be able to complete one task at a time before impulse urges him to veer off into other unrelated activities. This configuration denotes one who has a vibrant, stimulating approach towards mental activities that are typically of immediate self-concern. However, the stress involved with the T-Square pattern in general could imply a nervy, high-strung disposition too much prone towards mental irritability to efficiently settle down and work long and hard.

Usually, the main problem is that boredom, distraction, and intermittent attention prevents this apex Mars from becoming whole-hearted in its energy expenditure. Although the individual is stimulated to initiate a wide range of enterprising activities, he will need to coordinate himself intelligently, since well-managed mutable energy helps us connect and assemble energies with practical versatility. The individual normally needs (mental) rest periods in order to revitalize himself. If this is not recognized, then he is apt to expend nervous energy to the point of exhaustion or incompetency (especially if Mars falls in Gemini or Virgo).

When the tension of this T-Square has been resolved, the individual is able to initiate action in the proper, well-planned manner that insures effective results. His personal efforts prove successful due to the constructive, creative manner of their execution. This person is better able to inaugurate changes or new starts that are pioneering and refreshing, plus that which he straightforwardly initiates tends to invigorate others in a manner in which they assert themselves productively. His dynamic thrust of vital energy stimulates rather than repels others. Impulse to act is balanced with awareness of the consequences of action. This individual finds himself well-suited for being in charge of activities that energize social enterprise. While he still tends to want to head any project, he is now able to vitally express his drive in a manner that instigates new beginnings for those he acts for.

APEX JUPITER

The Apex Jupiter suggests an individual who becomes actively involved in the ongoing search for greater meaning in life, and who naturally approaches worldly affairs from a broadened, philosophical point of view. He is driven to subjectively question the rightness of current attitudes towards social morality, religious orthodoxy, ethics, and political theory. Life *encourages* but does not force him (due to the benevolence principle of Jupiter, even under the intense pressure of a T-Square) to learn tolerance, acceptance, and charitability in this lifetime if he is to develop a personal belief system that does not have to be defended from social attack. Thus, thru the development of wisdom, he will find that he does not need to moralize or proselytize in order to communicate his personal faith to others. Nevertheless, a mismanaged Apex Jupiter over-promotes all personal causes too loudly, using poor judgement or a lack of common sense. In addition, this individual is susceptible towards unrecognized self-aggrandizement.

While his prime concern is the upgrading and enrichment of his own life, he also tries to uplift and enlighten others thru his special capacity to inspire according to his personal social vision of how things *could* potentially be. Current actualities are less important to him. Life often ushers him into adopting the role of a natural teacher or general spokesman for the ethical, educational, political, or spiritual direction of his community, society, or world-at-large. But he will need to also practice what he preaches, since Jupiter can easily recognize an ideal social model but often is too undisciplined to become a prime example of that idealized model. Therefore, this individual tends to have an internal struggle trying to effectively apply the idealistic concepts he freely espouses, regardless of his sincerity. Nevertheless, he shows an above-average urge to broadcast his revelations on a large-scale basis regardless of his own personal short-comings. (*Oliver Cromwell - Immanuel Kant - Annie Besant - Eleanor Roosevelt - Madelyn Murray O'Hair - Jimmy Carter*).

In a *Cardinal T-Square*, the individual tends to approach his self-driven quest for understanding higher truth in an energetic, vigorous manner. He can show much zeal and fervor here. In his search for outlets allowing him a personal sense of expansion, this person can be very aggressive and headstrong. He is apt to become highly impatient with social restrictions imposed upon him by his environment and tends to want to confront such limitations openly and directly. Due to the initiating drive of the cardinal mode, the individual could channel his inspirational energies into areas requiring social leadership. He can be the pioneering type who can reveal fresh new concepts concerning social growth, and can charismatically awake the sleeping masses. Yet he is likely to experience short-lived enthusiasms and has trouble sustaining his faith over long periods of time.

On a more personal level, Cardinal Apex Jupiter denotes impractical impulsiveness that unwisely encourages this individual to over-extend himself in many areas without first reflecting upon his realistic capacity to properly manage such activities. He optimistically considers the immediate benefits shown in any enterprise, but seldom has the foresight to envision the long-range consequences. This Apex Jupiter is likely to be the most physically active, and thus travel is normally a natural outlet for the expression of the individual's exuberant energies. Although he is driven to look far ahead into the future with much self-confidence and enthusiasm, life will teach him to use better judgement in trying to improve his own social condition here-and-now.

If in a *Fixed T-Square*, apex Jupiter describes an individual whose social ideals have more long-range application and are more persistently pursued. He is less prone towards broadcasting his own faith and beliefs with the ongoing missionary zeal of the more crusading Cardinal Apex Jupiter. Yet his broader theories or philosophy of life tends to be as opinionated and dogmatic as those he stubbornly resists. He can benefit his own inner growth immensely by becoming more open-minded, flexible, and eclectic in his world-view. If not, his intensity and one-trackness (fixed mode) coupled with Jupiter's innate confidence and sense of ultimate rightness could manifest as bigotry and prejudice. The rigid, emotional orientation of the willful fixed quality here could be suggestive of intolerance concerning the belief systems of others that are contrary to those he unquestionably values.

As fixed signs are prone to accumulate resources and retain power rather than freely disperse it out towards the environment, this type of individual is often overly-indulgent, immoderate, and excessive in his expectations (normally wanting too much of a good thing and feeling little inclination to curb his expanded sensual appetites). Being more habit-bound and hard to change, this individual's ability to dissipate and waste vital energy can result in inertia and dullness of the senses. In general, this Apex Jupiter seeks expansion and extended control in financial areas or investments, and is prone towards having much faith in its wheeling-and-dealing potential. Although he tends to overcommit himself, this individual has the stamina to endure in all activities he firmly believes in.

If in a *Mutable T-Square*, apex Jupiter can denote a "guru chaser," or one who enthusiastically flits from one ideal, theory or philosophy to another rather restlessly. Inspiration here is basically mental, but is usually not directly acted upon in the manner of Cardinal Apex Jupiter. Nor is it sustained as productively as Fixed Apex Jupiter. The urge to have instant wisdom, speedy enlightenment, or special social benefits and privileges without having to exert much effort to merit them is often a central problem for the individual. His false hopes in receiving betterment without having to struggle and earn it usually leaves him constantly disillusioned, disenchanted, and aimless. It may be hard for him to sustain his faith in matters or commit himself to ideologies over an extended period of time. Jupiter's natural urge to wander and explore is further emphasized by the variety-seeking mutable mode. However, this roving spirit prevents the individual from establishing security with others. Irresponsibility and indecisiveness often triggers partnership conflicts that the individual tends to ignore, side-track, or wish-away. The vacillation tendency of the mutable quality can be amplified here.

The individual's inner drive for freedom and expansion causes him to seek constant variations in his associations, in which he wants to be casual and informal rather than structured. As a result, he tends to establish few, if any, long-term unions requiring lasting commitment. However, if this T-Square is used constructively, it can mark the development of an exceptional teacher, spiritual guide, intelligent administrator, or enlightened political spokes-man for the populace. The individual is better able to clearly translate and promote his acquired insight and wisdom with much versatility, adaptability, and even a sense of humor (quite often a necessary asset for spiritual growth). His tolerance allows him to openly and sincerely respond to all levels of social mentality.

When the tension of this T-Square has been resolved, the individual is more specifically motivated to contribute a philanthropic benefit or whole-heartedly support the progress of a socially-elevating cause. He aspires to bring his community or the world-at-large closer to fulfilling a collective ideal. Due to Jupiter's inclination to provide big opportunities that often extend one's social influence in life, fame and notable praise or recognition may result (even if not consciously sought after by the individual). His entire life then seems protected and further nourished by benevolent higher forces. He appears to be blessed and somewhat sanctified. Every true need can be provided for by the generosity and kindness of others he contacts. Meanwhile, he can joyously administer the moral and ethical nutrients needed to inspire others to improve and upgrade their social consciousness. He can play an important part in helping others understand the creative life principles guiding human evolution along a path of even greater inner enrichment.

APEX SATURN

The Apex Saturn indicates an individual who takes a practical, realistic approach towards establishing serious, long-term objectives in life. However, he often first must undergo delays and setbacks while still striving to gain recognition, social prominence, professional success, and general respect from others. Life forces this person to understand the wisdom of patience, proper planning, timing, and maturity. Ambition is likely to be an overwhelming motivation for this individual, who normally starts off in life feeling frustrated, held-back, and fearful of exposing any personal inadequacy to others (or even himself). Self-doubt and discouragement tend to block him from smoothly relating to others who otherwise could help him structure his aims early in life. He is apt to appear on guard, highly reserved, painfully self-conscious, and generally distrustful of intimacy in his encounters. Although attempting to protect himself from vulnerability by controlling others, he is also inclined to utilize their practical resources for the attainment of his concrete goals, which could eventually become abusive.

The pressure of responsibility typical to this T-Square often drives this individual to function in key positions of power, control, management, supervision, and all regulatory activities in which he can exercise authority over others. He often has a special capacity here that needs to be evoked and used sensibly. His above-average talent for organizing matters and formulating plans according to large-scale goals can be very effective when channeled in business enterprise. In addition, he can shrewdly calculate his moves and exert a high degree of discipline and self-control whenever required. However, due to his intensified need for ego-fortification, it is difficult for him to relax, feel at ease, and become expressive in close relationships. He tends to avoid or low-key unions where warmth, tenderness, or demonstrative lovingness are expected of him. Instead, he attempts to rule and command with an iron fist. Generally, this person must trust more and share himself with others upon a deeper, sensitive level. (*Theodore Roosevelt - Chaing Kai-Shek - Charles De Gaulle - Fidel Castro - Hugh Hefner - Lyndon Johnson*).

In a *Cardinal T-Square*, apex Saturn denotes an individual who often experiences *acute* frustration, anxiety, and apprehension due to the outer resistances he directly meets whenever he pushes too hard for immediate achievement. Life seems at first to deny fulfillment in his self-driven personal activities, creating periods of great pressure and discouragement. Still, the energy contained within this T-Square helps to fortify this individual's vital ambition, enabling him to dynamically confront difficult challenges head-on until he successfully defeats his opposition. Under critical periods in his life, he is normally able to focus and direct his managerial powers towards controlling issues needing immediate resolution.

Executive ability is very well-developed here as a rule. However, the assertive tendency of the impatient cardinal mode suggests a certain domineering, takeover quality in which the individual demands total supervision over all activities he personally initiates. He is quick to resent anyone who attempts to directly interfere with his plans of action, or who slows down the momentum of his plans. Nevertheless, he is usually lacking in staying power (even with enduring Saturn involved) and may have to apply greater self-control and patience in order to stick to plans that demand thorough organization and time to structure themselves properly. If his self-generated plans of action are delayed or postponed temporarily, it is teaching him to more carefully consider the long-term consequences of his here-and-now objectives.

In a *Fixed T-Square*, apex Saturn denotes an individual who can be rigidly organized, intensely purposeful, but willfully unyielding or resistant to the nth degree. There is suggested here a fixated, almost compulsive drive to establish lasting security and safety thru exercising tight controls over people and situations. The individual is one-pointedly determined to preserve the structure and order he values whenever possible. He desires to totally overpower and manipulate all matters under his authority and is unlikely to willingly share the control seat with others. It is probable that at some time he has consistently subjugated others in past lives to explicitly carry out his orders, and now experiences great internal conflict whenever challenged to surrender his indomitable will to another. Doggedly, he seeks to always have the upper hand in life, and can become somewhat ruthless in how he calculates to secure power.

Although usually uncompromising and obstinate, this person can become a reliable fortress of strength for others during crises, and seldom will back down from duties and obligations he is prone to concentrate his enduring attention upon. He can endure all struggles and persistently hang on until his well-defined aims are achieved. He may feel it is his sole responsibility to build permanent foundations and consolidate them with exceeding care, and thus is able to patiently work long and hard to attain tangible results. Nevertheless, he will have to become less absolute in his ambitions and less dictatorial in his relationships. His defensive inhibitions are apt to draw him into partnerships that are emotionally stifling for all parties involved.

In a *Mutable T-Square*, apex Saturn demands more discipline of mental interests and less scattering of nervous energy. Life is to force this individual to learn how to concentrate his intellectual energies and apply them in a practical manner with greater discernment and selectivity. This can actually become a very beneficial T-Square for mutable Saturn. The individual often experiences frustration and insecurity in many areas of communication until he works hard at developing proper focus and direction. Ambitions here can ultimately be geared towards profound mental achievements, in which the individual eventually becomes expert at carefully constructing mature thought-systems that can make an enduring impression upon social consciousness. However, he first must work at ridding himself of negative, pessimistic attitudes to prevent his concepts from becoming too narrow or cynical.

This pattern normally depicts the overly-rational skeptic who mistrusts the power of the imagination or the emotions. He tends to have to make a great personal effort to establish an educational background he feels secure with, since he typically fears or is embarrassed about appearing inept in areas he is mentally serious about. Life will present him with challenges involving authoritative positions that emphasize the dispersal or distribution of purposeful data and specialized information. He is to discipline himself to organize or synthesize the knowledge he patiently gathers. Mutable Apex Saturn is excellent for scientific work, technological studies, or scholarly analysis which all demand painstaking detail-consciousness. Once he can harness and control the versatile powers of his mind, he is capable of masterful technique in all areas of mental creativity.

When the tension of this T-Square has been resolved, the individual is keenly ambitious to undertake serious duties and social obligations without resorting to power plays, control tactics, or overbearing domination of others. His consistent efforts towards the building of true law, order, and justice within his existing society are highly respected by others. His display of personal authority and leadership indicates much integrity, strength of character, and fairness to those who judge him. Obstacles are now met without fear, discouragement, or a self-defeating sense of inadequacy. Responsibility in intimate and social relationships is never avoided or ignored, but approached with a level of maturity and constructive self-control that enables all involved to better structure their purpose for involvement. The individual can achieve an important and timely position in life due to his earnest, unselfish efforts at helping to solidify collective goals. His diligent devotion towards serious world issues can inspire him to organize his own strengths and priorities. In addition, he learns to share more of himself in intimate partnerships without trying to thwart the spontaneous expression of others. His inner foundation is so strong and hard to shake that he becomes less compelled to prevent others from having a deep impact upon himself.

APEX URANUS

The Apex Uranus indicates an individual who can act as a social catalyst for collective reform and general social progress. He often feels a strong inner drive to instigate sudden and radical disruption of the current status quo. He is urged to promote needed social awakening, according to how he perceives this need. However, the tremendous energies implied by this powerful T-Square pattern often pressure him to behave in too extreme or socially explosive a manner to comfortably attune himself to others. Apex Uranus denotes an above-average capacity to experience an enormous overload of nervous-electrical tension, resulting in a high-strungness requiring a vast amount of stimulating mental outlets to prevent the inclination towards violent, destructive action from manifesting. The urge to break down and shatter whatever impedes the individual from actualizing his unique ideals or aspirations is exceptionally strong and needs controlling.

When mismanaged, this pattern often marks the social misfit who is willfully out-of-tune with the established order of his current environment. He here tends to be a law-unto-himself type who defensively detaches his will from all outer pressures. Although highly self-willed and unpredictable, this magnetic individual can be very intuitive concerning other people and may use his insight to expose their human frailties to themselves in a manner that compels them to radically alter their lifestyle. His ability to penetrate outer structures and reach deeper facets of truth can be phenomenal at times. Constructively, this individual can become the much needed social visionary who possesses the charismatic power to liberate the mass consciousness from obsolete collective patterns of expression. (*Emily Bronte - Thomas Becket - Winston Churchill - Rudolph Steiner - Gurdjieff - Jim Jones*).

In a *Cardinal T-Square*, apex Uranus points toward a highly impatient, overly-stimulated individual who energetically throws himself into the self-proclaimed role of social activist or head crusader for some current group cause or mass movement. He is at least prone to want to spearhead his vision of progress in all personal relationships. However, due to the abruptness of his self-generated actions, he tends to alienate or intimidate those he imposes his aggressive reform upon. While he is apt to pursue his goals with much vigor, straightforwardness, and even excitement, he tends to make sudden moves that logically appear inconsistent and contrary to the plans already set into motion. When mismanaged, Cardinal Apex Uranus denotes lawlessness, social defiance, and one who can impulsively disrupt and unsettle the organization of any group endeavor. This is especially so if Mars is also involved as a base planet in this T-Square, intensifying the potential for wayward, self-generated impulse or reckless personal action. While Saturn tied into this configuration could provide a measure of restraint and self-control, it also implies a dangerous build-up of active, compressed pressure that eventually must vent itself in an authoritarian manner.

As the cardinal mode thrives upon change and movement in the outer world, and as Uranus is driven towards radical reform, Apex Uranus here can constructively denote the social innovator, freedom fighter, or active experimentalist who can evoke collective mental archetypes that inaugurate sweeping social changes within existing world structures. On the other hand, it could also represent the outer-fringe rebel whose compulsive, socially-directed activities shock and jolt established conventions. Cult leader Jim Jones' Cardinal Apex Uranus squared his natal Saturn (in Capricorn) opposing Pluto, suggesting an inordinate need to control others according to highly personal insights seldom shared by others. The need for ultimate management is further indicated by the natal presence of both Saturn *and* Pluto.

In a *Fixed T-Square*, apex Uranus indicates an individual who can be a determined law-unto-himself type. This uniquely self-willed individualist can mentally detach himself from the influence of others and instead independently pursue his own original course of action. While not as prone to actively defy existing authority figures, he is more likely to ignore established rules and regulations in favor of his own valued insights. In other words, he is not likely to dynamically initiate social changes in the urgent manner of one with the Cardinal Apex Uranus, but can more consistently persevere with established outer conditions until he is able to reform from a more secure position. His awakening insights are often attuned to his sense of values, and can often create intense turmoil within his relationships. While he can build up electrical tension over long periods of time, he eventually is compelled to suddenly release his overload with unnerving power and force.

Life will demand that he adapt to new, unprecedented experiences that literally force him to sharply alter his own value structure. On an interpersonal level, he demands to have the privilege to constantly express freedom the way he desires. Yet due to the dynamics of this T-Square, if his vision of "truth" is not all-inclusive, it will break down eventually and lose its structure entirely. The result could be disorienting for this person for a long time until he uses his will to reform his life in a manner that allows him to center upon new objectives. In general, the fixed quality here helps tone down the urgent excitability of Uranus, rendering its expression less erratic and unstable.

In a *Mutable T-Square*, apex Uranus can promote the

development of a radical thinker who often defies traditional systems of knowledge. Although often highly original, this individual's genius is typically misunderstood or intensely criticized by his contemporaries. He can be considered as either an intellectual misfit or an eccentric social crank espousing subversive ideas that could threaten current conventional thought. This person is often too erratic and non-directed in his approach to actualize his ideals on a workable basis. He can suddenly drop one ideal for another without explanation or apparent reason. Due to the natural variability of the mutable mode, Apex Uranus here can display a wide range of idiosyncrasies. The nervous system is often too electrified to function without a constant state of excitation and sporatic flux, giving this individual a high-wired temperament that is too unstable to effectively cope with mundane activity. Although eager to alter and modify whatever he puts his short-lived attention upon for the moment, he can become willfully restless when dealing with ordinary systems or routines.

Unpredictable Uranus working thru the changeable mutable quality here suggests that the individual has much difficulty focalizing his stimulating skills and mental abilities in any one area long enough to accomplish lasting reform. Or he may keep all his revolutionary insights strictly in his head and fail to manifest them in a practical, tangible manner. Although highly perceptive and keyed into the innovative alternatives and options available to his social environment, he tends to be blunt and almost too frank in his observation concerning others he either magnetically attracts or generally theorizes about. He best channels his driving, mentally explorative energies thru all communication fields that allow for exciting innovation and complete freedom of intellectual expression.

When the tension of this T-Square is resolved, the individual can truly become a light-bearer for the darkened world. He becomes a progressive agent for universal betterment, helping to actively disperse timely, socially-liberating knowledge. As he is now able to make a more conscious connection with the higher mental plane, he can effectively use his intuitional perception to energize others to tap into their own unique capacity. He demonstrates a more open, honest, and positive friendliness to all he encounters, enabling him to unify all group movements that endeavor to progress social causes. He becomes a dynamic model that awakens and liberates the potential for social freedom, often in a manner that allows him to creatively express his inventive spirit and originality. He is given the special privilege of contributing extraordinary benefits to society that further humanitarian enterprises. While he still may not completely identify with those he idealistically supports, since squares to Uranus defy standard organizational patterns, he sparks their dynamic potential for accelerated growth while still remaining a free agent.

APEX NEPTUNE

The Apex Neptune indicates an individual who is hypersensitive to all sensory stimuli, and is able to experience almost boundless emotional states of consciousness. Normally, he has highly refined sensibilities and is prone towards being deeply inspired on the feeling level. Yet his delicate inner nature can lack the ego-structure enabling him to cope with the ordinary rigors of mundane life. Dealing with practical realities may seem too demanding and unfulfilling to him. With two squares from Neptune involved in this tenuous configuration, the tendency towards self-deception and escapism is emphasized. There are usually hidden psychological weaknesses or blind-spots that must be faced objectively and analyzed if this individual is to ever clarify his needs in partnerships. His natural inclination is to cloud and color his perception of others in an over-idealistic manner due to his reluctance to accept human imperfection. The realization of inadequacy in others he attracts makes him become painfully sensitive to his own human frailties, and he unrealistically attempts to protect himself from such awareness thru denying their existence. He is apt to defend himself from the threat of harsh reality by distorting whatever filters thru his emotions.

Although impressionable to a fault, he will be forced to learn how to become more discriminating and selective about what he absorbs from the environment. Vulnerability only increases when he avoids the disciplines of self-analysis and discernment. By choosing to remain ignorant about his deeper levels (even if such choosing is predominantly unconscious), he leaves himself wide open to relationships where others subtly take full advantage of his feelings. Whenever he appears to be what he intrinsically is not, he magnetically draws people to him who are deceptive and dishonest in their intentions. When these unions are finally seen for what they are, the individual is deeply disillusioned and feels driven to withdraw into himself negatively. (*Beethoven - Lord Byron - Henri Matisse - Tchaikovsky - Artur Rimbaud - Voltaire*).

In a *Cardinal T-Square*, apex Neptune indicates an individual who is susceptible towards taking impractical, poorly-organized action when initiating dynamic issues in his life. He approaches immediate objectives unrealistically and jumps impulsively into weakly defined activities with blinders on. Often, he feels emotionally driven to energetically (as much as passive Neptune can) move towards ambitions that are very idealistic, but seldom does he tend to the finer details involved (he may not even realize there are finer details). Life will force him to slow down and organize matters with patience and care, since he can become too disillusioned quickly when plans seem to meet up with obstacles or snags. Without disciplining himself to adhere to some practical system or method, his poorly-coordinated efforts may leave him devitalized, confused, and even acutely depressed for the moment.

Cardinal Apex Neptune is often too impatient to concentrate long enough to manifest its inner dreams and beautiful ideals. In partnerships, this individual may actively withdraw from commitments if too much responsibility is required of him. His lack of staying-power, coupled with his active imagination, tempts him to design short cuts, schemes, easy way outs, and shaky plans that appear to promise the most the soonest with the least amount of effort involved. As the Cardinal signs deal with various expressions of identity, mismanaged Apex Neptune could denote self-negation *or* an exaggerated self-concept.

Constructively, the individual can be inspired to inaugurate new styles of art and music, or pioneer in the realms of creative expression, since these areas are highly suitable for him to better channel his other-worldly temperament and acute sensitivity.

In a *Fixed T-Square*, apex Neptune indicates an individual who is prone towards harboring deep emotional yearnings that are hard to gratify thru ordinary mundane outlets. Due to the tendency of the fixed mode to establish set habits not easily broken, the individual may have illusions about him and others that resist alteration, regardless of the plain facts presented to him. He is able to delude himself for a long period of time, due to the fact that his distortions are often self-satisfying, and thus he stubbornly blocks out whatever threatens his valued misconceptions. However, once he realizes his emotions have given him false messages, and that what he devoted himself to has no real substance, his intense disillusionment could trigger an enduring craving to escape from the inner pain generated. Since both Neptune and the fixed quality share sensuality as a common denominator, the individual may try to avoid self-confrontation thru heavy indulgence in substances that numb his sensibilities, or distort sensory awareness. The less creative he feels himself to be, the more gross and physical his cravings become, and the more unsatisfying.

Often, the individual feels a profound inner loneliness and lack of emotional connection with others (since the incredible resistance power of the fixed signs could here become blown out of proportion to the point that the individual is unable to feel affected in any way by his outer environment). Life will force him to dissolve his inflexible self-will so that he can yield to the deeper needs of others who need his strength. By surrendering his ego to a valuable social cause outside of himself, he may find himself able to draw from a wealth of inner resources that can be used to build ideal external structures in the world. He is pressured to show the will-to-serve and release the spirit of compassion he is capable of deeply feeling. Activities that help him dramatize the senses are excellent for him, in that it helps him get in touch with intense inner feelings that need to emerge to the surface and express.

In a *Mutable T-Square*, apex Neptune can express itself in its most disoriented manner. Usually, the individual can become mentally confused when under stress and doesn't interpret messages or signals in the environment very accurately or clearly. His own fuzzy thinking tends to interfere with his ability to directly communicate with others. He may, however, be able to indirectly communicate subtleties in a highly creative way. The urge to remove oneself from the every day pressures of life by escaping into his head is very strong. He is apt to feel more protected by living in the imaginative world of his own mind. This could result in poor outer observation ability, impractical distractions, absent-mindedness, and undue daydreaming. Although he may have a sponge-like mentality, able to absorb and retain a wide gamut of impressions, this individual is often too disorganized to structure the ideas he develops in a logical, sensible way. Life will teach him to carefully analyze his concepts to see if they contain misinformation or faulty data before he can arrive at any definite conclusions.

This T-Square denotes a lack of willpower plus a tendency to give up or give in easily rather than meet obstacles head-on. He may not even make an effort to work around problems, but could simply ignore or underestimate his difficulties. Highly influenced for the moment by the people around him, he is likely to be credulous or gullible until he stops taking people at face value and allows himself to objectively judge and evaluate. Otherwise, his naive and trusting nature may be readily manipulated by stronger egos. Mutable Apex Neptune indicates a chameleon-like ability to change self-expression so that it reflects the immediate environment (versatility is combined with Neptune's capacity to imitate), giving the individual an inclination to mislead people unintentionally or be misinterpreted by them completely. Constructively, he may show a variety of artistic, literary, or communication talents that need to be further cultivated thru self-discipline, concentration, consistent effort, and practical organization.

When the tension of this T-Square has been resolved, the individual is better able to use his inspirational energies in a more concrete, practical manner in his ambition to manifest the dreams and lofty ideals of his society or the world-at-large. He can become a creative fount from which the world receives healing, soul comfort, emotional enlightenment, and a greater sense of unification. He is able to influence thru the divine power of love. His compassionate heart renders him capable of wisely sacrificing his temporal interests in order to promote and nurture universal betterment, often thru the social services or the fine arts. In addition, his ability to open up to the sensitive needs of his environment is now balanced with an ability to know how to screen out undesirable forces that could throw him off his emotional center.

APEX PLUTO

The Apex Pluto indicates an individual who approaches his life with much intensity, strength of focus, and psychological stamina. He is naturally drawn towards investigating the complex undercurrents of life and can readily probe into subtle life matters with great depth and insight. He feels driven to expose their inner workings to the surface for better or worse. However, he tends to be relentlessly one-tracked in his aims here. This individual tends to have powerful, all-consuming obsessions that can tax his emotional energies when not understood for what they are. This is perhaps the most difficult of all apex planets to have operating in the chart, since Pluto forces the individual to undergo a complete metamorphosis psychologically before he can safely and humanely handle the compressed power of this T-Square.

Paradoxical Pluto implies here that this extreme individual can feel torn apart inside between his willful desire to fulfill ambitions thru force, manipulation, or subversive actions...and his willing desire to purge himself of all temptations to abuse power in order to gain control over others. He often swings from both poles for a long time until he finally allows one to possess him. This individual is quite complicated and very private. Not many are allowed access into his inner world, and those who are allowed are still not permitted full access. In his relationships with others, he may be puzzling and mysterious since here he can either show much cool remoteness, distance and emotional self-control, or passion, possessiveness, and great emotional intensity. And he is often battling within himself in trying to comprehend these forces. (*Goethe - Aleister Crowley - J. B. Rhine - Ralph Nader - Gloria Steinem - Anita Bryant*).

In a *Cardinal T-Square*, apex Pluto indicates an individual who is an intensely self-driven individualist, but often a loner who doesn't integrate with others easily. He may almost defiantly reject the assistance and support of others when directly pursuing his immediate objectives, and usually due to a fear that they will try to take control over these matters. Hidden strengths within him compel this individual to confront and overwhelm opposition in a forceful, ruthless manner when challenged or threatened. He is able to quickly gather and activate his power reserves and apply them towards crisis situations demanding immediate, decisive reactions. Cardinal Apex Pluto thus could be excellent for those involved in high-powered executive positions demanding penetrating insight into all crucial phases of operation.

This person can have a chip-on-the-shoulder attitude that makes cooperation with others almost impossible at times. His natural take-over inclinations make it psychologically difficult for him to willingly share power, or relinquish it to another without at least feeling an acute sense of resentment and even open contempt. This Apex Pluto, more than the others, is most prone towards showing its intensity on the surface due to the upfront, overt nature of the cardinal mode. This suggests that the individual's Plutonian energies are more readily picked up on by others or the environment in general, perhaps explaining why he is apt to find himself embroiled in active confrontation more than would be expected of Pluto. Life will force him to undergo explosive endings of one phase of his personal development in order to make fresh new starts in another phase.

In a *Fixed T-Square*, apex Pluto indicates an individual who can be deeply fixated and stubborn concerning his desires. He has tremendous staying power on the emotional level and does not break down easily. This individual can be remarkably determined to stick to any course of action he inwardly commits himself to, regardless of the imposing obstacles he knows he will have to confront. Anita Bryant's personal crusade for sexual morality is a prime example of the persistence and strength of conviction typical of this T-Square. The individual is able to consolidate his power reserves slowly but with great organization, allowing him to work towards a difficult future goal without letting anything or anyone interfere or block his enduring efforts (provided that he values this goal unconditionally). Sensuality and sexuality are often accentuated here, and often have a powerful influence over the individual one way or another. However, it is common that with Pluto squares, the repressive elements of sex are more evident. Free expression in this area may be problematic, due to the inclination to over-control the natural manifestation of the individual's libidinal drive.

With the opposition involved in this configuration, intense frustration could also pressure the individual to control the sexuality of others, leading towards power-struggles in partnerships. If he is to purge himself from internal negativities that often eat away at him, he is more pressured to do so from forces inside him rather than circumstantial dilemmas. Apex Pluto here enables the individual to undergo complete and enduring transformations concerning all unlit areas of his personality that otherwise enslave him psychologically and keep him alienated from the greater world around him.

In a *Mutable T-Square*, apex Pluto indicates an individual who can be revolutionary upon mental realms. Here is one who is malcontent with general surface knowledge, and instead is intellectually driven to explore the underlying fundamentals of whatever he applies his intense mental powers toward. Life often challenges him to struggle with comprehending complicated fields of study (i.e., nuclear physics). He can become quite stimulated to pursue any outlet that allows him to investigate, probe, research, or unearth relevant but normally obscured data. At best, he may be able to use this purposeful information to transform social consciousness. However, Mutable Apex Pluto can also indicate a hair-trigger nervous response to life, due to the intense degree of alertness suggested. The individual feels strong urges to tear down and destroy concepts and theories he feels lack depth, ultimate meaning or absolute truth (as he perceives it). Yet because of the powerful intellectual resourcefulness of this configuration, this individual seems compelled to give birth to profound new thought-systems that at least help regenerate his mentality. Life will teach him that his thoughts have incredible power and need to be directed out towards his environment with much self-control and mastery.

Mutable Apex Pluto can depict the socially-effective propagandist or potent radical thinker whose concepts can have a deep, unsettling impact upon society. His abilities can be most easily realized when focussed upon communication or educational fields. Political theorist Karl Marx had a natal Mutable T-Square with both Pluto *and* Saturn as apex planets. He obviously felt compelled to defy authority with his intense concepts concerning a more ideal balance of *power* within the hierarchy of social structure. His need to strengthen the political force of the working class seems quite fitting, since Pluto and Saturn were posited in Pisces (sign of the oppressed, suffering underdog). The individual will need to discipline himself to turn off his mental processes from time to time, since his inclination to scrutinize and break down thought could lead to nervous breakdowns or total mental collapse when allowed to continue past the point of normal endurance (Pluto overstrains the mutable mode here, which characteristically lacks stamina and needs periodic rest). He will need to apply his above-average perception of things to help him understand his emotional needs.

When the tension of this T-Square is resolved, the individual is able to constantly rejuvenate himself on all levels of his being. He has an increased ability to tap into his potent creative reserves where highly concentrated power is found. However, now free from hidden compulsions and deep pockets of negativity, he will be better able to utilize his inner powers for the benefit of himself and all he encounters. Although still prone to run up against intolerance and even violent resistance from others who may try to impede his objectives (Pluto represents stark reality, and just because this individual has undergone a dramatic transformation of self does not mean that his environment automatically does), he eventually can be totally accepted and recognized for his efforts to uncover some fundamental truth that has been hidden from the world previously (recognition could sometimes occur even after death, since Pluto can indicate exceedingly slow but timely fulfillment). For some, apex Pluto could suggest the ability to rise to a power position after developing himself during a long period of obscurity. On some level, the individual helps the world effectively utilize *collective* power.

ADDITIONAL CONSIDERATIONS

Sometimes you will find that, because of natal conjunctions, there can be more than one apex planet to consider just as there can be more than two base planets. There are no cut-and-dried rules for determining which of the two apex planets will be the more dominant influence. According to suggestions by Tracy Marks,[2] the strength of impact any apex planet could have may be gauged according to whether it falls in its own sign or house, conjunct an angle (of course, with two apex planets, the one more closely contacting the angle takes prominence), or is stationary, or is at the midpoint of the two opposing planets. All these factors should certainly be considered. In addition, I feel it is important to note if the apex planet rules an angle (ASC or MC in particular), or if it is the natural ruler of one of the base planet's sign position or the sign of the empty leg. This would add more support and reinforcement to the principle that planet represents. Actually, conjuncting apex planets will work together in action for the most part. If emphasis seems to shift from time to time, it is likely due to the fact that the actual situational challenge triggered by the

T-Square is more conducive toward evoking the principle of one planet more than the other. But even if one planet's theme is more accentuated at any period in time, the other one often provides sidelight, background issues operating simultaneously. It may be very important to note whether an apex planet is retrograde or intercepted. Future chapters to be covered should give helpful information regarding such phenomena.

References:

(1) Tracy Marks, *How To Handle Your T-Square*, Sagittarius Rising, Mass., 1979, p. 9.

(2) *Ibid*, p. 23.

8
The Yod

This not-too-common configuration occurs when at least two planets sextile one another while both quincunx a third planet, creating a large "Y" formation across the chart. This third planet (the apex point of the Yod) represents a highly significant principle requiring clearer and more purposeful focus of expression before this pattern can become actively triggered at some time in the life. Similar to the dynamics of the T-Square, this apex planet becomes the prime focal point of the Yod. Its basic nature reveals much about the characteristic motivation determining the outer manifestation of this configuration. The Yod has also been called the "Finger of God" pattern.

In my opinion, the ideal Yod is created by the apex planet in *lower* quincunx phase with one of the sextiling planets, while also in *upper* quincunx aspect with the other. However, in actual practice, one may come across a potential Yod that is instead formed when the apex planet is either simultaneously in lower *or* upper aspect to *both* sextiling planets. This would be determined by the natural rate of orbital motion of the planets involved. Al H. Morrison feels that a "true" Yod can only occur when "the focus point is the slowest in motion of all three bodies. Where the focus planet moves faster than the other two, it cannot be a Yod, but is only a back-to-back quincunx, or double quincunx."[1] Morrison's true Yod would thus involve the apex planet in both upper and lower phase with the sextiling planets. I am not qualified to make any absolute statements regarding the other two alternative formations, since I have not researched these configurations to any relevant degree. However, my own concepts concerning the Yod's main dynamics would suggest that Morrison may very likely be right. If he is, then a "true" Yod would *always* be found when Pluto is at the apex point, since this planet orbits slower than any other established member of our Solar System. And interestingly enough, Pluto's principles closely parallel the characteristics of the Yod quite well.

For the most part, all Higher Octave planets at the apex

point will normally denote an ideal Yod for the majority of charts in this 20th century. To continue further along this line of thought, the Sun, Moon, Mercury, Venus, and Mars as apex planets would then normally denote the "double-quincunx" version, since they are the faster-orbiting planets. And especially the Sun, Mercury, and Venus since they are not technically able to form quincunx patterns with each other. Morrison implies that the non-Yod, double-quincunx pattern denotes merely difficult (perhaps non-directional) lives in contrast to the more purposeful destiny indicated by the true Yod. While I find this distinction very interesting and food for thought, I have nevertheless included some examples representing those who have the "double-quincunx" pattern.

Considering what was said in Chapter One concerning the upper and lower quincunx aspects, it should be apparent that the combination of *both* influences expressed in the Yod could be quite a special challenge to constructively alter and bring into clearer focus that which impairs or hinders the *total* functioning of the individual. Here, inner *and* outer forces are working together to stimulate subtle but heightened pressures which may eventually release themselves during a timely crisis in self-awareness. This turning point could take years before it emerges and presents new alternatives to the individual. But when it does, the individual is then ripe and ready for a very fated change or destined new outlook in his life. The course of action he then takes at this time can completely reprogram the entire focus of his life pattern.

A Yod ready for activation is very much like arriving at a fork in the road and nevertheless having to proceed further in one direction or the other without securely knowing where either route is definitely going to lead to. We are simply aware that we must veer off onto another path. This change of course is not really a matter of conscious, deliberate decision-making due to any full awareness of the potentials involved (unlike the challenge of the opposition), but instead is one due to unrecognized necessity. Although this new direction, once embarked upon, may appear abrupt and unaccounted for, it has been accumulating strength and definition for a period of many years. Yet once the time for the Yod to be activated is right, the individual typically drops or psychologically lets go of certain interests and habits in order to become involved in enterprising attitudes and activities coming upon the horizon. And although he may at first feel a bit uncertain or even inadequate in dealing with his new, unaccustomed focus, this person often is soon surprised to find out how much ability and know-how he actually has in this area (no doubt due to all those former years of inner preparation upon subjective levels).

If his preparation has enabled him to operate at a more effective level of consciousness, the potential energy of the sextiling planets can allow him to make intelligent and innovative adjustments in the social environment. Or at least in those personal areas of life ruled by the houses involved in the Yod. And especially the house occupied by the apex planet *and* its opposite house, where the culmination of such alterations set into motion by the apex planet is normally found. But if he has not adequately adjusted to the pressures of the double quincunx emphasis, his *maladjustments* are also prone to surface at this time and actively struggle with the environment.

The reaction point directly opposite the apex planet is very sensitive. It pinpoints that focussed area where the individual's new orientation will center itself for better or worse. The passing of transits or natal progressions over this reaction degree should be noted carefully, and particularly so if slower-moving planets are involved. The Higher Octave planets, which already are motivated to be self-transformative, should be keenly observed. Sometimes a natal planet will be found at this reaction point in opposition to the apex planet. Until the Yod is fully activated, this reaction planet can create imbalance, vacillation, and contrasting conflicts for the individual regarding his ability to direct the apex planet. But once he has undergone the complete reorganizational process typical of a constructively mobilized Yod, this reaction planet can offer further awareness and perspective concerning more transformative ways of using both this fourth planet and the apex planet. The reaction planet is initially a conditioning agent that eventually becomes a prominent catalyst for inner illumination.

Richard Nixon has a mutable Apex Mars opposed by his 10th house Pluto as part of his Yod structure. This Yod (which also involves Saturn sextile Neptune) would be an example of Morrison's double-quincunx pattern. Yet in my estimation, it was fully triggered into overt expression in a particularly fated manner during the testing period of the entire Watergate affair, and perhaps intensely so for Nixon when *transiting* Saturn conjunct his Reaction Pluto. The course of events during this trying time of his life was certainly representative of an abrupt, unexpected turnabout of affairs that drastically altered his former status-quo. The culmination of events that led towards his enforced new direction was definitely fitting of power-leveling Pluto operating thru the 10th house of public judgement. Regardless, Apex Mars can open up a new life path involving an alternative form of personal expression centering around self-identity in action. Reaction Pluto here forces a deeper inner purge of interpersonal values which could result in a rebirth of priorities concerning Nixon's personal expression of power and will. The mutable element involved in this apex-reaction axis could denote (in this context) transformed mental awareness of creative options and alternatives regarding new avenues of self-expression. The rehabilitative potential of Reaction Pluto plus the initiating quality of apex Mars tells me that ex-President Nixon will probably not be out of the public eye for too long, if I am interpreting the potential of his Yod accurately.

Usually, the orb I would allow for a valid Yod is 7° for the sextile planets, and 3° for the apex planet. However, any seasoned astrologer is well aware that ideal orbs must be extended from time to time for various reasons. For example, I would stretch the orb if there is a planet at the reaction point, or if a planet is at the shorter-arc midpoint of the two base planets. Any planet at this midpoint ties in the energies of these base planets more closely together, strengthening the overall structure of the Yod. I would also stretch orbs when the apex planet rules one of the signs of the base planets, or vice versa. Thyrza Escobar (Jones) in her highly stimulating *Side Lights of Astrology* (one of my all-time favorite publications in Astrology) states that "the three arms of the 'Y' should contain *planets*, not just house cusps, nodes, or other sensitive points."2 I strongly advise you to read her succinct chapter on the Yod.

On the other hand, authors Helen Paul and Bridget Mary O'Toole in *The Yod And Other Points In Your Horoscope* state that their research has shown various sensitive points as part of the Yod's structure to be effective (i.e., the angles, the nodes, arabian parts).3 However, knowing the potential for astrologers to rationalize any point they so wish to using a myriad of factors in the chart, I would advise those wishing to do budding personal research on the Yod to first stick with actual planets before venturing into other chart factors. This is not to imply that I discount the work of Paul and O'Toole, but instead is to suggest that students first test the validity of Yod configurations formed exclusively by planets.

It may be good practice for any astrologer (especially one lacking a natal Yod) to compose a separate chart from his horoscope which only lists all natal sextiles in their proper house positions. All you need for a potential Yod to be formed natally, by progression, or tranit is a sextile! But unless you have *exact* sextiles (within a degree of orb), I recommend calculating the midpoints of each sextile for more accuracy of timing. Then note what degree, sign, and house the midpoint of the longer arc occupies. For it is precisely here that a temporary Yod can be formed. A transiting planet such as the Sun, Moon, Mercury, Venus, or Mars is not likely to stir up anything too noticeable or particularly "fated" in one's life at the time. However, these faster-moving planets in their progressed cycle should be noted and observed. Yet if a Higher Octave planet is to transit this sensitive degree, then pay special attention to this temporary Yod. At the same time, should the progressed Moon also conjunct or square either the apex degree, the reaction degree, or a midpoint of the natal planets in sextile aspect, really start taking notes (since the progressed Moon is the most important timer in secondary progressions)! For at this point, *any* other transiting planet conjuncting or squaring these points could evoke a noticeable response from your temporary Yod that may time an unexpected, mildly fated change of conditions for that particular year.

Temporary Yods have been known to operate in charts during the time of death, the onset of illnesses of long duration, serious injuries, and during separations (often by force or circumstances beyond anyone's control) in relationships. In general, these Yods denote all unforeseen turns of destiny. Of course, many other vital aspects (seemingly stressful *and* easy-flowing) may be operative at this time. Death in particular is fairly impossible to predict, thank goodness! Like any other multiple aspect configuration (or any aspect phase for that matter), the Yod or temporary Yod will function according to the level of understanding that the individual has concerning the basic principles of the planets involved.

COMPOSITE YODS

If another person's natal or progressed planet(s) conjuncts the individual's reaction degree within orb, this person may be very much linked up with the fated changes of the individual for better or worse. Such a person can either complement and share in the nature of these new changes at the time the individual must undertake them, or can antagonize situations by acting as a separative influence (in other words, he can induce balance or imbalance). Two other notable synastric patterns to observe are (1) another person's natal planet conjunct the individual's apex planet and (2) another person's natal planet becoming the apex planet, thus quincunxing the individual's natal sextiling planets. This latter pattern seems theoretically valid, yet it suggests that such individuals are only driven to experience the Yod's dynamics thru their often chance encounter (since neither individual experiences the energies of the Yod as part of his personal character structure). This second pattern is what I refer to as a *Composite Yod.*

Notorious gangsters Clyde Barrow and Bonnie Parker may
have had such a joint Yod, with Bonnie's Sun as the apex
planet (since I've only used their solar charts, the actual
existence of this Yod depends upon the exact degree of
Clyde Barrow's Moon). Yet due to the chance nature of
their encounter plus the dramatic and drastic chain of
events that followed after, it does seem probable that this
Composite Yod was operative. Another infamous couple,
mass child-murderers Ian Brady and Myra Hindley, had a
prominent Composite Yod. Myra's natal Pluto sextile
Saturn (two power-control planets capable of severity) was
in close quincunx formation with Ian's *three* apex
planets...Venus, Mercury, and Sun (all in Saturn-ruled
Capricorn). Barbara Watters, who gives a grisly account of
their criminal relationship in her explicit *The Astrologer
Looks At Murder* (a book definitely not for the squeamish,
impressionable Neptunian types, but more fitted for the
hard-core Plutonians like myself), states that Myra was
"fatefully in love"[4] with Ian (apex Venus). Watters also
implies that Myra was almost totally possessed by his calculating mind and indomitable will (apex Mercury and apex
Sun respectively). Naturally, there were several other
prime factors in their synastric profile to explain the
negative influence they had upon each other. But the
Composite Yod with its triple apex emphasis does seem to
stand out to me as one major factor.

Now understand that I am *not* suggesting that Composite
Yods bring out the undesirable, lower potential of a
relationship in the extreme manner of these two given
examples. I have merely used them to exemplify the Yod's
characteristic trait of sometimes unforeseen but often
extreme alterations of individual life direction, with its
proclivity for fated turning-points. For those inclined to
further research Composite Yods, I advise analyzing charts
of famous couples who, by suddenly joining forces together,
brought about completely new or unprecedented elements
of a notable nature into their combined life pattern that
could not be as readily evoked independently. Their
association should be marked by accelerated change in
circumstances of a somewhat unexpected nature, rather
than by slower, carefully structured development.

Most observers would admit that the fateful encounter between the Duke of Windsor and Wallis Simpson should qualify as a classic example of the dynamics of the Composite Yod, considering that their union eventually completely altered both their accustomed lifestyles and resulted in dramatic, crucial turning-points (especially for the Duke). In addition, the entire course of events following their first meeting progressed very rapidly to an inevitable conclusion, with the Duke abdicating the throne as King of England to marry the American divorcee. A momentus crossroads for sure. There *was* a Composite Yod formed between them, although with orbs a bit too wide for a "classic" example. Yet the nature of their destined encounter fit the pattern of the Composite Yod too closely to discount. The Duke's natal Moon as the apex planet formed this Yod by quincunxing the Duchess' Jupiter sextile Moon. The reason why I felt justified in stretching the orbs was due to the fact that Mrs. Simpson's Jupiter was also co-ruler of the Duke's apex sign (Pisces). And in this particular Yod, I felt the apex planet gained more significance since the Duke's Moon fell in his 1st house (prominence thru angularity) and was the ruler of his 5th house Sun sign. And of course, with the Moon as the triggering apex planet, the Duke was forced to move from England to Paris, being almost totally ostracized by the royal family (implying definite Moon adjustments on many levels).

Liz Taylor's magnetic encounter with her then co-star Richard Burton was as fateful as that of Antony and Cleopatra, and it resulted in surprising, although abrupt, turning-points for both of them (especially for Richard). And indeed, there were *two* separate Composite Yods formed between them. Liz provided both the apex planets. Perhaps the individual with the apex planet here is commonly the psychological activator of the Composite Yod's dynamics. Anyhow, Taylor's apex Jupiter helped form a Composite Yod with Burton's Jupiter sextile Uranus. At the same time, her apex Uranus formed a Composite Yod with his Moon sextile Saturn. This to me implies that Liz Taylor's impact upon Richard Burton's destined life direction had Jupiter-Uranus undertones. Of course, this proved quite true at the time of their meeting, since his eventual marriage to her brought him almost overnight world recognition in the acting field. Until then, his popularity was relatively confined to the British Isles. And although Burton's extraordinary talents would enable him to inevitably receive the acclaim from the public he now enjoys, Liz' attraction to him certainly proved catalystic.

Another famous couple whose sudden attraction and unexpected marital decision surprised the world was Jacqueline Kennedy and Aristotle Onassis. Their union seemed to have more distinctly changed the course of life direction for Jacke, since she had to make greater personal adjustments concerning her accustomed American lifestyle by marrying this influential Greek shipping magnate and living abroad. This fact alone should incline the astrologer to suspect that Ari would provide the apex emphasis. And sure enough, Onassis' apex Mercury *and* apex Uranus formed a Composite Yod with Jackie's Sun sextile Jupiter. But his Neptune was also conjunct the reaction point, adding a more complex dimension to this Composite Yod. I'm sure astrologers could have a field day interpreting the ramifications of this configuration! In general, pay special attention to those couples whose own individual charts show a multitude of natal sextiles. While Composite Yods statistically may not be that unusual to find, they still may prove to be particularly enlightening in defining the nature of those seemingly chance encounters that radically alter the lifestyle of at least one of the parties involved.

The following are interpretations of each natal planet at the apex point of a Yod. They do not take in account the nature of the base planets, the apex sign, or house positions of all three planets:

APEX SUN

Apex Sun may denote an individual whose central purpose in life may revolve around continuous personal adjustments and major self-correction. He normally is pressured to make needed alterations in the manner with which he demonstrates his will, power, authority, and self-pride.

Objective self-examination will be very important for his
proper growth, since maladjustments here are often due to
unrecognized self-centered attitudes. The individual may
have difficulty establishing his personal center. His
ego-drives are not expressed in a direct, outgoing manner
but tend to internalize and bottle up. This person can start
out in life with a low self-concept and a sense of inferiority,
making him feel out-of-tune with his early environment. He
may seem ineffectual and powerless for some time, leading
him to sense he is insignificant in the eyes of others
(especially authority figures).

Quincunxes to the Sun could generally be ego-deflating.
The individual is usually struggling inside with his
awkward self-consciousness. However, once this Yod is
fully activated, the individual may undergo a dramatic
change in character due to new major conditions that are
essential to his primary karmic theme, and that cannot be
avoided. Objectives now on the horizon could require his
full attention, inner strength, and outgoingness. He may
even have to mobilize his vital forces on a physical level. He
can gravitate towards a new field of experience that
permits him to exteriorize himself with confidence and
self-assurance. This incarnation could grant him the special
ability to reorganize his central core of being in a vitally
productive, creative fashion. The individual may now have
the conscious power to transmute the force of his will in an
almost alchemical manner. Once embarked upon, his new
direction could allow him to command many facets of his
outer life situations with much success and flair, resulting
in favorable recognition from the general environment. His
years of inner preparation have helped to fully individualize
him.

But if evoked and still mismanaged, this Yod may release
the power to abuse personal will and authority. The
individual may be able to powerfully dominate the affairs of
his new path, but often with fateful repercussions he
assertively brings upon himself. The only example I could
find of a well-known figure with an Apex Sun was the man
who helped put the term "sadism" into the dictionary...the
Marquis de Sade. This domineering, power-obsessed

individualist had his natal Sun quincunxing Pluto sextile Uranus. Obviously, the nature of these two willful base planets had much to do with de Sade's distortion and intensification of his ego-drives. With Pluto quincunx the Sun, power struggles could take on extreme forms of expression, yet seldom are direct or overt in the manner of their execution. With Uranus quincunx the Sun, de Sade had above-average mental abilities but was more representative of the "mad" genius. Added support here concerning the power-control theme comes from Pluto's position in Scorpio and Uranus' placement in Capricorn. Further reinforcement came from natal Mars in Aries (also co-ruler of Scorpio) squaring Saturn (ruler of Capricorn). De Sade died in an insane asylum. (*Marquis de Sade*).

APEX MOON

Apex Moon denotes an individual whose inner, emotional development is in need of sensitive adjustment. This person can still be caught up with disorganized, distorted impressions of the past that need to be objectively observed and clarified before his feelings can be free to further grow and thrive. This is a very personal, private apex planet. Potential emotional maladjustments are seldom evident on the surface. The individual may even be unaware of these conflicts due to the subconscious nature of the Moon plus its capacity to condition behavior in a very subtle, subjective manner. His instinctual response to impressions from the environment can be out-of-tune with what would normally be expected, since this highly reactive individual does not easily decode the emotional messages he receives from others. He may even attempt to screen them out in an obliquely self-protective manner. There may be some emotional trauma from the past (perhaps stemming from previous incarnations and then repeated in *theme* again in early childhood) that can keep this individual too defensive, unadaptable, and vulnerable to effectively deal with security needs in the here-and-now.

Apex Moon suggests faulty assimilation of impressions that nevertheless trigger this person to react in a habitually self-defeating way. Although he needs a great amount of closeness and intimacy from those he can trust and allow himself to feel nourished by, he typically can feel out-of-focus with others and may withdraw into a psychological shell in an attempt to find shelter and refuge whenever he fails to adjust to the emotional realities of any union. I would imagine the Apex Moon undergoes its most strained period during the individual's early developmental years, implying that this Yod may be activated as soon as the person reaches adulthood. Perhaps less so with a Fixed Apex Moon but very much so with the Cardinal Apex Moon. The Mutable Apex Moon is less decisive in acting out the Yod's challenge. In addition, Saturn and/or Pluto as base planets would suggest a longer period of time needed before constructive adjustments can be made.

Once this Yod is fully activated, the individual is to embark upon a destined change of life patterning that could leave him free from negative images of the past. Due to subtle yet constant reorganization of the feeling nature, he has inwardly prepared himself for a life direction enabling him to soothe or nurture others. His maternal instinct has undergone needed regeneration, so that a new path may open up permitting him to attend to the basic needs of the populace, to defend the interests of the weaker, or help others establish fundamental securities. Regardless of what life now presents to him, this individual finds himself strengthened by his inner foundation and advantageously nourished by his reassembled emotional resources. Personal needs are more clarified, directly expressed, and easily fulfilled. (*Alexander Graham Bell - Thomas Jefferson - George Gershwin - Grant Lewi*).

APEX MERCURY

Apex Mercury indicates an individual who first must reorganize all scattered loose ends on the mental level before this Yod can be activated. He normally starts out in life curicus about the workings of the mind, but he himself can appear out-of-tune with the environment in the area of personal communication (behaving somewhat like one with Mercury retrograde). With Apex Mercury, there is usually an inner drive to understand the stimulating surface of life, but with personal difficulty expressing this drive in a clear, direct manner. The individual can be quite an introspective thinker but often cannot assemble his thoughts in an effective way that could allow him to productively act upon such thoughts. He might put too much attention upon redefining his concepts by first taking them apart and carefully studying each facet in detail. The trouble here, however, is learning to reassemble them in a workable fashion. At times, the individual may tend to combine too many concepts in a haphazard, disjointed way and fail to establish coherency.

The quincunxes to Mercury demand that one unclutter the thought-processes of superfluous factors and streamline concepts so that they are structured with meaningful simplicity. Otherwise, the mind tends to further veer off into unnecessary tangents in an attempt to gather more information than can be sensibly applied. Intelligence is not apt to be affected, but merely the way in which it is utilized. Inner preparation typical of the Yod may be a bit more conscious here, since the individual is prone to recognize that he has an almost compulsive urge to seek out a wide range of learning tools and educational outlets. Due to the dynamics of the Yod, the individual is being trained to utilize his mental energies in a more thorough manner that allows for greater efficiency and consistency so that he can better comprehend the nature of his objective world. Once this Yod is properly activated, this person is likely to find himself operating upon a more purposeful intellectual level. At this time, he is apt to be directed towards new, stimulating communication avenues enabling him to have a greater educational impact upon both himself and his environment. Being now much more able to focus his mind, he may specialize in one area of mental interest where he can become totally absorbed. Constructively, the individual may find himself playing a destined role as an influential teacher, masterful communicator, or social enlightener. (*Helena Blavatsky - Werner Erhardt - Angela Davis - Marcel Marceau - Guru Maharaj Ji*).

APEX VENUS

Apex Venus describes an individual who starts off feeling out-of-touch with the values of his social environment. Due to his introspective evaluations of people, this person tends to view relationships from a different perspective than others (similar to Venus retrograde) and is usually not able to directly associate in the comfortable, easy-going manner typical of Venus. The individual is likely to feel awkward and out-of-place in ordinary social situations where he is expected to openly and freely participate. He is not able to easily establish a sense of equality with others, resulting in some degree of alienation. Nevertheless, this individual can inwardly be very reflective and ponderous concerning others, and is more analytical and scrutinizing than he appears on the surface. Although seemingly distant and almost anti-social at times, he is capable of much depth of understanding concerning the subjective nature of people. As he learns to constructively adjust facets of his own love nature thru careful self-examination, he may be better able to emerge from the background and express his feelings with greater upfrontness and clarity.

Once this Yod is activated in expression, the individual shows a heightened interest upon functioning from the social level. He feels driven to direct his energies towards the cultivation of collective values. Once he has arrived at his destined crossroads, partnership involvement takes on a new meaning, and relationships attracted at this time can assist him in purposefully fulfilling his objectives. Sometimes this fated turning-point can be catalyzed by the realization of an encompassing social goal that can be brought to fruition thru the advanced development of some personal talent or attribute that the individual has been subjectively refining for a long period of time. He may discover that he is able to have a marked influence upon the value structures of others, affecting their sensibilities in a way that helps them improve their own welfare. Since his own affectional nature can now be brought into better focus, the individual may also discover at this appointed time that his personal love life is markedly more satisfying, and that now he is better able to share himself more deeply and more enjoyable with others. In addition, his constant efforts at inner adjustment and reorganization enables him to establish a fuller capacity for self-love and appreciation of his true worth, resulting in a more lasting degree of contentment and security. The new direction stimulated by the Yod may involve individual participation in the fine arts, social enterprises, counseling fields, or legal affairs. (*Friedrich Nietzsche - Yves St. Laurent*).

APEX MARS

Apex Mars denotes an individual who starts off in life inefficiently applying his physical energies, or having difficulty initiating personal matters in a direct and open manner. The method in which he asserts himself may often be in need of correction and alteration. His active efforts may miss their mark for quite some time until he learns to bring his inner drive into clearer focus with his actual capacity to act upon situations with greater organizational intelligence. Otherwise, this individual is prone to plunge into activities without any sense of purposeful direction, resulting in non-productive energy expenditure. He is also likely to have to make adjustments concerning his aggressive instincts. He typically tends to try to control the external release of strong passions, but then can turn these urges back on himself in a self-defeating manner. Or else he may exhibit displaced anger, aiming his hostility at inappropriate targets. With Apex Mars, the individual may feel uncomfortable with his sexual tensions, and may not find adequate outlets for their needed release. In general, he can be out-of-tune with himself due to his indirect approach towards satisfying his desire nature.

Once this Yod is ripe for activation, the individual can find himself centered upon a new life course requiring him to mobilize his vital forces in an externally demanding manner. This new period of his life may manifest somewhat suddenly, perhaps under an acute crisis situation, compelling him to undertake dynamic, pioneering new starts involving courage and daring. At this point, he may become keenly aware that he must independently take full charge of his life and demonstrate complete self-sufficiency. His life's tempo now no longer allows him to waver, vacillate, or be indirect in action, but instead forces him to respond with much vigor and decisiveness. As an apex planet, forceful Mars could suggest that this individual might have to sever ties from the past or directly break away from former comforting securities during this appointed time of self-confrontation. He is to one-pointedly focus all his attention upon this new path and learn to adapt rapidly. Once he establishes a clearer view of matters here, this individual could become quite energized to work hard and become industriously busy with this enterprising phase of his life. He is normally able to operate alone, unhampered by others to a great extent. A mismanaged Yod with this apex planet, however, could result in fateful consequences of a crucial nature due to rash or disruptive actions on the individual's part. He needs to learn corrective ways of channeling his self-will. (*Friedrich Nietzsche - William Blake - Emily Dickinson - Carl Jung - George Bernard Shaw - Richard Nixon*).

APEX JUPITER

Apex Jupiter denotes an individual who is subjectively expanding his consciousness, broadening his social vision, and enriching his moral development in a reflective manner for many years before he is able to become fully awakened by this Yod. He may start out his life feeling out-of-tune with social laws, belief systems, and moral codes that he nevertheless is expected to abide by. He innately yearns to personally experience inspiration, uplift, and mental freedom plus put his faith in something workable. However, he is seldom able to find satisfying role models in the external world and thus is forced to turn inward and question why this is. Usually quincunxes to Jupiter operating on this lofty mental level are seldom troublesome, and often can be beneficial. The constant intellectual adjustments one undergoes while pondering upon such abstract matters can keep the mind open and receptive to all new theories and probabilities. However, on a more mundane level, Jupiter quincunxes can prove quite disorganizing and impractical. The individual normally does not manage his daily affairs very well. He tends to be inconsistent in his efforts and fails to pay attention to necessary details. His expectations almost always fall short of their promised potential and usually because he tends to procrastinate, use poor judgement, or even over-reach. While his inner faith in the ultimate fulfillment of goals is seldom lacking, his approach towards the application of his faith needs correction. He is learning to realize that his idealistic plans for improvement require patience, proper timing, and enduring personal effort. Plus a greater measure of common sense.

Once this Yod is activated to express, the individual will often find himself at a period in life where he is ready to drop a former belief or long-held ideology, and instead adopt another world view that inspires him to become more effectively aligned with the needs of his inner spirit. Usually due to a seemingly providential twist of fate, the individual is presented with greater opportunities to take part in a larger social pattern of ideal development. He now can find himself having extended social influence, and is motivated to use his new level of awareness in a benevolent, unselfish manner. Tolerance will be required of him if he is to benefit from this Yod. Life may allow him the privilege of broadcasting his own social or abstract concepts in an effort to stimulate the mass mentality. Jupiter's natural optimism and urge for expansion suggest that the individual is able to adjust very well to this destined transition, and often feels confident and positive about the new course of events he is to deal with. He rarely doubts the rightness of his direction here, acting as if he is operating under some higher guidance and protection. Sometimes this turning-point is triggered by opportunities for extensive travel (a pilgrimmage of sorts) or advanced education. However, if evoked and mismanaged, this Yod still allows him to have a strong impact upon the mass consciousness, but ultimately with fateful consequences often brought upon by the individual's own self-aggrandizement. (*Charles Dickens - Andrew Carnegie - Kirpal Singh - Adolph Hitler - Werner von Braun - Pat Nixon*).

APEX SATURN

Apex Saturn could be considered a very karmic Yod, with

Saturn giving more support to this configuration's characteristic "fated" undertone. It indicates that both proper timing and inner maturity are crucial determinants regarding the individual's readiness to approach this turning-point, and that he would probably fail miserably if he attempted to unwisely force such a new direction before all necessary qualities have ripened. But until he comes to this special forked road in his life, the individual normally starts out making continuous adjustments concerning his need for ego-security and self-preservation. He is apt to experience anxiety and uncertainty in his struggle to satisfy his safety urges, and perhaps because authority figures in his early environment were ambiguous or inconsistent with their attempts to provide structure for this person. The individual is often out-of-tune with his ability to structure and define his own identity while growing up, and may feel at times like an unwanted outcast in the environment. Self-defeating attitudes here can be quite entrenched and further reinforced by harsh outer conditions. The two quincunxes to Saturn denote that the individual initially feels very inadequate, insignificant, and may be painfully aware of any deficiencies he has (economic as well as psychological). However, due to the corrective nature of the quincunx plus Saturn's natural drive to overcome obstacles, this Yod is very well suited to undergo whatever is required in terms of reorganization in order to insure stability and efficient functioning in the world.

The individual may inwardly be preparing himself for a new level of inner strength with this testing Yod, but one which can free him from negative, burdensome attitudes that have long weighed heavy on his soul. Once this Yod is activated, the individual is firmly pointed toward a timely life direction where he is able to display his special capacity for social responsibility and purposeful activity. At this point, his ambitions are now allowed to fully surface and become more effectively realized in the outer world. Major turning-points in life are likely to occur when this person has shown suffiicent self-discipline, steadiness of focus, and fortitude. He now is to embark upon a destiny that may be highly important for his soul growth, and one in which he is to confront with much resolve and commitment. The new path tends to have serious implications and is one not to be approached lightly. From this appointed time onward, the individual is likely to work hard and with much dedication to a singular life goal that may unfold itself slowly but purposefully. With Saturn at the reins, he is seldom allowed much leeway in how he is to handle his duties and obligations. Fateful consequences are highly emphasized here, especially if the individual chooses to ignore this demanding path once initiated. Fateful here is not meant to imply tragic doom, but it can denote increasing frustration, all self-induced, resulting in a sense of failure and personal despair. It seems reasonable to assume that this Yod could be triggered off sometime during the individual's 28-30th birthday, when he also experiences his first Saturn Return (which can be quite a momentus turning-point in itself). At this time, he may adopt a new life direction enabling him to attain a significant and well-respected social position. (*Johannes Brahms - Anton Chekhov - Thomas Jefferson - Lewis Carroll - Maxim Gorki - Alfred Lord Tennyson - Leon Trotsky - Bernard Baruch - Marcia Moore*).

When the apex planet of the Yod happens to be one of the Higher Octave planets, it might be indicative of a more special turning-point for the individual. His new path in life may actually designate he can become a magnetic channel for promoting the ongoing unfoldment of collective destiny. This individual may personally undergo a major alteration of life directives that can enable him to have an outstanding impact upon the world at large, helping humanity undergo its needed social adjustments. This is similar to the potential shown by a Higher Octave apex planet of a T-Square. The difference is that the individual with this pattern is not consciously driven to manifest this destined role in the forceful, tensional manner of one with the T-Square configuration. Instead, it is almost as if he is chosen by a quirk of fate to play out such a cosmic role. Unconscious factors are highly operative here. It is interesting that most of the examples of well-known personalities who had natal Yods also had the apex point involving a Higher Octave planet. Compare this to the sole example given for a Yod with the apex Sun. Perhaps this suggests that since Higher Octave planets are already highly impersonal, transformative, and collective in their focus, those with such apex planets have less difficulty gravitating towards a destined direction that can be known and felt by the whole world. This should not suggest that such apex planets cannot be used in less altruistic, selfless ways or even used for the highest good of the individual (since any Yod can be mismanaged). However, in general, these types of Yods are less prone to center exclusively upon the individual's personal sphere of activity. They instead compel this person to extend his interest into vaster and more encompassing fields of activity.

APEX URANUS

Apex Uranus describes an individual who starts out in life feeling very different and markedly out-of-tune with his early environment. He is often making constant, and sometimes erratic, adjustments in his attempt to cope with his own uniqueness while learning to integrate with others in a prescribed conventional manner. Since Uranus is a planet of quickened mental energy, this individual's accelerated nervous and intellectual development may be such that he can have problems communicating with others on the average, mundane level. He views everything from a unique angle and is seldom able to be moulded and structured to conform to even ordinary, established procedures. Often contrary and rebellious, the individual is to learn to alter his willful mental temperament before he can expect to freely handle the new direction indicated by the Yod. His innate detachment from involvement in everyday activities needs to be transformed into an impersonal yet humanely-concerned drive to reform for the betterment of all. The conditions that often prompt his fated change in life directions are apt to emerge suddenly, unexpectedly, and with a measure of disruption of all carefully formulated plans that may have already been set into motion previously. It is normally manifested as an unaccounted for turnabout of activities which can be jolting at the moment, triggering new, experimental ways of expression. The individual's destined path is likely to bring his originality to the forefront and allow him more personal freedom and liberty concerning self-expression. He may find himself more directly active in improving the welfare of a group or progressive collective enterprise.

The role he plays at this appointed period in his life is in itself catalystic, or at least extraordinary in some way. All his years of inner preparation have enabled him to become liberated from the mainstream of mediocrity so that he eventually has the unique privilege of helping to step-up the social consciousness and encourage greater collective cooperation. If this Yod is used on just a personal level (since the heightened energy of the Higher Octaves cannot always be sustained by the individual's nervous system, and may thus have to be stepped down from its universal application to strictly personal expression), the individual is likely to embark upon an exciting new path allowing for a greater degree of independent spiritedness. He tends to be a trailblazer, and normally in a highly creative manner, and thus handles his new life path with much inventiveness and innovation. But if evoked and mismanaged, this Yod suggests sudden repercussions coming from the environment that radically alter the individual's lifestyle, and often against his will. This turning-point can be brought about due to the individual's intolerance of convention, his excitable yet disruptive behavior, his active rebellion against the norm, or even his lawlessness. The sweeping changes that can occur during this appointed time seldom leave him the same as before, but are apt to make irrevocable rifts within his environment. (*Franz Schubert - Oscar Wilde - Aleister Crowley - Upton Sinclair - Alfred Adler - Aldous Huxley - Yogananda - General Douglas MacArthur - The Duchess of Windsor - Dag Hammarskjold - John F. Kennedy - George Wallace - Henry Kissinger - Barbara Walters - Johnny Carson*).

APEX NEPTUNE

Apex Neptune indicates an individual who begins his life pattern feeling out-of-touch with the ordinary mundane realities of his environment, and who inwardly longs to be elsewhere where life is more calm, peaceful, and beautiful upon all levels. He would rather ignore needed social adjustments by staying within his emotional ivory tower and view the harshness of the real world from a safe and comforting distance. Obviously, his interpretation of situations outside of himself is subject to error and distortion, keeping him in a state of much subjective anxiety and even fearfulness when life cannot sustain his ideal vision. With this Yod, this person must undergo constant adjustments in his emotional attitude if he is to psychologically survive and adapt to the environment he must otherwise submit to. Emotional disorganization is apt to cause him great internal suffering and confusion, pressuring him to eventually seek corrective outlets if he is to ever find peace within himself. By working hard at examining his vulnerabilities, he can eventually learn to avoid seeking out escapist, non-productive avenues of expression. The two quincunxes to Neptune represent facets of his character that are markedly out-of-focus with the realities of current circumstances and thus need greater structure and definition. His personal inner adjustments are quite subtle and may not be clearly seen for many years by either himself and/or others. While imagination is very strong, it is seldom applied in a constructive, workable manner. Self-defeating feelings of unworthiness further aggravate problems. However, during these sometimes lonely and unfulfilling years, the individual is nevertheless preparing himself for a new life path where his vision and sensitivity can be put to more productive use.

When this Yod is fully activated, the individual arrives at that promised forked road in his life and begins to almost magically flow in the new direction presented. His destined life orientation at this point encourages him to devotionally search for an emotional ideal, ultimate love, unearthly beauty, or the discovery of a universal unity of life that combines all forms of manifest energy in a manner that emphasizes a sense of a creative whole. He can embark upon his path with a great amount of inspiration, dedication, and selflessness. Sometimes this path will demand that the individual work quietly behind-the-scenes or underground for some time before he surfaces and presents his contribution to the world. He at least adjusts thru undergoing periods of needed seclusion and privacy while drawing upon his inner spiritual resources. This Yod is usually triggered when the individual has effectively developed his ability to sacrifice temporal desires for some greater and often more intangible ideal. This fated change of course may still seem fraught with uncertainties, illusions, or deceptions (especially in areas where the individual still remains maladjusted), but it nevertheless could put the individual in closer attunement with the Universal Heart. His role could be that of the compassionate healer or defender of the socially neglected, the inspired artist, or the illumined one who is able to deeply delve into the mysteries of life. But if evoked and mismanaged, this Yod could also denote the social martyr or victim of society whose inner malcontent draws unto himself unstabilizing experiences that further weaken and undermine his total being (and normally due to his reluctance to confront and resolve the painful emotional elements buried within his psyche). (*Leonardo da Vinci - Isaac Newton - Yogananda - Meher Baba - Marlon Brando - Richard Burton - Robert Kennedy - Christine Jorgenson*).

APEX PLUTO

Apex Pluto denotes an individual who may begin his life having a great amount of depth-awareness and emotional intensity, but is rarely able to present these qualities to the surface. The penetrating perceptions he may have are not normally shared and understood by others. Thus, the individual may tend to withdraw even more deeply into his interior self and find himself out-of-tune with the superficial worldly activities of his environment. Maladjustment may be emphasized here more than any other Yod pattern, since attitudes in need of correction run deep and tend to be fixated for long periods of time. The individual eventually becomes aware that his inability to be directly affected by anyone has a profound, disturbing effect upon him. Although he may start off with a somewhat anti-social behavioral pattern, he is able to keenly observe and retain subtle details of others that most people overlook. Even the commonest of mundane interaction may reveal inner patterns to him, symbolizing a more powerful interchange of energy. This introspective individual is not prone to simplify his view of life, but can become quite engrossed in its potential complications. However, as objectivity is usually lacking and as his extreme perspective can be out-of-focus, he is to learn to temper his observations with greater moderation, flexibility, and emotional balance. This Yod has strong karmic undertones similar to one with the apex Saturn. For one thing, the established conditions operating previous to the full activation of this Yod prove non-essential for the ongoing growth once the new path has been undertaken. Thus, they are likely to be destroyed or completely abandoned in the course of this destined change.

New, often momentus situations existing at the adoption of this direction pressure the individual to surrender unto them, suggesting that he psychologically must accept these conditions. They may seemingly be forced upon him with little or no other options in sight. Typical to Pluto, something from his past pattern of expression must die or regenerate before this transition can be advantageously undertaken. In other words, this individual is often not meant to return to any previously desired objectives after coming to these crossroads. Inner preparation during his obscure, underground years have now allowed him to adapt to a new level of power, enabling him to purge himself of all former vulnerabilities...and become reborn in the process. This Yod can propel one into a high-level authority position, sometimes giving him organizational control over super-structures in society. He is either able to be in charge of matters that require complex planning, or else is involved in reducing issues to their basic fundamentals. His appointed role could be that of an agent for exploring the unknown, potent resources available to humanity. Or even ushering in the new order of things to come and thus revolutionizing the world-concept. If used upon a personal basis, this Yod puts the individual in contact with a field of operation in which his mental depth and penetrating insight can be used creatively. He may follow a specialized path that enables him to uncover inner meaning with little distraction or interference from the external world. Yet if evoked and mismanaged, this powerful Yod could suggest inevitable changes which may de-elevate the individual to a more frustrating level of obscurity and isolation. This may be brought upon by the individual himself due to his self-destructive passions, his futile attempts to manipulate or coerce others, or simply his open defiance to undermine existing authority at any cost. (*Ralph Waldo Emerson - Stephen Foster - Admiral Byrd - J.P.Morgan -J.Edgar Hoover - Gerald Ford - Charlie Chaplin*).

References:

(1) Al H. Morrison, *Mercury Hour* (7th Extra Edition), Jan., 1980, p. 62.
(2) Thyrza Escobar, *Side Lights of Astrology*, Golden Seal, Calif., 3rd Edition, 1971, p. 44.
(3) Helen Paul, Bridget Mary O'Toole, *The Yod and Other Sensitive Points in Your Horoscope*, Vulcan Books, Seattle, WA, 1977.
(4) Barbara Watters, *The Astrologer Looks At Murder*, Vahalla Paperbacks Ltd., 1969, Washington, D.C., p. 115.

9
Unaspected Planets

Although the main focus of this book so far has been aspects in the chart, it may also prove important to consider a planet in the horoscope that appears unaspected. The term "unaspected" can be misleading, since a planet will invariably make some aspect pattern...either thru minor aspects, connection with the angles of the chart, midpoints or thru harmonics. However, an unaspected planet is commonly defined as one which makes no *major* aspects within reasonable orb (although what determines "reasonable orb" is still a matter of controversy and debate). Astrologers will run across such planets from time to time. Perhaps the finest resource available offering a selection of various astrological opinions concerning unaspected planets is Geoffrey Dean's *Recent Advances In Natal Astrology* (published by The Astrological Association, England, 1977). Dean devotes an entire chapter discussing this phenomenon. In general, astrologers feel that while not necessarily weak, an unaspected planet does not integrate itself easily with other components of the psyche (represented by the other planets). This is also my attitude concerning unaspected planets. Yet although these planets may not interrelate very well, their prime distinction is that they can at least retain their truer nature more markedly so than aspected planets, for better or worse.

An unaspected planet can appear quite intense and one-pointed in its expression, since its energy is not colored by other planets functioning thru other signs. And since other houses are not involved, this planet is apt to concentrate its circumstantial manifestation in one emphasized area. There are no blending of principles found, and thus no apparent modification of the innate expression of that planet. Yet without aspects, planets are not encouraged to express themselves in the multifaceted manner of aspected planets. Dr. Dean, in a personal two year study, established that while unaspected planets *do* express themselves in an individual's character (he disclaims that they are "dumb notes" 1 in the chart), they seem much harder to control in their expression than aspected planets. 2 He also states that "the principle of an unaspected planet tends to be either switched on or off with no halfway measures allowed, and the native oscillates between on and off. Hence, 'all or nothing' is another fair general description." 3 He concludes that because of this oscillation feature, the unaspected planet's strength is very difficult to ascertain.

Thyrza Escobar suggests that an unaspected planet can be "highly outstanding" 4 in its influence. Doris Hebel views such planets as "important, distinctive, erratic; and the direction of their influence...beyond prediction." 5 This distinctive yet erratic quality is supported by Eugene Moore, whose theory on unaspected planets is very interesting. In a workshop he gave in Atlanta to the *Metro. Atlanta Astrological Society*, 6 he described an unaspected planet as behaving in a manner similar to *Uranus*. Moore feels such a planet shows where an individual stands alone. The direction of action the planet here takes can be uncertain, spasmodic, and irregular. Although the planet tends to lack stability, it could be representative of genius. For example, Moore interprets one with an unaspected Sun as being highly independent and detached from external influences, making this person a virtual island-unto-himself type. If the birth data given of the Ayatollah Khomeini is correct (May 17, 1900), he would have an unaspected Sun. Eugene Moore's description would aptly fit this willful patriarch. In addition, it is interesting to note that Moore's view of an unaspected planet as being "spasmodic and irregular" would correlate with Dr. Dean's findings that unaspected planets have a "switched on and off" quality about them.

To interpret what an unaspected planet could natally signify, it may be first important to ask why aspects are relevant to begin with. In my opinion, aspects enable any planet under consideration to further undergo experience in consciousness thru involvement with other planets. Aspects stimulate a planet to test out its potential, and thereby develop its innate capacity to express itself thru a diversity of experiences. Aspects allow planets to combine forces together in a manner that introduces new dimensions for *both* planets involved. Therefore, if any planet is unaspected, it is less psychologically driven to branch out into a fuller range of activity normally typical of aspected planets. Although unaspected, such a planet (by virtue of not associating itself with other planets) should behave in a highly *self-contained* manner. Unaspected planets may manifest like *exact* conjunctions in terms of intensified single-mindedness of impulse and interest. Yet *unlike* a natal conjunction, an unaspected planet is apt to experience a sense of *isolation* in dealing with its basic principles. Since only one planet is involved here, it has no sense of blending or synthesis with any other planet. Without the dynamics of the conjunction involved, self-awareness thru personal action is not readily evoked. Unlike planets in conjunction, this planet expresses its nature more totally, but usually in an intensely automatic yet unregulated manner. Other planets help modulate a planet's expression thru aspect connections, which here is not found.

Does anything modify an unaspected planet? For one thing, the sign an unaspected planet falls in becomes more emphasized and therefore influential. The house placement *may* take on unique prominence *if* no other planet is posited there...unique at least according to how the individual personally relates to affairs of that house. Without squares or oppositions to it, an unaspected planet does not undergo the stress of common challenges in life, nor does it experience the extra momentum of force typical of that same planet under tensional configurations. Perhaps this planet is working out a special level of development that cannot be afforded otherwise if strongly aspected. While creative, self-expressive outlets (suggested by trines and sextiles) may prove harder to attract or even appreciate, the unaspected planet might still be able to manifest its potential with great impact within one exclusive area of life (indicated by its house position and thru the dynamics of its sign). It might also express much of itself thru the houses(s) it rules in the chart.

An unaspected planet could take on the nature of a
singleton in that it can become a conspicuous focus of
attention. Yet unlike a singleton, it is not able to filter the
composite blend of the other planets in the horoscope. I feel
one trait of an unaspected planet that seems to stand out is
its unpredictable nature. Usually our estimations of how
any planet might act out its impulses are prompted by the
presence of aspects to that planet. But with no aspects to
consider, what is an astrologer to expect in terms of that
planet's expression? There are probably other unknown
factors in existence that regulate the manifestation of life
principles beyond what is presently realized thru the
structure of astrology as it has now *evolved.* Astrology is as
subject to the evolutionary process as is everything else
(which should be evident every time a new planet is
discovered and added to the structure). We should not
assume that all that *is* is exclusively contained within solar
system based astrological archetypes (as we typically do
when describing life processes indicated by the Zodiac).
What if earth-based astrology is simply the necessary
springboard for human beings to eventually tap into
completely alien concepts of being? What if even more
powerful galactic archetypes unknown to us nevertheless
direct the mechanism of earth-based astrological phenomena? Frankly, we just do not know if the astrological
formulae we apply to our human condition *are*
unconditional. Thus, if an unaspected planet tends to show a
periodic lack of control in its action or moments of
oscillating expression that are hard to account for, it could
be prompted to activate this way due to processes that we
are not ready to know about yet. These planets have been
shown to undergo periods of spurtlike activity for no
apparent reason (*i.e.*, not because of transits or
progressions). With our limited knowledge, it is hard to
explain how these planets are generated into expression
without any aspect stimuli.

Theoretically, it would seem important to note whether the
unaspected planet under consideration is retrograde, at its
station, intercepted, or conjunct an angle (since all such
phenomena can occur regardless of aspect contacts from

other planets). Research and careful observation are needed before astrologers can arrive at concrete conclusions. The following delineations are strictly suggestions of *some* of the ways an unaspected planet might influence individual character when found in the natal chart. Although the sign and house of an unaspected planet are important to consider (since they add more complexity to the expression of the planet's urge), their influence will not be considered in these interpretations:

UNASPECTED SUN

Eugene Moore's interpretation that an unaspected Sun individual behaves like an island-unto-himself type seems right to me. When unaspected, the Sun's autonomous, self-governing nature can be even more emphasized. This condition should accentuate an independent spirit, but not always in a wholesome, well-balanced manner. A heavily aspected Sun natally would suggest one who is driven to gain recognition and honor in the external world thru a vibrant, confident display of one's abilities. Such an individual makes an effort to attract attention and be openly admired or praised for his achievements in order to feel ego-fulfilled. Thus, he consciously attempts to radiate his energies in a manner insuring a direct impact upon his environment. However, the unaspected Sun individual seems less driven to exteriorize himself. He appears less overtly glory-seeking, and thus makes little effort to secure center-stage positioning. Nevertheless, he is motivated to focus upon his own self-importance, holding himself in high regard. Self-esteem and self-pride are important to him, whether reinforced by his environment or not. As his strength and integrity come from a subjective source, he is less dependent upon outer relationships for ego-support. He can be very rooted within his own inner core of being, regardless of how unstable or chaotic his external surroundings are. Such intense self-centeredness may make him appear unresponsive and aloof, almost as if he is totally absorbed within his own self-made world.

The inner nature does not associate itself very well with other facets of the character, determined by the other planets. Thus, one's individuality is seldom stimulated into *full* expression, although it may be one-pointedly evident in a singular area of one's life. Planets connected with the Sun by aspect gain a greater sense of their own purposeful strength. Being thus tied in with one's vital ego structure, they are brought more into conscious, creative expression and given a firmer sense of direction thru the positive activation of the will. With an unaspected Sun, the remaining planets still function, but without a dominant central life theme to revolve around. They neither help nor hinder the individual's main objectives, but only because they are not directly related to such objectives. Perhaps the drives of these planets are forced to take the back seat, in which they are experienced as mere secondary needs given less attention and development. Instead, the individual may be more intent upon the exclusive development of his pure solar characteristics.

UNASPECTED MOON

In my opinion, the Moon (representing the receptive, nurturing principle) is one planet that needs to connect itself with other planets in order to function properly. The Moon deals with the drive to attach, and to absorb energy thru such attachment. Aspects to the Moon help condition the individual to make constant functional adaptations within his immediate surroundings, allowing him to adjust his center continuously in order to effectively cope with the stresses of the environment (the Moon is the natural helpmate of the Sun in this regard). But when unaspected, this isolated Moon inclines the individual to feel an unnatural sense of disconnection with the immediate environment, especially on the emotional level. Perhaps the individual has difficulty acclimating himself to any environment over a long period of time, and therefore appears restless, unsettled, and very much *not* at home with his current conditions. He may undergo spurtlike periods in which restlessness greatly accelerates and moods change rapidly, resulting in emotional highs and lows. The Moon is also readily colored and given definitive structure by the other planets. Without aspects, the Moon would remain formless and indistinct as a process of personality.

Plus other components of our nature (shown by the
remaining planets) would be less able to be nurtured and
supported by natural, protective instincts. The individual
may show a less caring concern for the development of
those other parts of his nature. With an unaspected Moon,
the individual's feeling nature is not necessarily weakened,
but it is less able to be demonstrated on the surface. But
since emotions are less likely to be evoked and openly
expressed to any notable extent, this person may be at a
loss in trying to recognize what triggers them into action
(since aspects to the Moon help us objectify and pinpoint
our needs rather than keep them buried and indefinable).

In Dean's study, he found that the psychological effects of
an unaspected Moon "could be the most personally
traumatic of any planet."7 Obviously, since the Moon helps
an individual feel sheltered, secure, and nourished within
his environment, one with an unaspected Moon could feel
markedly unstabilized or uncommonly vulnerable, which
could be traumatizing. It would seem reasonable that this
solitary Moon could accentuate the lunar principles of
enclosure and insulation, suggesting that the individual
tends to overly contain his feelings and impressions rather
than allow them to freely interact with other facets of his
nature. And since underdeveloped due to a lack of active
expression, they may remain in a state of immaturity.
While one's range of open emotional expression can be
diminished, there still can be great intensity of feeling and
concern in the area of the chart where the Moon is located.

UNASPECTED MERCURY

Like the Moon, Mercury is another planet that benefits
from a variety of aspect connections with other planets
(although, considering its abstract nature, it is less
dependent in this context). Representing the principle of
clear, unbiased objectivity, Mercury can be a neutral
influence. It does, however, function more effectively when
it is able to combine itself with other planets, since it
develops best thru the stimulation of a diversity of
influences. Mercury is energized to further express its
innate potential due to its curiosity about what is unfamiliar

(it is driven to want to know how all of life works). Other planets can provide Mercury with the essential learning experiences it eagerly seeks out. But unaspected Mercury, lacking in this educational opportunity, could represent one whose mental development is seldom well-rounded. Although the mind often is quite powerful and capable, it can become one-tracked in its application. And while the individual may be able to intelligently gather information in areas that attract his interest (indicated by Mercury's natal placement), he may not comprehend as much about himself. Mercury offers us the ability to apply the light of reason to all facets of our human nature, at least in a manner that prompts us to question our impulses. One with unaspected Mercury might be less driven to direct his mental power towards the observation and analysis of the other components of his personality. Thus, these other parts of his psyche are unlikely to develop and express themselves thru the benefit of logical, objective evaluation (unless they fall in Mercury-ruled signs and/or houses). However, the individual can exhibit an extraordinary mental facility in a singular area of life, suggested by its placement.

What is perhaps beneficial about unaspected Mercury, unlike a heavily aspected one, is that it is less inclined to become scattered and distracted (since it is not being simultaneously activated in a multitude of areas). Yet, by being less diversified, this type of mind could become less flexible and adaptable to change (and especially so if posited in a fixed sign). The individual is less inclined to weigh all sides of an issue, since he is less familiar with all sides. Not necessarily stubborn or rigid, unaspected Mercury is simply not as prone towards recognizing options and alternatives of thought, as would be a well-aspected Mercury. According to Dean's study, the urge to communicate is unlikely to be diminished. Yet it does appear to operate in moments of spurtlike activity (although often in a brilliant manner), in which the individual can appear hyperactive (mentally and verbally). For the most part, I'd imagine the individual feels isolated and disintegrated on the mental level.

UNASPECTED VENUS

Perspective may be less characteristic of an unaspected Venus, since the lack of aspects from other planets offers little sense of contrast, a factor essential for the development of perspective. And while contrast can be experienced thru natal oppositions in the chart involving other planets, it here is unable to be evoked thru Venus processes. Contrast involving the *Venus* principle may at least be experienced thru variances according to the sign and/or house placement. Otherwise, it tends to remain latent. Since unaspected Venus is not able to branch out and associate itself with other planets, the outgoing, socially adaptable side of this planet has difficulty expressing itself (at least with a sense of coordination, balance, and poise). This placement may describe the wallflower Venus whose social instincts are too self-contained to have an impact upon the environment. Venus represents the attraction principle. Without aspects, the capacity to attract is limited to a singular focus of interest, which could prove to be obsessive and single-minded. Affectional interests are not apt to be actively pursued. The individual can be very passive here, yet very intense in his response. The sensual, appetite-fulfilling side of Venus could be more accented, since one can remain self-contained and socially-uninvolved while still pursuing these personal urges.

When unaspected, Venus is less driven to reflect and evaluate before acting with the degree of deliberation or vacillation typical of a heavily-aspected Venus. The individual is less impelled to consider other needs within his psyche, denoted by the other planets, and thus is less urged to establish balance in self-expression. Venus here may tend to fulfill its impulses in a sporatic, almost compulsive manner showing little restraint or moderation. The individual can become very one-pointed in the satisfaction of his desires. But for the most part, affectional needs remain latent and unevoked or else are rarely displayed openly. This Venus can be quite undemonstrative, although quite reactive on more subjective levels. While the individual may feel quite divorced from receiving the common pleasures of social interaction (making him more of an observer rather than a participator in social functions), he still may attain intense satisfaction from an exclusively valued area of his personal life, usually indicated by Venus' house position. He may be able to internally balance himself in this area and achieve a sense of inner harmony that can seldom be acquired thru the usual external Venus activities.

UNASPECTED MARS

Psychologically, the planet Mars innately is driven to separate itself and act apart from outside influences in favor of independent self-expression. Headstrong Mars does not seem to enjoy having its impulsive urges modified by the often contrasting needs of the other planets. Perhaps when heavily aspected, Mars feels more hampered and confined. Unaspected Mars is more able to function in its pure form, which could be quite uncompromising. The individual's ability to act on his own personal behalf may operate without the coordinating support of other factors of his make-up. Although the active drive of Mars is limited to applying itself in fewer areas of the individual's psyche, this drive can be expressed with much strength of focus, one-pointed interest, and energy expenditure. In Dean's study, he found that unaspected Mars produced effects that "were the most outwardly marked and distinctive of all..."[8] Individuals he observed did not appear to lack initiative or seem listless. One's sense of drive was not reduced. In fact, most were notably energetic and active on some level of their being, almost in a non-stop manner. Perhaps unaspected Mars, functioning according to its truer nature, could reasonably suggest constant activity, untempered or unmodulated by the other planets. The urge to be on-the-go, or in continuous motion, or always doing something, thus, could be compulsive at times. The sign involved should help to determine upon what level of experience the individual is most commonly active.

Unaspected Mars may tend to be more self-centered than heavily aspected Mars. The capacity to act according to one's sense of self-interest may be emphasized. Aspected Mars is challenged to undergo a wider range of experiences in consciousness, enabling it to become more adaptable to the pressures of life. Without aspects, Mars tends to have a singular focus lacking the guiding benefit of other components of the personality. Unaspected Mars can act out its energy in an unrestrained and almost boundless manner, since constructive limitations that could be provided by other planets are absent. All tensional traits typical of Mars (such as anger, aggression, violence, etc.) may suddenly flair up and actively vent themselves from time to time. The raw, unrefined energy of Mars is here less able to become modified. Because the individual is not motivated to apply his Martian impulses towards the stimulation of other parts of his nature (which could help release energy), an excess of pent-up energy builds up until the psyche can no longer contain it. Negative manifestations of Mars here are likely to be very unconscious, and thus are apt to seem quite irrational at times, since actions taken are not influenced by facets of the nature which could lend reason, control, insight, perspective, and awareness of consequences.

UNASPECTED JUPITER

Jupiter naturally seeks out active social participation rather than solitude. Jupiter is the planet of outreach and breadth of scope. When unaspected, it is apt to be less gregarious and socially expansive. Or else it behaves so in spurts of enthusiasm. Jupiter's innate spontaneity is unlikely to be fully brought out, except during erratic moments of expression. The individual may temporarily display unbridled exuberance which tends to die out as quickly as it manifests. Planetary aspects help Jupiter further develop its judgemental abilities, since a variety of aspects motivates the individual to seek out experiences that promote these abilities. Unaspected Jupiter attracts less situational affairs in which judgement must actively be applied (suggesting then that it may be undeveloped). Other parts of the nature are not able to grow thru the process of inspiration and uplift typical of Jupiter energies. Lacking buoyancy, the individual may feel very weighted down by the gravity of life (unless there is strong support from Sagittarius placements and activity in the 9th house). However, according to Jupiter's house position, the individual can show a great amount of zeal and self-encouragement. Instead of candid and casual, the individual may appear detached and mentally remote (since Jupiter, like Uranus, deals with far-awayness themes).

Unlike the more worldly-wise aspected Jupiter (whose broadened life opportunities assist in the development of wisdom), the individual is likely to be highly idealistic, yet innocent and unassuming in many areas of his existence. This condition could denote the ivory-tower dispositon. Unaspected Jupiter may feel more disconnected with socially observed moral or religious standards. The individual is less prone to follow belief systems or world views that are expected of him due to cultural pressures or early conditioning. Even if intensely philosophical, his self-containment here suggests he is a loner in his search for higher meaning or ultimate truth. However, his vision could be very unique because of this. Betterment is nevertheless to be found operating most evidently in the affairs of Jupiter's house position.

UNASPECTED SATURN

Like independent and self-reliant Mars, Saturn might also function with less difficulty when unaspected. In its unaspected condition, Saturn's inclination towards solitude can be emphasized. However, since Saturn develops structure better when being tested thru rigorous life experiences, its lack of aspects here could suggest that less circumstances are available to properly test out its strengths and weaknesses. Saturn in aspect with another planet allows that planet (or part of the psyche) to become productive in a sensible, responsible manner. The planet is more grounded and better able to function realistically. But when unaspected, this normally dutiful planet can become more indifferent or unconcerned about processes outside of its own singular sphere of operation. Structure and definitions are found only in limited areas of life, and are not related to the remaining components of the overall nature. Therefore, this could imply that the individual is not motivated to take direct, conscious control over many parts of his nature. Self-discipline and organization of needs may be markedly lacking as well as caution or self-preservation

(Saturn is the safety urge that establishes all necessary limits upon the will in order to preserve the integrity of our being).

Although rigidity and crystallization may be less problematic with an unaspected Saturn (unlike one making a multitude of contacts), the individual can become too receptive to many random influences in a non-directional manner, without the usual benefit of the normal brakes and controls of an aspected Saturn. Attempts at ordering one's life may be at least inconsistent, and one's conscience may be less applied in life situations. The individual is apt to float thru life for the most part, establishing no set guidelines for living or abiding by few inner laws (no matter how outwardly successful and accomplished). Patience and long-range planning may be less evident, while timing can generally be off. However, Saturn is quite inclined to enduringly concentrate itself in one area at a time rather than scatter its focus. Thus, there may be a notable urge to control and manage affairs in the area of life shown by Saturn's house position with little susceptibility towards distraction. Yet the individual has to be careful not to become too unadaptable to the potential variations of self-expression.

UNASPECTED URANUS

All Higher Octave planets are too intense and awesome to be expressed in their pure, undiluted form. They especially need aspect contacts to help step down their quickened energies if they are going to be used safely. When unaspected, they can prove too much for the ordinary human system to handle effectively. Thus, they either will operate in an exclusively unconscious fashion (with occasional spurts of unpredictable and unusual behavior), or perhaps not at all (remaining totally latent on the character-level, and thus projected onto people and situations). Yet for some individuals, for unknown reasons, an unaspected Higher Octave could indicate extraordinary capacity far beyond average human expression (almost as if these people are constantly plugged into unlimited sources of cosmic power). When unaspected, Uranus becomes most self-contained and independent of outside social influence. It tends to be less driven to inaugurate breakthroughs in the outer world environment in the more open, rebellious manner of a heavily-aspected Uranus. The detachment quality of unaspected planets can be accentuated, since Uranus by itself already tends to be impersonal. Without sufficient outlets for channeling (which aspects would provide), nervous-electrical tension could build up and intensify, creating periods of much restlessness and discontent. The individual would thus experience bursts of energy expenditure for short periods of time. Uranus' potential for presenting one with unsettling conditions or abrupt turnabouts of outer affairs, however, is for the most part limited (confined only to the affairs of its house position) without disrupting other features of the individual's life. In other words, the individual's capacity to experience chaos or disorder is reduced (which may seem like a blessing for some). But as Uranus helps to accelerate human growth thru *meaningful* disruption, its lack of aspect connections could hamper soul progress in the long run. Without the electrical stimulation of Uranus charging up various facets of his nature, the individual is less galvanized to shatter rigid and stifling patterns of behavior. Therefore, progress is slower. Flashes of genius or sparks of intuition may be specifically felt in the house area, where the individual can feel quite unique and unmatched, for better or worse.

UNASPECTED NEPTUNE

By its own very nature, Neptune tends towards withdrawal, seclusion, and privacy. It prefers to remain absorbed in the inner worlds of consciousness and has a harder time adjusting itself to manifesting in concrete, solid terms. The more aspects it has, the more likely it is to be challenged to manifest itself thru external experience, regardless of the level or quality shown. It is forced to come out of its closet, so to speak. Unaspected Neptune could perhaps represent a most passive condition for this other-worldly planet. Without the driving stimulus provided by aspect contacts, this unstimulated Neptune could encourage the individual to keep his search for ultimate emotional ideals to himself rather than develop them in the environment. He may be able to find inner comfort and tranquility by creating beautiful images within the realm of his fertile but unplowed imagination. Neptune's fantasy ability could be markedly powerful and intense, since this faculty does not necessarily have to be supported thru active involvement with the environment to operate. But imagination, fantasy, revelation, and inspired vision all tend to have few tangible avenues for their expression, unlike heavily-aspected Neptune. Dreams may thus seem quite unattainable for this individual. Normally, the less active Neptune is in the chart, the less the individual is prone to act in a way that promotes self-deception (illusions here could be described as self-contained. And those that exist may be found manifesting according to the affairs of Neptune's house position.) When unaspected, Neptune is not able to directly influence the drives of the remaining planets, denying them the benefit of spiritual insight. For some, this means a more material world view devoid of visions of ultimate perfection and unity. The individual may have a harder time believing in miracles, and thus is less able to directly experience or recognize them. Nevertheless, he is less apt to feel confused or disoriented with the world he does give credence to.

UNASPECTED PLUTO

Pluto is the planet of the isolationist. It represents a part of our psychological make-up that is remote and distant from involvement in the mainstream of ordinary life activities. At least in the natal chart, it often operates in a highly subtle, underground manner, and from an intensely subjective point of view. When unaspected, Pluto's tendency to isolate itself and stand far apart can be even more emphasized. The individual may have subterranean forces within his psyche that are completely fragmented from other facets of his interior make-up. And with Pluto, these buried forces normally have great power no matter how hard they are to tap and bring to the surface of one's consciousness. Unaspected Pluto suggests spurts of compulsive and almost overwhelming desire-expression that could appear quite foreign to what the individual's normal, conscious awareness of his being is. Pluto needs aspects to help reduce the level of its power and intensity, and to allow the individual to become more consciously aware of what otherwise would be his deepest, most obscure drives. Aspects are the necessary agents which allow such primal urges to emerge to the borderlands of consciousness and better undergo the necessary struggle required to transform themselves into renewed powers. Yet without aspects, Pluto could limit the individual's ability to establish proper outlets for regeneration. He is therefore less tested to develop self-mastery (especially on the emotional level), or purposeful control over his life-expression. He can become quite over-shadowed by his shadows. Other parts of his overall nature (the remaining planets) are not allowed the benefit of regeneration upon their most fundamental levels. They are denied deeper insight into themselves, unless perhaps planets fall in Scorpio or the 8th house. On the other hand, unaspected Pluto (being more latent in expression) can imply that this individual is not as likely to attempt to gain power over others, at least in the more dominant, overbearing manner of heavily-aspected Pluto. But if so, such power-plays are less recognized and objectively analyzed by the individual. Periodic honest self-examination is needed, especially as related to Pluto's house activities. Otherwise, one with unaspected Pluto has less life-opportunities to confront and overcome his darker nature, no matter how disturbing these facets of his nature prove to be.

Before closing this chapter, I want to emphasize that what I find important about an unaspected planet is not so much the nature of the planet itself, but how a lack of that planet's influence affects other parts of the personality. Other planets are not able to directly connect with the unaspected planet in concern, and thus cannot take on some of its coloration. Thus, interpretation should not only be based upon the intensified, self-contained temperament of the unaspected planet, but also upon the condition this creates for all remaining planets. This allows the astrologer to view the whole process involved with the unaspected planet phenomenon. It allows for a more holistic delineation. For the most part, if a planet makes no major aspects in the chart, I would then look for the closest minor aspect (especially the tensional ones) made and give that particular aspect more attention than otherwise.

References:

(1) Geoffrey Dean, *Recent Advances in Natal Astrology*, The Astrological Assoc., England, 1977, p. 356.
(2) *Ibid*, p. 356.
(3) *Ibid*, p. 356.
(4) *Ibid*, p. 356.
(5) *Ibid*, p. 357.
(6) Eugene Moore, "Unaspected Planets," M.A.A.S. Workshop, Jan. 16, 1977, Atlanta, Ga.
(7) Geoffrey Dean, *Recent Advances in Natal Astrology*, The Astrological Assoc., England, 1977, p. 363.
(8) *Ibid*, p. 364.

10
Retrograde Planets

There are periods in the cyclic orbit of a planet when it appears to slow down, come to a halt, and then proceed to reverse its orbital direction. This is known as the retrograde phase of that planet. Accustomed to the stability of its normal daily rate of motion, the planet now manifests the urge to withdraw from further forward motion (symbolizing the gaining of new experience) and instead begins to cross over previously transited degrees (symbolizing past experiences). Yet in between is a period of almost no motion called the stationary phase, in which there is a rare stillness and inner composure of the planet. All this apparent phenomena is very essential to the astrological interpretation of retrograde planets. Actually, no planet is able to move backwards in its orbital path. Yet the fact that this retrograde condition is in reality an astronomical illusion, created by the accelerated motion of the Earth, does not invalidate the *psychological* influence retrograde planets have upon human personality.

Life principles represented by retrograde planets are more likely to express themselves upon an individual's inner level as deeper facets of his character that are not easily observed on the surface. Being more submerged, retrograde planets denote qualities operating from a more subjective point of view. Consider this image: the initial point of the Zodiac is 0° Aries. The starting point for the twelve houses is the ASC. A planet at 0° Aries or the ASC is symbolic of the emergence of conscious expression, and thus announces the commencement of a new cycle of experience for that planet (whether thru attitude or circumstance). But if that planet was to turn retrograde, it would re-enter the 12th house, crossing back over the last degree of the sign Pisces in the natural wheel. In this respect I view retrograde planets manifesting urges similar to the principles of the sign Pisces, the 12th house, and the planet Neptune (as ruler of both). They also seem to imply the karmic implications of the 29th degree.

This, then, is to suggest that retrograde planets stimulate a returning to previous conditions of awareness or "unfinished business" originating in the hidden depths of the personal unconscious. The principles represented by a retrograde planet require less conscious involvement in the outer world. They seek more reflective, contemplative experience to work out the planet's urges. Retrogradation activates those not-too-obvious facets of personality that remain "behind-the-scenes" for the most part. This condition can result in inner illumination when well-managed, or much self-undoing when poorly handled. As the unconscious components of one's selfhood are even more inaccessible than are his subconscious factors, the function of a retrograde planet is obscured and harder for the individual to objectively recognize. The gradual slowness of the planet's retrograde motion implies that there is something from the past that needs to be carefully re-studied or patiently reconsidered, and thereby more thoroughly assimilated. There is a degree of awareness already present here that needs to be reviewed in a less hurried manner. Retrograde planets could pinpoint principles that were either dealt with too superficially and applied without much depth of understanding in past lives (and now they need enrichment), or else were misapplied to the point of distortion (and now they need to be regenerated upon inner levels before they can be used constructively on outer levels). To insure the proper growth and psychological maturation of the individual, the essence of that retrograde planet must be grasped and realized more fully before the individual can proceed further with his evolution.

On a conscious level, the individual may have difficulty outwardly directing the urges of the planet in concern. It seems these planets respond in a passive manner regarding external activities. They at least tend to apply themselves in more subtle, indirect ways. Although highly receptive to inner currents, they are apt to be reluctant to demonstrate their capacity freely upon the surface of life affairs. Retrograde planets, in my opinion, do not lose any strength of expression. They simply suggest a focalization upon more internal developments than do direct planets. Yet the individual may need to establish a clearer and more well-defined understanding of what that planet means on its deeper and more profound level before he can expect to utilize the principles indicated in a productive manner. Because of this, matters represented by the planet involved (according to its natal sign and house position) are often delayed from reaching fruition or fulfillment until the individual has deepened his awareness. He tends to operate at a slower pace psychologically to insure a more complete and thorough sense of comprehension...and thus must often learn to adjust or adapt to limiting conditions that sometimes can occur.

Authors Virginia Ewbank and Joanne Wickenburg have formulated a very unique concept concerning retrograde planets. In their equally unique book, *The Spiral of Life* (self-published, Seattle, Washington, 1974), they feel that for planets Mercury-thru-Saturn (the luminaries are not able to have retrograde phases), the retrograde condition operates as though working thru the latter sign the planet rules (since these planets all have dual rulerships according to traditional astrology).1 In other words, Mercury retrograde is more descriptive of Virgo processes rather than Gemini. Virgo is apt to carefully study and analyze what Gemini readily gathers unto itself. Mars retrograde acts in a manner more fitting of Scorpio rather than Aries. Venus retrograde is more attuned with abstract Libra instead of earthy Taurus. Retrograde Jupiter ties in with Pisces principles rather than Sagittarius, while Saturn retrograde expresses more like Aquarius instead of Capricorn. I strongly advise reading this insightful book, since it covers many dimensions of astro-psychological delineation in a very sensitive and clearly-defined manner. The authors are very consistent with their presentation of astrological principles, which is a rarity to find in most available literature.

If the individual has four or more planets retrograde (especially when they are personal planets...Mercury-thru-Saturn...and not mainly the Higher Octave planets), he may begin life internalizing many of his urges. He may become more attentive to his subjective world. John McCormick, in his *The Book of Retrogrades* (self-published, U.S.A., 1973) refers to four planets retrograde as a "quadron" and states that this natal condition reflects "a tendency upon the part of the native (with a Quadron Retrograde) to withdraw and seek expression in private."[2] I feel that the more planets retrograde in the chart, the more the individual is apt to view life differently from others with few, if any, retrogrades. Retrograde planets can be suggestive of unique and highly individualized abilities, since they are more motivated to draw from resources within one's deeper self. Originality of one's life approach could be indicated by one having several natal planets retrograde, and this is likely due to the fact that the individual is less moulded or shaped by external social structures. Instead, he may be more able to develop himself according to his inner promptings, which may not always be understood or accepted by others. Much of this person's true nature is typically kept from direct surface exposure until he has learned to know the essence of his urges thru careful, subjective focus. Due to the natural introspective nature of retrograde planets, their full expression is often held back in one's early years until they have been more fully explored and reflected upon.

Many natal retrograde planets could denote the "late bloomer" type of personality, exhibiting unexpected talents and abilities in one's more mature years (similar to any singular retrograde planet). However, if many of the retrograde planets are involved in stress configurations (especially squares or quincunxes, which tend towards indirectness of expression), the individual is likely to avoid direct participation in the worldly events around him, and may shun purposeful challenges requiring active response in favor of retreating within. He tends to operate upon a different wave-length from elements in his personal environment and thus may feel awkward or somewhat out-of-place in general social situations. His difficulty in relating to the mainstream of life may make him feel inadequate at the start of his life, as he learns to adjust to standard ways of behaving. This could be particularly so when retrograde planets make stress aspects to the *ruler* of the ASC, to the ASC *itself*, or to one of these planets if it is the ruler of the ASC. If stress patterns here are left unresolved, the individual may feel quite detached or disconnected from his surrounding, thus feeling very lonely and isolated.

On the other hand, many well-managed retrograde planets can indicate one who is adept at transferring all drives and urges to a more sublime level, giving one more ability for spiritual development or greater self-awareness upon inner planes of consciousness. The individual may be better able to attune himself to the power and wisdom of his unconscious. He therefore can more effectively transcend the apparent limitations of his personality. Retrograde planets seek answers *within* to conditions direct planets prefer to discover thru overt activity in the manifest world. These planets can be best used for very lofty purposes by one who attempts to gain a greater understanding of the needs of the Higher Self. I do not completely agree with those schools of astrology who claim that retrograde planets *exclusively* represent negativities we have brought over from past lives due to errors of conduct. Perhaps sometimes this is the case, but I don't see this as being a general principle of retrogradation. Direct planets can obviously be equally descriptive of undesirable traits of character, and perhaps even more so since they are likely to express themselves more directly out into the environment. However, retrograde planets *do* seem to operate more compulsively at times, following their own course of action regardless of pressure in the external environment. But again, this does not have to be perceived as negative activity.

KEYWORDS FOR RETROGRADE PLANETS

CONSTRUCTIVE	NON-PRODUCTIVE
meditative	withdrawn
profound	inhibited
depth awareness	blockage of outer awareness
inner strength	maladjustment

KEYWORDS FOR RETROGRADE PLANETS

CONSTRUCTIVE	NON-PRODUCTIVE
reformation	regression
humility	timidity
universal identity	thwarted self-identity
self-knowledge	morbid self-absorption
subtle	evasive
self-attunement	self-undoing
reflective	repressive
spiritual power	health problems (often psychological)

STATIONARY PLANETS

One very important phase for any planet during its natural cycle occurs when that planet reaches its station. By this is meant the period shortly before a planet either turns retrograde or direct. A planet at this special point of its cycle is dramatically slowing down in its motion. Tracy Marks suggests that a planet can be considered stationary "if its speed has decreased to less than 1/10th of its normal motion."3 You may have to use your own judgement as to when a planet begins to become stationary. Normally with slower moving planets (like the Higher Octaves), a planet is stationary when it remains at the same degree and *minute* before changing direction. For faster moving planets, I consider them stationary when they remain at the same degree only before changing (at least concerning the natal chart, not necessarily progressions). What does a stationary planet mean in natal analysis? Perhaps the best clue describing its nature is shown by its most obvious feature: it is concentrating heavily in one singular degree area of the chart. Stationary planets could be said to exhibit an intent interest (according to the nature of the planet), and thus could also suggest much intensity of drive.

In general, a stationary planet is not easily thrown off course from the area of its one-pointed focus. Being virtually motionless, it tends to firmly entrench itself, and this may denote strength of application plus dogged persistence. For better or worse, a stationary planet has much *impact* upon the nature of the individual. However, due to all these above traits, a stationary planet might also depict characteristics that can become immobilized within the personality. The individual can become too set in his orientation here to allow for adaptation, resulting in a stubborn, inflexible manner of expression. On the other hand, the fixity of the planet's condition constructively indicates much stamina and endurance. Aspects to this planet should help determine whether the stationary phase tends to make one firm and resolute in a purposeful way, or rut-bound and static. Usually, it will manifest both ways from time to time. This planet often needs to be thoroughly absorbed in something worthy of its above-average attentiveness if it is to feel satisfied. Nevertheless, the individual will also need to exercise more objectivity in this area to insure that he is not becoming overly-fascinated with the processes of this planet to the exclusion of developing other components of his make-up.

In a natal chart, a stationary planet will either be about to turn retrograde (called stationary retrograde) or turn direct (called stationary direct). This will prove significant in delineation. A *stationary retrograde* planet will take on a more subjective, internalizing disposition, as the individual is about to begin to focus upon the psychological implications of the planet with growing concern. This phase of the planet simply shows more concentrated intensity, creating greater *inner* impact than would that same planet when merely retrograde. A *stationary direct* planet has already assimilated the urges of the planet upon deeper, more introspective levels and is now ready to emerge to the surface of awareness and utilize what has been subtly developed. Stationary direct planets may appear more enterprising, since they are ripe for inaugurating new starts concerning the principles of the planet in concern. They could reveal a degree of anticipation, expectancy, or urgency not commonly found with mere direct planets. However, as both stations still represent a planet that is hardly in motion, efforts towards inner examination or outer utilization will have to be approached with patience, thoroughness, and steadiness of focus. Awareness of subtleties may be important. These same dynamics may also be applied to transiting planets at their stations. However, as with all transiting factors, current outer conditions (rather than ingrained facets of character) stimulate individual response during the stationary periods. Transits need to be interpreted within the context of the individual's existing environment.

A retrograde planet in the chart may eventually, by progression, reach its stationary point before turning direct. The faster-moving planets will most likely do this within the normal lifespan of the individual (Mercury and Venus in particular, and sometimes Mars). For all other planets, much depends whether the natal retrograde planet is already sufficiently close enough to its station within a reasonable time period. Just as the stationary phase for some planets can last several days, a stationary progressed planet's influence can also be in operation for several years. Unlike transits, progressions deal more with the timely *inner* unfoldment of character potential (which may or may not be projected thru relationships or events). I feel the less projected a planet, the more that progression has been properly assimilated and allowed to become an integral part of the inner nature. But even if a well-assimilated progression expresses thru the projection mechanism, what is projected becomes constructive and harmonious to the needs of one's character. However, transits are normally likely to represent existing conditional elements within one's current environment, operating more thru concrete, situational affairs. But even these energies may not always be expressed thru the individual's circumstances (since transits do not always relate to personal events or the urge for action). One of the mysteries of astrology is that no one can predict with any absolute certainty the level upon which any individual will express principles, since this is determined by the evolutionary status of each personality (plus one's ability to effectively use free will). In general, the more self-aware an individual is, the more prone he is to first experience *any* planet (natal, progressed, or transiting) thru attitude and behavior rather than thru concrete, mundane circumstances. Of course, any well-integrated individual should be able to more easily transform attitudes into productive, creative activity without much difficulty.

When a progressed retrograde planet reaches its station and is about to finally turn *direct*, the individual (during that specific progressed year) is reaching a major turning-point in his inner growth pattern. This particular year could mark a significant shift in one's attention, described by the nature of the planet involved. It might symbolically mean that the individual's internal preparatory period of deeper assimilation and integration is reaching completion. He is to now center his inner focus upon the objective world once again and begin to use the energies of this planet to influence external matters. The individual can now mobilize such energies outward from his own center and create a greater impact in his surroundings. Although he may show much depth of understanding concerning this planet, it is likely that he might apply its principles with a bit of awkwardness and uncertainty for the first few following progressed years (since he has not been conditioned since birth to openly function in the direction now presented to him). However, he may tend to show eagerness and expectation in his attempt to demonstrate his awareness in this area. For some people, this condition is akin to being released from a state of stifling confinement and finally being allowed to freely express and expand in the world. Authors Sakoian and Acker feel that when a progressed retrograde planet has reached its station and eventually *re-crosses* over its initial natal retrograde degree, "the individual begins a new cycle of experience with regard to things ruled by that planet."4 I speculate, however, that the sense of a new cycle is first initiated at the station degree, but reaches a peak period for activation when the progressed planet reaches that sensitive natal degree (since this usually occurs many progressed years later after the transition period, giving the individual enough time to develop his capacity in the outer world). But as I have not put this concept to the test, my claim is strictly theoretical.

When a progressed direct planet reaches its station and is
about to turn *retrograde*, the individual (during that
specific progressed year) also undergoes a turning-point in
development. However, this condition could prove to be
more difficult an adjustment for some, since one is now to
begin to turn within after being conditioned from birth to
function upon the worldly surface of mundane life. This
transition could thus appear more like a crisis for those who
have never considered the urges of the planet from a more
introspective view. The individual tends to feel this
transition more deeply since energies are now directing
themselves towards his personal center and away from
normal external interests. Things seem to come to an
abrupt halt and make a sudden turnabout psychologically,
which could be very intense. Constructively, this pattern
denotes a time period when the individual can deepen and
enrich his awareness of principles indicated. He may begin
to come into contact with inner resources that were not
encouraged during his life before this time period (in other
words, potentials not stimulated during the powerful
formative years). He may not even have been aware that he
had such resources until now at this progressed phase,
suggesting that he is slowly coming into more direct contact
with the contents of his unconscious. From a
reincarnational level, the individual may be reintroduced to
levels of awareness from past lives that have been held in
abeyance during his early years (for evolutionary reasons
astrology may not be able to explain). What has been buried
or submerged within the individual's psyche may now be
confronted upon subjective states of consciousness, for
better or worse. But I'd imagine the intent here is for the
better.

Similar to a progressed retrograde planet reaching its
station, turning direct, and crossing over its initial natal
degree...a progressed direct planet reaching its station,
turning retrograde, and re-crossing over its natal degree
could mark a peak period for the individual. At this time, he
may find himself having profound insights related to the
principles of the planet in concern (insights that may help
him re-alter his entire approach to matters symbolized by
the planet). He could be indelibly impressed to adopt a more

spiritualized, in-depth attitude in this area during this period of his life. While it is not common, there are times when at least two planets *simultaneously* turn retrograde or direct on the same progressed day. If this is the case, then dynamics described here should be even more accentuated. There are also times (albeit rare) when as one planet turns retrograde, another turns direct on the same progressed day. This particular progressed year should certainly be noted and observed, since the individual will feel quite in flux with himself and may exhibit contradictory behavior (depending upon the planets).

Astrologers often wonder how a natal retrograde planet is affected when that same planet in *transit* temporarily turns retrograde. I don't think anyone in the field has a pat answer for this situation. Nevertheless, I have heard many with Mercury natally retrograde claim that whenever transiting Mercury goes retrograde, their minds appear to work better, with personal plans and decisions manifesting with more satisfying results than otherwise would be expected. Naturally, these Mercury retrograde types would have something to eventually communicate in this regard, due to the thought-provoking nature of this planet. I have not heard as much about other planets in this regard. Perhaps if a natal retrograde planet turns retrograde by transit, the individual is more attuned with himself during this time period. He thus may find himself more outwardly active and expressive in those life areas denoted by his natal retrograde placement. This makes sense, considering that during all other transiting direct periods, the individual is apt to feel out-of-tune with what he is experiencing in the immediate environment surrounding him, and accordingly behaves differently. The attunement felt here would suggest a degree of inner fulfillment for such a person, even if outer conditions would typically be described as otherwise. He probably has a stronger connection with himself upon deeper levels in this regard, and therefore feels more synchronized with outer events during this brief period.

There are many more conditions that could be speculated upon concerning retrograde phenomena, such as: do they work with *converse* progressions, or by solar arc direction (which markedly speeds up the movement of the Higher Octave planets making them more accessible in forecasting), and how are they to be regarded concerning composite charts (especially when one person has a planet retrograde and the other does not)? But at this point, I wish to cover the effect retrogradation may have upon the planets. The following delineations will cover each planet retrograde natally, by progression, and during transit phases:

MERCURY RETROGRADE

NATAL:

Natal Mercury retrograde can indicate a mind that is innately introspective and prone towards various levels of contemplation. The individual appears less driven to outwardly communicate in a direct, to-the-point manner (especially when it strictly concerns himself). These individuals may start off in life appearing reserved in speech, apparently slower or more deliberate in response, and even a bit dull or non-expressive by common social standards. On the other hand, I have known people with natal retrograde Mercury who were quite fluent and quick in speech when discussing impersonal subject matter or universal, abstract concepts. However, the more personalized their thoughts became, the more they tended to become almost tongue-tied and hesitant, seldom elaborating or volunteering detailed information. Perhaps here, what is initially experienced upon mental levels is not always easily related back at the next moment upon outward levels (and this seems very much the case when Mercury is in stress aspect with either Saturn, Neptune, or Pluto---all ponderous planets). Thus, it can be safely assumed that this person perceives and inwardly evaluates or reflects upon more, at all times, than he is outwardly willing or able to tell (at least until a later date, after some mulling over of matters). He is not likely to reveal his thoughts about many personal issues unless directly asked. And even then, his natural mental reserve inclines him to give minimal response. Yet for some, such response can be concise and succinct.

Because retrograde planets normally do not put as much an emphasis upon external development, they sometimes can seem handicapped when forced to deal with strictly mundane circumstances...especially on the social-interaction level. In this instance, one with Mercury natally retrograde is prone to think and analyze problems differently than would one with Mercury direct. Here, this person's solutions to both major and minor predicaments are more individualistic, since logic and reasoning abilities are often more readily directed towards the observation of subtleties and less obvious factors that others normally would overlook or ignore. Such an internal focus of the mind-force makes this an occult mental position, in which the deeper workings of the thought process are given more stimulation. The rational mind establishes a closer connection with the unconscious and all its powerful contents. Yet from a strictly practical viewpoint, this condition may also be a sign of mental obscurity in which the private thoughts of the individual are unable to clearly structure themselves or be well understood by others.

There is usually less ability of the Ego (shown by the Sun) to direct and control the expression of the mind (since Mercury retrograde is symbolically turning away from the direction the conscious Sun is advancing toward). Thus, this person may be less confident in activating his mental energy toward his main objectives or central goals (as the unconscious here holds greater power over the concrete, rational mind). This individual tends to absorb information without being as consciously aware of doing so. He absorbs more data from the environment than is apparent. Yet on the surface, he may appear to learn things at a slower pace than others. This could be because attempts at knowledge-gathering stir deeper levels of inner awareness, and thus data has to be analyzed carefully, re-analyzed, and thoroughly reflected upon before this individual is able to effectively apply such knowledge in the external world.

Mercury retrograde is often found in the charts of highly self-critical individuals, as the selective and discriminating

facets of Mercury easily turn inward. Subjective
self-examination is accented. It seems harder for these
people to make quick, on-the-spot decisions or think in
terms of absolutes (since the retrograde condition keeps
them in mental flux, constantly preoccupied with modifying
plans, revising former thoughts, or continuously adapting
to outer changes that are often unforeseen). Normally, this
individual has to work harder at paying closer attention to
immediate details in the environment. Especially in regard
to written material. There is a strange absent-mindedness
observed here mingled with incredible recall of subtle
matters most other people neglect or fail to spot. Although
the mind may seem harder to stabilize on the worldly level
(since it is less apt to pay full attention), it can often become
more aligned with the dictates of the Higher Self (especially
when Mercury is well-aspected). The abstract components
of the conscious mind are more readily stimulated in this
respect. What this mind fails to receive in terms of direct
communication, it makes up for in terms of indirect, subtle,
non-verbal response. The depth of understanding
potentially found here should not be underestimated because of this individual's tendency to appear awkward and
uncertain about demonstrating his mental abilities upon the
surface. (*Nostradamus - F.A.Mesmer - Frederic Chopin -
Alan Leo - Israel Regardie - Salvador Dali - Erich Fromm -
Howard Hughes - Norman Mailer*).

PROGRESSED:

When Mercury turns *retrograde* by progression, it
demarks a period in the individual's life indicating a gradual
and subtle turning away from his accustomed mode of
objective, intellectual fact-finding. The individual is now apt
to experience more vividly the subjective power of his
mind. Of course, much depends upon the exact age one's
Mercury turns retrograde. The earlier this occurs, the less
impact it seems to have upon his waking consciousness at
this time. The later it occurs, the more the individual can
become intensely attuned to the depth of his mental
processes. At this point, he can appear increasingly
self-absorbed concerning his personal communication with
others, since he now is more sensitized to the response he

receives (and often because such responses do not always align themselves with what he is initially attempting to communicate. As the gap widens, he is forced to become more thoughtful and reflective). At best, he finds that only few individuals are able to pick up on what he is trying to express. There is now indicated a growing readiness for more profound self-analysis, which can lead this individual towards a focus of attention upon all mental self-development programs or educational interests that can aid him in his search for inner meaning. Age is still an important consideration in delineation. For example, at age seven, this retrograde transition phase could denote a tendency towards reading problems, trouble with numbers, difficulty in speech, or less general interest in school studies that demand precise thought structure or detailed retention of facts (as applied to math or science, for example). However, this young individual may do better with those studies that help him further develop his understanding of visual images or symbol association (since imaginative processes are often stimulated and heightened).

The individual may find himself more uncertain about making major life plans and thus can experience an inner restlessness that may keep him in a state of mental flux for some time (although this is usually less evident on the surface). As this retrograde period lasts about 24 progressed years, it slowly conditions the mind to become more contemplative and philosophical. In some cases, depending upon natal aspects, it can denote a period of mental frustration or learning difficulties. Often this person now requires more time to thoroughly comprehend things and therefore may have to put more effort into assimilating his outer studies and external observations. His unconscious mental contents may rise more to the fore and divert his attention from mundane thought processes. He may be less consciously alert to the outer details of his immediate environment, which can make him periodically more forgetful, absent-minded, or just plain careless in thought and speech. On the other hand, he can become increasingly sensitive to subtle changes he might otherwise normally overlook. He may also be acutely sensitized to inner adjustments within his own nature, almost as if his unconscious is instructing him to understand in a manner different than his conscious mind ever could. Check the natal house Mercury occupies as well as the houses with Gemini and especially Virgo (being more reflective) on their cusps. These are likely to be circumstantial areas of needed mental changes, of new outlooks, or of reconsidered thoughts that are bound to help this individual come in closer contact with his inner self during the duration of this progressed retrograde phase.

While the individual can begin to respond to Mercury's progressed retrograde phase starting on the exact year it turns direction, he may react to this shift in consciousness a few years before, during this planet's stationary phase. For those who have not made sufficient contact with their subjective inner self previously, this progressed change of direction is likely to manifest thru confusion or disruption in outer life circumstances in the first few years of this period. When Mercury turns *direct* by progression after being natally retrograde for some time, the individual feels as if his mind has been released from its subjective state of expression and is now able to be more active and effective in influencing his external affairs. Its preparatory period is officially over, and now the individual's mental energies must move back out into the outer world of experience to demonstrate its fuller capacity. He may feel more free and open with his communication potential, but now relates from an in-depth viewpoint. He tends to want to apply his intuitive understanding to everyday matters in his environment, in order to comprehend their truer nature. While seldom superficial in his observations, he is now less obscurely ponderous and hard to interpret. He himself becomes less self-conscious about his mental processes, thus removing blockages that might have developed in previous years. And he is more prone to want mental *exchange* with others on a give-and-take that seemed almost impossible before. Mercury's stationary period is apt to present the individual with a sense of inner crisis, in which he must come to grips with his mind and begin to develop new communication resources furthering his growth. The pressures during this stationary period build up until transformative mental release becomes imperative.

Aspects to Mercury during this progressed time period should indicate how such a release can occur.

TRANSIT:

This is a period lasting about 24 days, normally occurring about 3 times a year. Transiting planets are more apt to trigger outer events in one's current experience rather than activate inner conditions or attitudes. Still, these events will operate upon the level that the individual is experiencing the natal planet inwardly. Thus, when a planet turns retrograde by transit, it appears to interfere with the normal ongoing flow of activities represented by that planet in the outer world. This can create frustrating conditions, delays, setbacks, or last-minute changes of plans according to the individual's degree of susceptibility. When transiting Mercury goes retrograde, it is not the best time for making important decisions or signing documents and papers that are expected to finalize a long-range commitment or contract of some sort. This is because the normal communication emphasis of Mercury (along with its capacity for clear-headed perception, cool logical analysis, and objective reasoning ability) is temporarily turning away from expression upon the level of daily routine activity. It is instead urging for mental expression upon less tangible, structure realms. So one can expect all types of minor but irritating disruptions when dealing with any and all forms of communication or transportational channels. The more mercurial the activity is, the more vulnerable. And since Mercury rules so many little and seemingly incidental things in our daily life, trouble can crop up from many diverse areas at once during this period. The typical mundane disturbances to be found are those dealing with car repairs, telephone malfunctions, mix-ups in messages, mail delays, postponed deliveries, machinery breakdowns, suddenly cancelled appointments, or last-minute alteration of previous plans and negotiations.

If transiting retrograde Mercury makes stressful aspects to any natal planet(s) at this time, the individual should be especially sensitive and alert to any lack of clarity or logic in his thinking. He may not be as keenly attentive to details at this time, and might easily confuse or muddle affairs due to neglecting to observe minor and seemingly inconsequential factors (especially concerning work or chores at hand). Mistakes are made more easily and more repeatedly under this transit, and often can go unnoticed for some time. However, sometimes errors made in the past can now be brought to one's attention and corrected (I've seen conditions work both ways time and time again). Even objects lost or hidden can be found during this period. The general advice here is to never assume anything or take anything for granted when Mercury is retrograde. Double-check everything. Remember, this can be one of the hardest times for people to be aware of the smaller issues in daily affairs.

The house that Mercury is transiting thru is likely to be where its retrograde influence has its greatest impact, along with the natal houses ruled by Mercury, to a lesser degree. Any planet that Mercury makes exact aspects to during this period should be very important to note. The degree at which it turns retrograde is also very sensitive; natal aspects to this transiting degree often set the tone for the entire retrograde period, according to my observations. The transiting Mercury retrograde period is excellent for involvement in all mental activities such as research, editing, revising written work, proof-reading, etc. Due to the introspective nature of retrogradation, this period is also good for meditation, in-depth self-analysis, and various forms of psychological techniques for self-understanding. It is a good time for mental review in which the individual can gain from going back over previously held ideas and concepts, re-analyzing their present relevance and value, and then making all necessary corrections and modifications. Since Mercury is moving slower, the mind can be more deliberate in its evaluations and thus reconsiders matters more carefully. A constructive time for re-appraisal. New activities should be planned out in detail during this period but not executed, while unresolved matters from the past are best completed.

VENUS RETROGRADE

NATAL:

When a planet is retrograde, there is expressed a need for greater concentrated attention upon evoking the subjective facets of whatever that planet basically represents. Less focus is thus put upon the materialistic application of that planet. Venus normally gives us the urge to attract beauty, refinement, and comfort in the outer world. It prompts us to learn and value cultured interaction, and sensitizes us to the esthetic potentials of life. When it is retrograde in the natal chart, the individual's esthetic values are more personalized rather than socially conditioned. His social instincts at least operate along less extroverted channels. This means the individual is apt to be more reflective and subjective in his evaluations of love, beauty, and partnerships in general. He is able to appreciate and value things which are either overlooked by or are less appealing to those with Venus direct. This can suggest that one with a retrograde Venus may possess a fuller awareness of inner or abstract beauty, and therefore may not be as attracted by only surface physical appearances. He may be more harmoniously attuned to the subtler elements. The love nature can be more profoundly experienced, since emotions here can have a deeper impact upon his nature. But they are simply harder to express in open, demonstrative terms. In this instance, the potentially shallow, superficial side of Venus is less evoked. The individual is not as prone to behave in a conventional social manner simply to obtain approval and acceptance from others. He may be somewhat reserved or inhibited in the display of affection, and may need more time to develop himself here. He is often a late bloomer in romance (in terms of inner fulfillment).

On a relationship level, retrograde Venus is not as inclined to be out-going and gregarious. As it is more emotionally self-contained, it is less driven to actively seek out others for friendly, intimate companionship. This person is likely to withdraw from close involvement in favor of establishing relationship between the various parts of himself. While he may doubt his capacity to enjoy personal contacts with others, he tends to turn within for emotional fulfillment (valuing his own company more in most cases...suggesting a need for seclusion and solitude). Outwardly, he therefore may appear stand-offish and somewhat reclusive in temperament. Because of this, true satisfaction from love and other emotionally-based relationships may come later in life (if at all). The individual is obviously meant to review his personal values, tender feelings, and even dependency needs upon more introspective levels before he can feel comfortable and secure with others, and able to share the many parts of himself in a balanced and coordinated manner. He needs to examine the motivations that urge him to love or cherish another (since his attachments are seldom easy for him and others who view him to understand). Since unconscious factors are at work here, the individual's attraction can appear incomprehensible, irrational, or impractical. Upon a positive level, the refinement principle of Venus can be more penetrating within the psyche, allowing the individual to slowly develop a more mature, spiritualized expression of love. But this is normally only after ample self-evaluation. Venus here is able to love from a more abstract, universal viewpoint in certain cases.

Venus retrograde tends to have less interest in accumulating physical goods and possessions for strictly worldly value, and therefore the individual is less materialistic in the most pragmatic sense of that term. He becomes more concerned with the inner value of what he owns. Yet, in some instances, this condition could reflect one who has difficulty in dealing with building financial security in his life due to conflicting values (his own vs. society's). He may block himself from satisfying emotional needs thru physical resources. If very much under stress aspects in the chart, retrograde Venus could denote intense emotional frustrations due to limited affectional or artistic outlets. His ability for self-acceptance can also be blocked, which might warp and distort his expression of personal love and sociability. This condition could indicate one who does not feel worthy of receiving love, since he may have a muddled concept of self-value. Or, in some instances, the love principle turning its energies upon the self in a very subjective, instinctual manner could suggest a tendency towards some degree of unconscious narcissism (i.e.,

morbid self-attraction). All submerged or indirect feelings
will eventually have to openly surface upon a waking level
of consciousness before this individual can develop a
healthy objectivity and perspective concerning them.
(*Michelangelo - Gustav Mahler - Adolf Hitler - Pearl S. Buck
- Winston Churchill - Meher Baba*).

PROGRESSED:

When Venus turns *retrograde* by progression, it times a
period when there is much emotional flux, restlessness in
unions, and changes in values. There is normally a
subjective urge to withdraw from the level of social
participation that had been previously established. The
individual may begin to feel more self-conscious or
awkward in social interaction, and may ponder more about
the deeper values of partnerships from a reflective
viewpoint. One's inner perspective can widen, although due
to latent emotional factors that are now brought into closer
contact with conscious feelings. This progressed period
lasts about 42 years. It should thus be viewed as a gradual,
subtle conditioning factor stemming from adjustments in
the individual's inner make-up rather than a predominantly
event-producing influence. It has often been observed that
the year in which a planet turns retrograde by progression
as well as the year in which it turns direct (representing the
peak of that planet's stationary phase) are those sensitive
times disclosing major shifts in consciousness or inner crisis
points for the individual regarding the principles involved
and working themselves out thru the house occupied.
Venus at its stations can stimulate social uncertainties, a
blurring of values, or the awareness of previously hidden
love yearnings. From a reincarnational point of view, the
individual may now become more attuned to relationship
attitudes he may have developed in past lives, which may
prove contrary to those he has been conditioned to establish
in this life up to this point. Discontent is likely to be felt
upon the emotional level because of this, although this may
be registered as vague desires in the beginning of this
retrograde phase.

At this time, one with a progressed retrograde Venus may

become increasingly less concerned with appearing attractive or appealing to others in a socially conventional manner. He may be inclined to shun associations involving standard social interaction in favor of solitude. He is more likely to respond to his urge for *self*-satisfaction in this regard. The outer world of appearances becomes less appealing for him, suggesting he becomes increasingly less cooperative concerning what is socially expected of him. This is especially so if natal Venus makes oppositions in the chart, suggesting a greater urge to rebel against compromising with others. His tendency to intimately share himself may be diminished. However, the individual shows less inclination to exert his social drives in a frivolous, superficial manner. Being now more socially reflective, he may seem remote and aloof regarding others. He is to seek out human values that are more universal, although impersonal, in scope. His unconscious therefore has more power dictating his choices in unions. Thus, relationships he forms can have more fated undertones. People he intimately associates himself with at this time can bring him in touch with his emotional depths for better or worse (indicated by natal aspects to Venus). His reactions to such relationships should be indicative of unresolved emotional needs that now must be transformed. Because of this, love attitudes expressed at this time can become complex and hard to define.

The year Venus turns retrograde could coincide with eventful conditions involving inner realizations concerning one's ability to love if natal Venus makes stressful aspects at birth. Affectional impulses, previously kept hidden from waking consciousness, may begin to become subjectively experienced and analyzed. If Venus is decidedly more active as a "money" planet rather than a "love" planet in the chart, its retrogradation by progression can reveal a period of financial problems or poor management of goods and funds, since the individual's inner self is psychologically turning away from mundane experience in the realm of matter. The individual's growth pattern now demands that he attempt to spiritualize his material, worldly values thru inner balance. It can denote for some that a greater effort must be made to tap into latent resources that can be used

Returning the bird
tribes

for personal sustenance. For others, this could suggest the need for a more collective utilization of individual assets. But at all times, the individual is pressured to re-evaluate how he is to attune himself with the people in his life experience. Retrograde Venus enables one to reclaim talents and abilities once valued in former incarnations. The individual is now to find new ways of using such resources for the welfare of all rather than for merely self-gratification.

TRANSIT:

The transiting retrograde Venus phase is a period lasting about 42 days. It occurs approximately every 1½ years. This period most likely alters conditions involving our love impulses, attractions, conscious emotional response, personal values, and partnership considerations. It can also tie in with attitudes concerning current financial conditions and personal possessions. It is usually a time when there are circumstancial affairs enforcing changes in close associations. The house that Venus is transiting thru is important to note. For it is usually here that the individual is pressured to modify his evaluation of a person or situation in his life. The individual may be better able to get in touch with deeper, subjective feelings about such matters, although these feelings are less able to be directly shown upon the surface. This is a time of emotionally mulling things over in an attempt to feel more comfortable and balanced with affairs emphasized at this period. One is advised to carefully deliberate and weigh out all sides before making firm commitments in current unions. Thus, it is not an advisable time for entering a marriage or even beginning divorce proceedings. Both the individual and his partner(s) are characteristically more indecisive and fickle on the emotional level, especially when this transiting retrograde Venus makes stress contacts to natal planets (particularly so when Mars, Jupiter, or Uranus are involved). This trait should also apply to new alliances in business partnerships and all professional matters.

Since Venus is also a money planet, its retrograde transit can suggest a poor time to make major financial purchases or investments, as the true value of any desired product is apt to be harder for the individual to accurately assess. He may blindly over-value things during this phase. What is indicated here is a need to look below the surface of apparent beauty or charm (whether in people or objects) and more cautiously appraise an attraction's real worth. We are likely to be motivated by spurts of emotional idealism, rather than practical necessity. In general, one should be more discreet about what one chooses to buy or sell in the area of adornments, luxury items, jewelry, decorative pieces, fashion, expensive furnishings, or other fineries. Extravagance and impulsive spending may later be regretted when Venus finally turns direct and we begin to reconsider and re-assess our actions here. In some cases, there may be delays in obtaining desired possessions (perhaps due to financial mismanagement from the past that is now brought to our attention) or else a lack of current supply (desired items are out-of-stock often during this period), suggesting that our timing in purchasing is off. And since our esthetic perception is less keenly tuned into details, this is not a good time for judging color, tints, and shades (as trying to match up paint or fabric).

As Venus retrograde by transit suggests that conditions described by it are not in a state of balance, but are in constant flux, this period can denote a greater potential for having misunderstandings in unions. Misinterpretation of intentions is likely, and assumptions concerning the feelings of others prove faulty. Open confrontation can be awkward and indirect expression with others tends to complicate matters. Involvement with legal matters (especially involving the lower courts) may prove unprofitable or at least punctuated with delays and setbacks. Such proceedings are best begun after Venus turns direct if one must undertake them. On a constructive level, transiting Venus retrograde can be an excellent period for reconsideration of all existing relationships in terms of their true value for the individual before reaching any final conclusions involving decisions or commitment. We need to review our needs involving others more thoroughly. In addition, this is also a marvelous opportunity for going back and completing all artistic/creative works previously left unfinished before venturing into new projects. We usually can make welcomed improvements in this area, enabling us to feel more inwardly gratified with the results. We also benefit ourselves by reviewing financial matters of the past, evaluating the pros and cons of our actions, and establishing better ways of balancing our monetary affairs in the future.

MARS RETROGRADE

NATAL:

Mars rules the drive or urge to eject vital energy outward into the external world. It desires to directly activate conditions to suit personal impulses thru assertive and often rapid movement. It is one planet that functions most comfortable when it is free to thrust itself forward with much momentum into the manifest world in an attempt to dynamically face and overpower all impeding situations thru head-on action. Its psychological nature needs this type of challenge for growth. However, when it is found retrograde in the natal chart, Mars obviously has more difficulty externalizing aggressive impulses towards an outer objective with the open drive typical of direct Mars. Energy can internalize readily, giving the individual a surface appearance of calmness, composure, tranquility, and stability. Yet inwardly, this person is much less able to relax since energy is constantly being expended thru subjective tensions as well as internal body processes. Mars retrograde does not throw itself spontaneously into personal action in the accustomed manner of Mars direct. This Mars seldom energizes itself to face up to opposition in a straightforward manner. It is less overt in its moves. Individuals with retrograde Mars often behave more passively or non-combatively than they feel deep down inside. The main impetus of this Mars is decidedly more psychological than physical, more reflective than actional, and more deliberate than impulsive.

What motivates this person to act or do things is less obviously understood, since often he is triggered into expression by subjective, internal stimuli rather than external factors. He is motivated here by predominantly unconscious facets of his psyche, and may be at a loss as to why he is driven to act. Perhaps retrograde Mars is an opportunity for one to reflect upon the whys of action, encouraging activity to be thoughtful and purposeful rather than impetuous and poorly planned. His reflective approach could suggest a degree of uncertainty about taking action until he has internally reviewed the nature of what must be done. Thus, his apparent lack of initiative and enterprise can be misleading, since he is actually developing strategy (seeking thru careful planning the most advantageous moment to act upon a situation). Thus, it is typical that he will delay from taking action until a later time that feels inwardly right for him. He normally prefers to act alone in seclusion or solitude rather than in the presence of others. In a male's chart, retrograde Mars under strong stress patterns can lead to undue inhibition or misdirection of the sexual force, which potentially can result in impotence. There may be at least a general lessening of physical excitement thru the usual stimuli in favor of more complicated psychological arousal. In a female's chart, there can be frigidity or a deeper problem adjusting to the masculine principle within than is apparent. Women with this placement may further externalize this difficulty by attracting men who either sexually frustrate or psychologically threaten their identity. These men themselves may basically be maladjusted in their own expression of masculinity. For both sexes, sexual tensions slowly build up but are less recognized by these individuals.

Under natal stress patterns, this Mars can be harmful to the psyche, as energy initially generated from conflicts in the outer world first turns within towards the self. Hostilities, resentments, jealousies, and outright anger are seldom allowed to be released thru the most direct and immediate outlets available. They are instead capable of being pent up, stored inwardly, and permitted to dangerously concentrate themselves within the individual. Astrologer Mary Vohryzek, once in personal correspondence, referred to retrograde Mars as having a "seething" quality about it, with periods of unexpected eruption. My observations here have definitely attested to her insight about Mars retrograde. These individuals are often baffled about the intensity of their passionate, somewhat destructive reactions in this regard. For some who unduly repress their tensional forces, the physical body may end up being the focal point for such over-charged energy. It thus can suffer inflammations and infections of a more complicated, resistant nature than that same Mars would if natally direct. This seems particularly so if Mars connects in any way with Virgo, Scorpio, or the 1st, 6th, and 8th houses. Physical self-infliction can be strong (whether thru direct, yet unconscious, abuse or accident-proneness). Sometimes, physical vitality can be somewhat impaired, and perhaps due to the fact that the individual directs this energy towards energizing the more intangible, non-physical parts of his being. Exhaustion is apt to occur, although the individual may ignore his need for total physical relaxation. On the other hand, inner stamina can be stronger with Mars retrograde, almost as if one has a compulsion to be active regardless of the limits of his body.

For the individual who seeks to direct his energies towards spiritual development, a retrograde Mars can give one the stamina and inner strength needed to courageously explore less obvious inner conflicts and bravely combat all the "enemies" he may meet up against on the psychological battlefield within. And as his unconscious is more likely to direct his desire-impulses, the individual can find himself driven to act or work towards an impersonal objective or world cause, instilling an urge to crusade and pioneer for others altruistically; he may be detached enough to act without considering strictly self-centered needs. (*Toulouse-Lautrec - Sigmund Freud Beethoven - Lord Byron - Judy Garland - Al Capone*).

PROGRESSED:

If Mars turns *retrograde* by progression after birth, it will likely remain in that condition for the rest of the individual's life (as its retrograde phase lasts 80 progressed years). Beginning with its stationary period, Mars describes an emerging period of change concerning objectives, with a gradual moving away from pre-established methods of asserting oneself towards here-and-now goals and ambitions. The individual is apt to appear less aggressive in his approach towards acting out his impulses in his environment. He becomes less desirous of making a dynamic, head-strong effort in attaining certain needs. The house that Mars occupies in the natal chart often undergoes some conflict and inner friction as the individual begins to re-direct the direction of his vital energies. If he attempts to resist and fight against the pressing need to make internal changes in his style of action here, he is bound to undergo many experiences in his outer affairs that appear to hamper and thwart his self-willed intentions. He benefits by adjusting to the urge to release himself from all self-centered desires and allow himself to act according to the underlying direction of his unconscious (which now at this time is to be his inner guide). From this point on, he is less prone to display an openly competitive spirit. If anything, he will compete with himself more rather than with others.

This progressed phase can be a time when the individual seems less eager to work with worldly projects requiring a great expenditure of physical effort. Instead, he may become increasingly retiring or subtle in his actions. He is more prone towards focussing his energies upon less obvious challenges, or may assume work that requires him to retreat from public notice and attention. While not necessarily having less initiative, he may simply seek out fewer socially-demanding ventures to involve himself with. He becomes less fast-paced in the external world, but may accelerate his activity concerning his inner nature. Introspection can become a stronger motivating force. He is to become more in touch with the truer nature of his personal impulses. This long-term phase can give him deeper insight into what his desires are requiring of him in terms of inner growth. He therefore may be less inclined to act out of blind instinct. Although more subjective, the individual is presented with a fuller perspective by being more actively in contact with his unconscious. Conflicts, however, can now flare up with greater force from within, sometimes energizing destructive psychological tensions when left unresolved. Due to this internalizing focus of attention, there is likely to be delayed circumstantial activity or ongoing movement of an eventful nature in the house that Mars occupies (as well as those natal houses Mars rules).

For those who have been open towards seeking spiritual development, this retrograde condition can denote the ability to transmute the energies of the passions and self-centered instincts to a less egocentric level, whereby the total self is vitalized and renewed. The individual thus begins to understand *why* the battlefield of life must first begin within himself rather than from his external environment. Karmically, this is not a period in which he is to freely and willfully explore new territory or follow an uncharted path. Instead, the individual is more urged to complete work upon projects that may not have reached proper fruition in past lives due to impatience, a lack of staying power, or reckless actions. He is now to act according to previously laid down plans that lie buried deeply within his psyche. He is to fully complete that which he had started in the past, before confidently moving on to a new cycle of activity.

If Mars turns *direct* by progression after birth, it describes a phase of the individual's life in which he is to begin to release his vast storehouse of specialized energy back into the world at large. Although he at first tends to feel uncertain about his capacity to succeed in the outer world thru his self-driven efforts, life now encourages him to become more enterprising and assertive in a manner that has a more direct impact upon his immediate environment. He starts to behave in a more overt manner, thereby becoming increasingly adept at objectifying his inner impulses thru circumstantial activity. By being more direct and spontaneous in his actions at this point in his evolution, he is also more likely to stimulate activity with others he confronts. He may also have to learn how to adjust to a more quickened tempo in his life affairs. In many ways, this phase for Mars should feel like an opportunity for freedom of energy release and activation of personal ambition. The individual can begin to feel more alive and vital in the world he must function in, along with developing a greater degree of self-confidence and assurance that needs he most personally identifies with will find appropriate external channels for expression.

TRANSIT:

Transiting Mars will turn retrograde for approximately 80 days, and occurs every 2 years. Often a trouble-maker for many, Mars is perhaps even more so when retrograde in transit. The house position it is operating thru at this time is very important to note. Mars' energy normally impels us to instigate new starts of activity, sparking exciting events that keep us from falling into rut-like patterns or giving in to inertia. But when retrograde, it may seem as if the individual's new plans backfire, lose expected momentum, develop too slowly, or fail to sufficiently activate at all. We often feel as if we are moving backwards in a self-defeating manner instead of forging ahead. It is thus obviously not the best time for initiating activities that call for a notable degree of enterprising effort, daring action, adventurous challenge, or constant and vigorous physical energy expenditure. Matters related to the house occupied by this Mars just may not generate enough steam and power to sufficiently get things going at the pace desired or required for optimum results. This is because the energy of Mars is temporarily being diverted into activating upon less concrete, worldly affairs. The individual is being conditioned to reflect back upon previous actions, giving him the opportunity to re-channel his efforts in a manner that can present him with new ways of mobilizing his vital forces. Frictional experiences at this time are telling him that he has not aligned his energies properly, and that he needs to direct his physical attention to what he has formerly neglected, or failed to carry thru to completion. Mars transiting in retrograde phase urges for constructive alteration of an energy pattern that otherwise could end up becoming very self-depleting and non-productive.

If already vulnerable to health disorders, the individual may experience problems involving his vitality during this transit, and often due to unrecognized temper, irritability, impatience, or frustration of drives. Complaints normally seen here involve inflammations, scrapes, burns, cuts, or injuries due to sudden accidents. If in stress pattern to the natal Moon or the ASC, Mars here can denote minor or major surgery (yet of a psychosomatic nature that has slowly been developing). The individual may not be as consciously aware of the gradual build up of negativism in his force field, nor is he likely to be in full control of his energy utilization during this period. Therefore, this Mars phase can promote a greater susceptibility towards accidents, breakage, arguments, fights, and mishaps of varying degrees due to impetuous but irrational behavior, or rash and careless action on someone's part. Transiting Mars retrograde can indirectly stir up increased internal activity, manifesting outwardly as restlessness, a desire to suddenly change existing conditions without considering future consequences, and energetic moves lacking a sense of practical direction or purposeful commitment.

New beginnings hastily inaugurated at this time often prove to be premature, sometimes requiring that the individual start all over again when Mars goes direct or else abandon his plans altogether in favor of a new pursuit.

However, this transiting retrograde phase is excellent for initiating the planning stage of any important project, or going back and reworking on previously initiated projects, finally finishing matters of the past. It is also an appropriate period for taking a rest from demanding physical labors and instead directing such physical energies towards more introspective interests. It is best to wait and further plan, if at all possible, until Mars turns direct again before going forth and proceeding with pioneering new personal interests. By doing so, we are more likely to have considered the more subtle actions required to insure a more successful outcome. When used constructively, all transiting retrograde phases are periods of opportunity to retrace our steps and reclaim something of value.

JUPITER RETROGRADE

NATAL:

As Jupiter governs the principle of expansion and outreach in the social sphere when direct, its retrograde condition in the natal chart signifies an individual who is not as apt to seek his potential for abundance, enrichment, and prosperity from matters of the mundane world. Instead, he is more inspired to search within himself for opportunities for growth. He seeks to widen his horizons from a more subjective point of view. There is often experienced inwardly a fuller sense of protection, well-being, and inner peace. The benevolent expression of this planet is more psychologically realized. Thus, the individual is likely to be more internally contented and self-satisfied than he may outwardly appear to be. Of course, this could promote procrastination concerning making realistic use of tangible, practical opportunities presented to him by the environment (especially if they involve a committed effort on his part). The vision, scope, and foresight of this planet can turn towards inner needs, and thus are often channeled thru abstract mental objectives or spiritual development easier than thru strictly material aims. Interestingly enough, this individual tends to have a harder time being giving and generous on the material level with what he possesses (whether physical goods, talents, or other personal assets). He holds back from spontaneous expression in this regard. Yet he is likely to be more freely giving of his insight and inspiration. Being a more ponderous Jupiter, this individual can feel less casual and carefree than one would with a direct Jupiter. He is more attuned to abstract principles than direct Jupiter individuals are, but can feel less of an urge for active social participation.

This individual has strong philosophical leanings, but appears less enthusiastic or eager about broadcasting his beliefs and revelations to others...at least in the straightforward, self-promotional manner of one with Jupiter direct. He is rather more concerned with deepening his own personal comprehension of the lofty ideals he seeks, in an attempt to gain greater inner freedom thru wisdom and self-enlightenment. As the more universal, abstract side of Jupiter can be more readily tapped when it is retrograde, this person is motivated to establish a clearer grasp of extended life principles, theoretical propositions, cosmic realities, and absolute truth. Deeper insights can come to him thru dreams, inner visions, and inspired states of thought...although his interpretation of their import tends to be highly subjective. Yet this in itself could impair one's judgemental ability. This individual normally has more faith and trust in his own potential than in that of others. He is apt to believe more in himself than in anyone else, although he is not arrogant about it. This tendency may be the source of his inability to recognize the fuller benefits of most of the worldly opportunities that come his way thru the energies of others. His inner voice is more prone to direct him, suggesting that he is intent upon self-guidance. This can make him very dedicated to the path of growth he chooses for himself, regardless if this is a solitary or impractical path.

As Jupiter retrograde denotes one who is less content with common material comforts, physical luxuries, or mundane prosperity, this person is seldom impressed by worldly bigness or social affluence. He is less a preserver of class traditions. Even if he does attract material benefits in his life, his natural inclination is often to minimize their importance. He feels detached from them. The wealth and riches he instead yearns for are moral and spiritual. He wants to sense abundance internally. This could denote an inability to wisely handle or enjoy large amounts of money, or profit from elevated social status. He may even reject these if they should be bestowed upon him, in favor of pursuing a less socially valued ideal. Religious interests are likely to be expressed as internal states of consciousness rather than formal outer observances or traditionally organized rituals and ceremonies adhered to by the masses, since retrograde Jupiter is less concerned with form and structure within the social sphere. The individual often chooses to follow a faith or belief system that is more custom-tailored to his own inner calling. His world view can be very unique and unorthodox. He resists indoctrination, preferring to think for himself about the weighty issues of human existence. Another way of viewing retrograde Jupiter is that the individual can find benefits in areas that are less recognized as fruitful by others. He can be adept at tapping into hidden potentials and turn them into uncommon opportunities. Because of this, the natal house that Jupiter occupies may not appear as lucky or fortunate as would normally be expected unless one is willing to search for deeper and less obvious advantages. (*Raphael - Nostradamus - Thomas Jefferson - Herman Hesse - Gandhi - Oscar Wilde - Isadora Duncan - Rudolph Steiner*).

PROGRESSED:

When Jupiter turns *retrograde* by progression, it remains so for the rest of the individual's life (120 progressed years). The individual slowly becomes conditioned to gradually learn to discover those intrinsic truths about life he needs to seek out for his own expansive growth. The gaining of material abundance for its own sake, or the attainment of social benefits thru the elevation of worldly status becomes less desirable, and therefore increasingly difficult to externally attract. The individual becomes inspired to discover more subjective outlets for personal comfort and prosperity. Although the effects of progressed retrograde Jupiter can be felt by some when it reaches its station, the exact year it changes direction can pinpoint a time of new goals and ideals that alter one's philosophical attitude towards worldly success in some manner. He may find himself less inspired and thus growingly disenchanted with the mundane facets of the house where Jupiter falls, and instead begins to adopt a more broad-minded, idealistic viewpoint. Or he may attempt to explore the less obvious benefits of this house. If natal Jupiter is very much under stress patterns in the chart, its progressed retrograde condition suggests that wiser and more prudent analysis is even more crucial in the handling of matters here if additional errors of judgement or wastage of resources is to be avoided. This is because the individual is likely to be more other-worldly concerning this sector of life than ever. There can be shown a greater inclination to pay less attention to details that could prove significant for success. The individual could suffer losses due to a reluctance to apply practical, down-to-earth measures to issues at hand. This can result in many years of irresponsible business dealings due to general mismanagement of duties and obligations. Long-range dreams that can't seem to get off the ground are usually due to poor planning or a lack of organization, but not necessarily a lack of vision.

Karmically, the individual may be re-introduced to a religious, political, or intellectual value that played an important part in his growth pattern in a previous incarnation. One should be very alert to all sudden urges towards spiritual involvement or expanded mental outreach at this time (especially at the stationary period) as this could offer clues concerning one's link with his superconscious mind in past lives as well as his former moral, ethical, academic, and devotional leanings. There is now a new opportunity to resume a particular philosophical path that may not have been fully assimilated in the past. The individual may easily find himself drawn to an ancient system of thought or belief and might surprisingly be able to integrate it into his present lifestyle with relative ease. He now seeks personal inner enrichment in the house Jupiter occupies.

If Jupiter turns *direct* by progression after birth, it denotes an appointed time in the individual's life in which he is to bring his wisdom concerning life, his inspirations, and his inner ideals to the surface so that they can now be used for society's benefit. Life is encouraging him to open up again to the world at large and actively participate in social affairs that can support its needed growth and progress. While still not inclined to adopt materialistic values at this time, the individual is better able to attract material benefits that help him structure his social goals. He is now eager to witness in manifest, concrete terms, the expansion of those ideals he holds sacred. His humanitarian instincts are more active and need channels for their expression. His enthusiasm and exuberance about life is able to become more apparent to others. Rather than retreat and withdraw, the individual may now feel positive and optimistic enough to affirm the rightness of his active involvement in the mundane world. This is particularly so if progressed Jupiter changes direction after the individual has experienced his first Saturn Return.

TRANSIT:

The transiting retrograde Jupiter phase is a period lasting 4 months and occurs usually once a year. Its length of retrogradation implies that it acts more as an influence on character, attitude, and behavior rather than events. Still, this can be a poor time to travel abroad, relocate long-distance, or have any new important legal or financial deals to finalize. In general, extended travel and communication channels can prove frustrating, or be delayed, or cost more than anticipated. However, the greater import of this phase is that it can become a marvelous time for gaining deeper insights into spiritual or philosophical matters, as wisdom can flow easier from the superconscious and make contact with the conscious self. It urges the individual to seek out the underlying truths concerning current matters represented by the house Jupiter is transiting thru. This house can suggest where the individual may find an inner sense of contentment and support, even if the outer circumstantial situations at this time do not reinforce this. Due to his subjective feelings of guidance and self-assurance, the individual may be more optimistic about future potentials here than is apparent. Thru a reconsideration of ideals previously overlooked or underestimated, he has the capacity to broaden his vision of what could be. Belief in self could be reinstated.

Although the individual may find it easier to develop greater faith and a more hopeful outlook due to self-inspired contemplation, his outward expression of enthusiasm, exuberance, and joviality can be somewhat subdued at this time. By turning within for greater understanding, the individual may now gain a greater perspective concerning social values presented to him at this time by his environment. He may feel detached from what is socially expected of him during this period and may reject such pressures in favor of listening to his own inner calling. By examining his social affairs more carefully and deeply, he may judge and evaluate the rightness of such activities according to his own personal, unique guidelines for living (suggesting the need for more expansive self-examination of his truer, inner beliefs). Hopefully, when Jupiter finally turns direct again, the individual will adopt fresh, new attitudes concerning how he can enrich and elevate his associations with others in his community. His participation then can become more purposeful and fulfilling, in which he can gain greater social acceptance while still remaining true to the needs of his spirit. He is better able to separate himself from previous social standards, blindly followed, that have been stifling for his inner growth. If he can remain true to the revelations he has experienced during this retrograde phase and abide by them, he can be free to follow greater paths of social expression in the future. If transiting retrograde Jupiter is undergoing stressful aspects, inspirations may appear to be stronger and more intense, but it is often less reliable and should not be acted upon at this time, at least in regard to making dynamic changes in situational affairs. Judgement could be faulty.

SATURN RETROGRADE

NATAL:

Saturn governs all attempts at structuring the ego in order to secure the fortification and stabilization of the individual's status-quo in the social realm. When it is direct in the chart, its focus is primarily set upon the construction of enduring shells, barriers, and solid defenses that protect the individual from being overtaken by external forces outside of his control. It thus becomes the planet of self-preservation, urging us to establish safety patterns thru realistic functioning, which characteristically can be separative and power-control oriented. It attempts to insure that personal vulnerability is minimized by establishing appropriate limits and self-discipline in the outer world. However, when Saturn is natally retrograde, the individual's urge towards personal self-structuring and definition is not readily stimulated by external conditioning. Instead, this person may unconsciously attempt to preserve a limited psychological mould or image of himself that he may chronically protect and support, no matter how self-defeating. If Saturn makes many stress patterns in the chart, then this inner framework can be unduly rigid and unyielding to external influence. It is likely built upon subjective fears, compressed anxieties, inadequacy, and an all-pervading sense of personal unworthiness. Feelings of self-doubt and inferiority are more inwardly experienced than is apparent on the surface. Self-generated pressures are more emphasized.

Retrograde Saturn denotes one who turns all disciplinarian, authoritative urges typical of this exacting planet upon himself rather than in his environment for the most part. He can thus be overly self-critical and plagued with personal guilt whenever he fails to live up to his demanding expectations of himself. He becomes overly sensitive to any sense of lack or deficiency he perceives in himself. This condition can be the signature of a bruised and battered ego that repairs itself very slowly and hesitantly (since resistance to change can be very strong). The individual is apt to be self-negating or self-denying on a subtle level and can be prone towards a degree of psychological masochism that is rarely recognized or accepted on the conscious level. Positively, retrograde Saturn can indicate one who is well-equipped to withstand a barrage of circumstantial stress without appearing very threatened or fearful. However, he is likely to endure these outer pressures and struggles without instigating the dynamic changes needed to relieve them. The endurance and perserverance of Saturn here chooses to function inwardly in an attempt to control or harness the energies of the psyche. As a result, he is less willing to openly defend himself and assert control thru his will when confronted by stronger and more dominant egos (especially if Saturn makes stressful contacts to the Sun, Mars, ASC, or ruler of the ASC). Easily intimidated, he can outwardly appear to submit or bow down to the demands of others without much resistance. But inwardly, he may adapt poorly to such pressures and remain in a state of long-term frustration and resentment. Bitterness and depression can be acutely experienced yet rarely demonstrated upon the surface. He needs to set limits upon others in terms of what they demand or expect of him if he is to establish greater self-respect.

Often, this individual's conscience is so vividly experienced that repression can block or thwart the fulfillment of personal desires and ambitions. He may have a distorted sense of what he should or should not do. Perhaps one of the most important lessons to be learned here is the affirmation of one's personal self-importance. The individual needs to freely accept himself as he is (even his shadow parts) without emphasizing a sense of shame, self-rejection, or personal disappointment. Fearful of successfully making personal changes that could beneficially alter his self-image (he can be morbidly self-judgemental), he is often too narrow in self-concept to be tolerant of his innate weaknesses. He will have to overcome psychological obstacles from within before he can expect to comfortably function in a productive manner in the outer world. Ambition to achieve social status and merit can be less innate when Saturn is retrograde, as this planet's determination to accomplish and climb up the ladder of success can be diminished. Perhaps true success for this individual has a uniquely personal meaning that has nothing to do with commanding respect and praise in the world at large. He may be more attuned with the challenge of controlling his inner nature and sensing security and power upon this level.

As Saturn represents the inner image of the archetypal father-figure, its retrograde condition could suggest that the individual's father did not represent the standard role-model. While not necessarily weak, the individual's father may have presented himself in a manner that seemed distorted or disorienting for the individual during his formative years. Or else the individual's attitude towards his father contained subjective facets that did not align themselves well with the outer reality of what his father really was like. Both confusion and ambivalence could have resulted due to this. Regardless, what is important here is the individual's inner *reaction* to his relationship with his father, since this can determine how he deals with both inner and outer authority in the future. In many cases, one with Saturn retrograde seems to have difficulty wielding power and authority in a balanced manner, suggesting that it is normally underdeveloped (or over-developed for some, who attempt to compensate for feelings of powerlessness).

The individual may be tempted to withdraw from actively pursuing challenging tasks and duties in the world due to his underlying sense of incompetency. He may even be reluctant to accept maturity, a factor necessary for feeling capable of dealing with competition. Sometimes he would rather not even attempt to defend his social position if he must risk failure or public judgement. Nevertheless, when well-managed, this Saturn can denote great inner discipline, the ability to accept and work under limitations or denials without undue stress, and the stamina to face difficulties with more detachment and insight. The really harder issues of life are normally found originating within his own psyche. (*Peter Tchaikovsky - Franz Shubert - George Eliot - Ernest Hemingway - Richard Nixon - Greta Garbo - Marilyn Monroe - Emily Dickenson - Albert Einstein*).

PROGRESSED:

Once Saturn turns *retrograde* by progression, it will not go direct again within a lifetime (since it remains so for 140 progressed years). It denotes a time in the individual's cycle when he begins to forego seeking control and authority in the outer environment in the driving manner of direct Saturn. Rather than obtaining a sense of absolute security thru the ambitious management of social affairs that could afford him social achievement and elevation, he is to now concentrate upon first developing a more structured, well-defined psychological foundation. He is to reorganize the manner in which he has been attaining his position in the social realm up until this point in time. Thru such re-patterning, he may be better able to come in closer touch with what still needs to be sufficiently organized and restructured on his inner levels to insure proper growth. The house that Saturn occupies thus takes on added seriousness on the subjective level plus increasing depth of approach. The individual now learns to become more reflective and self-examining concerning the outer role he is driven to adopt in dealing with his dharma, or inner sense of social responsibility. He becomes more cautious concerning how he takes charge over external matters and makes changes more slowly, due to his thorough evaluation of the inner reason behind his actions. He takes time to consider the consequences of his long-range commitments before assuming obligations. Responsibilities assumed must now align themselves with his truer sense of inner purpose and meaning. Because of this, circumstantial affairs shown by the house Saturn occupies are likely to undergo situational delays, limitations, slow-downs, and mundane restrictions... all in an effort to put the brakes upon his ambition until he begins to impose needed inner self-discipline in this area. As more unconscious components of his psyche now directly influence the structuring of his ego, the individual can begin to recognize the universal implication of his urge to strive and achieve in the world.

Karmically, Saturn turning retrograde by progression may reintroduce the individual to negatively-constructed security patterns and safety mechanisms that played a significant role in his past lives. Because of this, he may now be better able to gain a more profound understanding of unconscious fears, inhibitions, and self-limiting attitudes that have stifled many subtle facets of his ego in this present lifetime. He is now given an opportunity to review his shadow (in the Jungian sense of the term) and take stock of himself in a way that allows him to apply a sense of order to those parts of his psyche that otherwise would remain fragmented and unintegrated. To accomplish this, he is likely to spend the rest of his life in a not-too-obvious state of self-contemplation. He may gradually shun public activity, worldly exposure, or outer recognition in favor of concentrating upon rebuilding an inner anchor for himself at the spiritual level. Seemingly less socially motivated and even hermit-like at this time, he may seek to simplify his life needs and limit his interests and pleasures to only those activities which aid in the type of restructuring his inner self demands. Much will depend upon the natal aspects to Saturn as to how he will focus upon gaining an enduring soul structure for the remainder of his life.

When Saturn turns *direct* by progression, the individual *gradually* begins to take on a more assertive attitude towards tackling responsibilities in the outer world. Although cautious about social involvement, he has a firm inner foundation to venture forth from. In many ways, this transition period should seem very liberating and self-releasing. The individual can now feel more responsibly in touch with the greater affairs in the outer world, as his ambitions are better able to manifest thru the existing structures in his environment. Since birth, he has been conditioned to take on a more in-depth approach toward authority and control. Yet at this appointed time, he is to move back out once again into the objective world to display his own sense of self-importance, authority, and control with greater purpose and direction when well-managed (since he has psychologically delved into the more profound reasons for his drive to succeed). He is now to work at building a better and more consistent sense of ego-structure and definition *outside* of himself, diminishing his innate tendency to unconsciously submit to the pressing demands of others in his environment. He becomes less dominated by external conditions not of his own choosing due to this, strengthening his sense of self-respect and autonomy. At the same time, the individual can now loosen the tight and rigid psychological reigns he has had over his inner self for much of his life, and thus begins to experience a growing sense of personal freedom from all self-imposed restrictions (most of which have been stifling and uncomfortable). Therefore, the individual becomes less anxious and self-condemning. The house that Saturn natally falls in is here activated with a renewed sense of ambition, whereby the individual exhibits an emerging eagerness to accomplish and achieve something worthy of social recognition and respect.

TRANSIT:

The transiting retrograde Saturn phase is a period lasting about 4½ months, occurring once a year. Passing temporarily thru a natal house, Saturn slows down the normal rate of current activity so that the individual is given a better chance to develop a more efficient and sensible plan or method enabling him to make the most *later* out of any realistic endeavor opportunity offers here. Outwardly, due to *both* the innate nature of Saturn plus the normal dynamics of retrogradation, worldly enterprises or expectations may undergo postponements or unaccountable setbacks. His immediate ambitions often seem thwarted unnecessarily (according to his limited perspective), and usually because unforeseen commitments and responsibilities enter his life and demand his time and energy. However, with Saturn retrograde, such obligations are likely to be an example of "unfinished business" neglected at some previous point that now must be resolved and completed (on some level of his consciousness) before the individual is permitted to forge ahead into new activity. Nevertheless, a less obviously understood but proper timing system is here taking place, and the individual will actually succeed with his interests best in the long run when he now accepts his present duties at hand with more patience, endurance, and inner steadiness of attention. While he still should continuously work at manifesting his current objectives in this sector of his life rather than give up, he should not push for immediate results or demand satisfaction. Saturn is teaching him here to slow down, apply the brakes on his ego, and become more thoroughly organized. Saturn retrograde allows him to become even more careful about wasting or misapplying any significant resource in the house it now occupies.

This phase is often a poor time for making any important *new* career changes, or impulsively attempting to disrupt and alter one's present status or standing in the community or the world-at-large (such as resigning from a long-standing position in one's profession). It is a better period for first attempting to make adjustments or alterations that could ideally relieve any sense of frustration. Yet although astrologers (sometimes naively) strive for the ideal, real life demands that one fulfill patterns that do not always satisfy our preconceived concept of what should be. What is demanded of each individual's inner growth pattern dictates this, not our formulae. As this period normally presents additional responsibilities which often can seem straining and time-consuming, the individual should not actively seek out extra obligations, since they could prove to be more burdensome and draining than anticipated. Saturn retrograde is trying to put one in touch with inner limits.

However, this can be an excellent time for taking stock of oneself and working upon building the inner structure needed to foster a greater level of psychological strength. In this cycle, Saturn should be more ponderous and reflective than ambitiously striving to achieve outer goals. If Saturn should make stressful aspect contacts with any natal planet(s) at this time, there may manifest the re-emergence of weak elements in the personality structure that have been avoided in the past, and that now need to be attended to and given corrective focus.

RETROGRADE HIGHER OCTAVE PLANETS

When Higher Octave Planets are in their retrograde cycle, their impact theoretically can be accentuated. This is because, like the retrograde principle, these planets already have a strong link with the unconscious elements of humankind (or the inner self). The Higher Octaves remain in their retrograde cycle for almost half a year, suggesting that approximately half of those existing on this planet have them retrograde. Compare this to the mere 23 day cycle of Mercury retrograde, and you can understand why it is absurd to make absolute, blanket statements concerning their *specific* natal traits when retrograde. Still, they may behave differently when retrograde. Perhaps much here depends upon how these self-transcendent planets integrate themselves within the total natal chart. If they are natally prominent (meaning that they make significant contact with the Sun, Moon, Asc. and/or other angles of the chart...or are unaspected, or if one is the *only* natal planet retrograde), their retrograde traits are more evident. The human psyche must, in some fashion, have more conscious connection with these particular retrograde planets if they are to be recognized and somewhat understood for the uncommon psychological functions they may represent. Otherwise, their influence might be too abstract and subtle to even consider in this context.

URANUS RETROGRADE

NATAL:

For those able to respond to Uranus retrograde natally, the workings of the intuitional sense can be very potent. However, because of greater unconscious attunement implied by retrogradation, intuition may operate so readily and rapidly that the individual might not objectively perceive its activity as something apart from his normal waking consciousness. He may take its existence for granted and thus could even cope with it better (his ego-structure is less threatened by it). In general, the individual's potential uniqueness, genius, or even eccentric behavior is likely to be held back from full expression in the outer world. Yet such qualities are apt to be more acutely experienced inwardly by the more self-awakened soul. He is prone to *react* on deeper, less obvious psychological levels in a more self-willed, rebellious, and defiant manner than he outwardly shows. He may actually be more intrinsically radical, unconventional, or original in outlook than is apparent. Thus, most would assume that this person is more orthodox and conservative (or more normal and ordinary by most social standards) than he subjectively knows himself to be. He closets much of his potential for colorful individuality. The normally disruptive force of electrified Uranus is less focussed upon outer realms of experience, but instead concentrates upon the inner planes of consciousness...providing the individual with sudden insights that enlighten him to first reform from within. It is almost as if the individual is unconsciously attempting to throw light upon pre-conditioned attitudes developed in past life cycles and, thru such insight and illumination, strive to free himself from binding pre-structures (especially of thought). Until he sufficiently can accomplish this, he repeatedly tends to turn attention away from *overt* involvement in progressive activities that could help change the social nature of current life affairs. His sense of future vision first depends upon successfully confronting and reforming elements of his own past. Thus, this is the more introspective, self-revealing Uranus. It is less driven to actively play the outer role of social activist.

If cataclystic Uranus retrograde should receive frictional aspect contacts from other natal planets, this individual may be uncomfortable with whatever triggers his rebellious impulse to unexpectedly tear down established structure. He may be at odds with himself, perplexed as to why he stirs up disorganization in his affairs (according to the house position). In this case, outer conditions symbolize the *readiness* for inner chaos. Sudden, unsettling changes in attitude are here stimulated from the unpredictable stirrings of one's own unconscious self rather than from stimuli in the external environment. If anything, situational affairs become those appropriate *symbols* needed to objectify changes undertaken by the inner nature. The outer circumstance itself is less important than the *inner* significance of that circumstance for this person. Expect unexpected explosiveness with this placement from time to time, since pent-up nervous tension finds fewer outer channels compared to Uranus direct. Volatile reactions appear to come out of the blue with no rational explanation (although often with subjective meaning for the individual so aroused). Of course, in some cases, this could mean that the individual is less understood in his personal expression of Uranian traits (which already are not easy for most to appreciate) than one with Uranus direct since he is catalyzed from within. His outer actions could seem even less appropriate for the occasion, and often are only comprehended (to some degree) by the individual himself. Wherever his special talent or brand of genius is to be found, this individual is likely to make even more radical departures from the norm, since he revolutionizes from a more subjective point of view that is uniquely his and his alone. This condition, in fact, could easily suggest uniqueness-plus.

The group of souls who incarnate together with Uranus retrograde may collectively find themselves karmically gravitating towards whatever first prompts them to restructure and reform their inner selves more thoroughly before they attempt to discover how to best revolutionize society at large. Initially, they may find themselves *psychologically* pulling away from the established order of things around them in an attempt to first explore their own inner nature. Remember that these individuals, being intently concerned with knowing their own individuality first, often feel polarized or alienated by the social standards they nevertheless are expected to submit to. Their desire is to know internal freedom before they work toward advancing social freedom. The inner path of liberation they tend to follow may therefore seem counter-productive to what society wants or demands from such a generation. Realize that these broad, sweeping statements do not apply to each and every member of this group but to those select few who are able to connect more directly with Uranian forces. For those who have learned to pay closer attention to the unfoldment of their individuality while also learning to broaden their impersonal goals and aspirations for society, Uranus retrograde can inspire these souls (often in an apolitical manner) to bring startling revelations and original thought to the awareness of the world concerning the expansion of human potential. Still, any sense of gaining relevant social insight first comes from being able to be enlightened from within. The individual is driven to awaken himself according to his own uncommon self-vision and at his own special pace. Although sometimes appearing highly active and vital in group affairs promoting social idealism, this individual is still inwardly prone to feel apart from the crowd he supports, more concerned about following the guidance of his inner self. (*Friedrich Nietzche - Karl Marx - Henry David Thoreau - Walt Whitman - Gertrude Stein - Alfred Adler - Evangeline Adams - Edgar Cayce*).

PROGRESSED:

When Uranus turns *retrograde* by progression, it remains so for the remainder of the individual's incarnation (155 progressed years). Thus, it should be very important to note the house Uranus natally occupies, for here is where a gradual turning within for greater freedom of self-expression plus an increased awareness of one's true individualism can be subjectively experienced. If this person is sufficiently responsive to Uranus to begin with, he now is being conditioned to become more personally inventive and experimental in dealing with these house matters than ever before. Therefore, he may start to become less willing to adapt to standard procedures or conventions he formally accepted without question. At least, he now questions social dictates more than before. For most people, subtle inner changes described by this phase will be hardly felt upon a conscious level. Or else they may become projected thru unusual outer events that periodically disrupt the inner status quo of the individual, often without any sense of rhyme or reason. This person can now feel inwardly at odds with what he is outwardly experiencing, as new attitudes about life are developing from within. He is less readily conditioned to behave according to the pressures of his environment. Karmically, this soul may be now reintroduced to the nature of former rebellious urges from past lives. He may re-contact and re-experience past personality quirks of temperament and idiosyncrasies he never knew existed in his nature. At this point, he may even have a more intense awareness of how and where he did not smoothly fit into the social structures of the past, for better or worse. Any sudden impulse toward liberating self-expression at this time (especially during the stationary phase) may offer clues concerning individualistic, yet unresolved, urges developed in former incarnations. One's humanitarian drives and/or occult understanding from the past may be better reviewed upon psychological levels. The individual may at least be able to continue to work upon a phase of individualization that was not allowed its most progressive, ideal unfoldment at some previous point in time. Progressed Uranus retrograde could signal a ripe time for the re-emergence of some free-form, unorthodox way of behaving that was an essential part of one's nature in ages past.

When Uranus turns *direct* by progression, Uranian energies are now apt to become less self-focussed, and instead can become more socially directed. Of course, this (like the remaining Higher Octave planets) can be very slow in its manifestation (except for those few who are triggered into expression during the stationary phase). Idealistically, the individual is now ready to forge ahead and experience life according to its more collective potential. But he is now better able to offer the world the fruits of his own self-illumination. However, this does not in itself guarantee that the world will understand and accept his insights, since he has initially come from a very subjective point that only he may comprehend and appreciate (due to all those former years of internal delving). But at least he is now driven to openly exteriorize his personally experienced insights, regardless of how they may be socially received or rejected. He is personally prompted according to his own sense of self-revelation, to now attempt to influence his worldly environment. For those few sufficiently attuned, this phase could denote a time of emerging genius and brilliant application of both knowledge and skill, according to the area of specialized interest the individual may have developed in this sector of his life. It could also imply the unearthing of willful and highly disruptive elements within the psyche, previously buried within, that increasingly engage in more direct and open conflict with the status quo and/or authority figures. The individual may more overtly attempt to brake all established rules of conduct or social protocol in favor of following the guidance of his own inner voice.

TRANSIT:

Transiting Uranus retrograde lasts about 155 days, occurring once a year. If it is to have any personal impact at this time, it is most likely to do so according to the circumstances of the natal house it is transiting thru. And also according to the nature of any natal planet or angle it strongly aspects...especially when aspecting at the degree of its station before turning retrograde. Near exact aspects should be quite noteworthy, since they tend to color the entire phase of this transit. In regard to aspects, especially note conjunctions, squares, and oppositions (since they all have a symbolic affinity with angularity, which in turn suggest open, and sometimes dynamic, action leading to turning-points in growth). Because most of humanity are not able to easily manage Uranian principles, its transiting effect is bound to be most immediately experienced as the disruption of the accustomed flow of affairs typical of the house it transits. Disruption here suggests sudden alteration of personal plans due to unforeseen new conditions in the environment that throw one's original intentions off course. Matters in concern tend to lose their structure quickly and break down as situations now bring forth unexpected elements which challenge the status quo of activities. But usually this is all for the individual's benefit, soul-wise. Uranus retrograde by transit can help put the individual in touch with needs for personal freedom of self-expression that may have been previously unrealized until this point in time. The individual is now given another opportunity to contact that highly unique part of himself that seeks more liberating forms of activity or fresh, new approaches for its optimum development. This may be particularly so if Uranus should make several aspect contacts to natal planets (rather than merely transiting thru a house).

Perhaps the Higher Octave planets are retrograde for so long because it is relatively harder for us to properly assimilate their special qualities without lengthy, periodic recapitulation. Their retrograde phases allow us to constantly review our progress here and learn to more thoroughly understand the purposes of these transcendent planets. As their motion becomes even slower when retrograde, perhaps they permit us to concentrate upon their qualities even more intently. With Uranus turning its intuitive impulses inwardly during this retrograde transit, the individual may be better able to stumble upon new avenues of expression that could result in greater self-illumination. He may reach a level of self-truth that can jolt him from ego-inertia or mundane stagnation in the area Uranus transits. The impact may not be that outwardly notable, but it can be stunning upon one's subjective levels. New insights gained suggest that the individual may reform his attitudes here and never see things quite the same way again in this department of his life. Although discontent does not openly show itself during this period as readily, it can be a thoughtful discontent that pressures the individual to change outworn patterns of behavior for the better. An internal sense of rebellion (normally directed against the self) can be felt before it surfaces and is directed towards the environment. Usually, outer situations at this time seem to operate beyond the dictates of our self-will (even more so than when Uranus is direct in transit), for we are now being conditioned to attune ourselves with universal will. When mismanaged, this retrograde transit can mark a period of strange mishaps for some that can rarely be analyzed or explained with any measure of success. Situations can defy all logic and reason, at least when strictly viewed from the surface appearance of things. Even out-of-the-blue opportunities are harder to account for. Uranus retrograde is prompting the individual to look below the surface of matters to discover deeper, hidden causes previously ignored...and to view such matters in the light of pure truth and objectivity. This is at least an ideal way of using such a transit. Whatever is suddenly brought to our attention represents what we must reform to help us better integrate a past cycle, left unresolved, before we can be free to forge ahead into the future. We are to focus upon such matters with great clarity. Unfortunately, very few of us are willing to be so honest and self-revealing about our life, and so we seldom receive the benefits of mental enrichment Uranus retrograde can grant us during this period.

NEPTUNE RETROGRADE

NATAL:

For those able to respond to Neptune retrograde natally, there can be a greater focus put upon the spiritualization of the individual's subjective world first and foremost before the individual directs his attention towards social obligations. Neptune here may focus its energies upon dissolving all existing psychological structures that have been over-crystallized. Its influence may thus be less problematic in the outer, concrete world since it prefers to nurture inner conditions developed in the past. As Neptune retrograde can be even more closely in touch with the power of the unconscious than Neptune direct, the individual's receptivity to subtle, emotional undercurrents can be heightened and intensified, increasing psychic sensitivity for some so sufficiently developed. However, if Neptune here is under severe stress patterns, psychic disorientation can be even greater due to the inability to objectively separate and recognize one plane of consciousness from another. Neptune's introspective nature; as well as its capacity for deep withdrawal, can be accentuated. Escapist tendencies, self-deception, and inner confusion are apt to be less apparent on the surface. Although imagination and visualization abilities can be very potent, they are less directed towards improving the social environment. They are not as often applied towards the advancement of future collective goals, at least in a direct manner. Instead, they tend to turn back towards the inner self in an attempt to visualize a more ideal condition of how things *could* have been. In other words, inspiration and revelation are applied more towards previous conditions that now only exist within the inner nature as intangible impressions. Although seemingly in conscious control outwardly, the individual may have a harder time exerting inner discipline and a sense of order. He may avoid structuring his internal world, suggesting that he can become highly susceptible to the powerful forces of his own unconscious. Neptune direct can be more resistant to the darker emotional contents of the unconscious, simply because it attempts to turn attention away from the unconscious and instead focus upon the glamour of the material world to a greater extent. With Neptune retrograde, the individual is more inclined to keep all energies of this planet unmanifested and undifferentiated. However, much here depends upon the evolvement of the individual as to how he copes with this condition.

This individual could be more devotional, self-sacrificing, or merely passive and psychologically non-resistant than he shows himself to be on the surface. Yet he may also be more vulnerable to the harsher realities of his existence, since he is tempted to avoid direct confrontation with those factors of his life that do not align themselves with those preconceived ideals inwardly he adheres to. There may be even more difficulty bringing visionary dreams down to a practical, workable level of functioning. Plus such dreams or visions may have little to do with the current circumstances of one's present life, but are more representative of past conditions that now represent "unfinished business." These subjective conditions, as intangible as they are, seem to have a strong emotional fascination for the individual. Disillusionment with outer world affairs can affect the individual more deeply than is realized, prompting him to safely retreat into his own self-made world of fantasy and illusion at times. Retrograde Neptune feels more at home upon immaterial, dream-like levels of awareness. Thus, when mismanaged, it could denote emotional distortions, unconscious complexes, or ingrained escape mechanisms that are harder for the individual to willingly bring to the surface, objectively examine, and satisfactorily resolve. The tendency is to be trapped in over-idealized past situational experiences that offer little opportunity for new inner growth in this present incarnation. The individual needs to realize that all experiences of the past are best used to promote the inspiration needed to give deeper purpose to the affairs of the present, as well as to offer added enlightenment concerning the potentiality of the future. The individual here must not allow himself to be forever locked into some previous emotional pattern that leaves him psychologically immobilized. Although apt to be very reflective, this individual should strive to establish greater balance by making an effort to channel his inner impressions into here-and-now objectives (especially in activities that allow for creative expression).

The lack of inner structuring ability indicated here can minimize one's capacity for psychological self-preservation. There can be much *internal* disorganization that frustrates the Ego and its functioning. The group of souls, however, who have incarnated together with Neptune retrograde may collectively be driven to express a greater non-interest in those material securities traditionally exalted. They may aspire more towards other-worldly or more abstract objectives in general for their security needs. Some of the more evolved and self-aware here can become illumined channels for spiritual refinement thru unique expression of love, beauty, or emotional idealism (often manifesting thru specialized self-expression in the fine arts or spiritual pursuits). On an individual level, Neptune retrograde can denote one who can unconsciously surrender his will easily to that experience which offers him a deeper sense of self-transcendence. He needs less tangible proof of the existence of Neptunian principles. When mismanaged, the individual may express a martyr-like attitude, in which he may punish himself emotionally in order to atone for something troublesome that is now hidden in the depths of his unrealized past. He is more sensitized to the essential root-problem that keeps him from feeling internally unified with other parts of his psyche, and cannot attain inner peace until he has redeemed himself. He needs to examine his feelings carefully here and finally forgive himself for any and all transgressions of the past. Otherwise, he may blindly continue to put himself in self-negating conditions that deny him the satisfaction of worldly accomplishment, material success, and human comfort. When constructively utilized, retrograde Neptune allows the receptive individual to take advantage of an almost mystical knack for uncovering those subtle spiritual realities that most of humanity are oblivious to. Remember, since half of humanity are born with Neptune retrograde, not all will respond in the manner described above. Since Neptune is already quite vague and undefined, most people will not recognize its process within their nature, regardless of whether it is natally retrograde or direct. The delineation I have offered should better apply to those few individuals who can effectively respond to the sublime impulses of this delicate, ethereal planet. (*Leonardo da Vinci - William Blake - Ralph Waldo Emerson - Walt Whitman - Pierre Baudelaire - Toulouse-Lautrec - Helena Blavatsky - Max Heindel*).

PROGRESSED:

When Neptune turns *retrograde* by progression, it remains so for the rest of the individual's mortal life (approximately 158 progressed years). The worldly affairs of the house Neptune natally occupies can now either gradually become increasingly spiritualized (due to the individual's growing awareness of underlying unity and oneness), or can become further disoriented and unrealistic, with the individual exhibiting a greater inclination to ignore, avoid, or retreat from openly facing up to the challenges and obligations of this house presented at this time. The urge to sacrifice the attainment of worldly benefits in favor of seeking inner understanding can now become emphasized in this sector of life. The individual may either begin to become more selfless in orientation and thus desirous of rendering impersonal service for the ultimate benefit of humankind (according to his own subjective vision), or he may instill additional confusion and personal disappointment due to self-deception if he attempts to willfully resist turning inward for self-examination. Life, at this timely point, is requiring that he now retreat back into a part of his inner consciousness that readily sees thru the veil of materiality and all its attendant illusions. The stationary period, naturally, should represent a time of confusion and uncertainty, especially for the earthbound individual who has never contemplated upon the spiritual origin of his manifest being. He now may be more vulnerable to the hidden forces of his inner soul nature.

Karmically, the individual may be reintroduced to idealistic dreams and lofty goals from past lives as well as personally unresolved blind-spots (especially on the emotional-feeling level). One should be very attentive to all emerging selfless impulses to heal, comfort, protect, and compassionately uplift the plight of the suffering of the world at this time, on whatever level experienced. This may give one valuable clues concerning one's previous experience with upgrading personal emotions to a more universal level of understanding. Also, any budding interest in devoting oneself to the advancement of the fine arts or beauty in general could be significant, since retrograde Neptune by progression could put one in touch with latent artistic talents. Illusionary feelings that may have led to self-deception in the past may now also be evoked to further test this soul. For the remainder of his life, this individual is to deeply ponder about the meaning of humanitarian love, often by putting aside his own materialistic desires and instead aiding others who are uncertain about their spiritual path, if true peace within is to be attained.

When Neptune turns *direct* by progression (similar to Neptune turning retrograde), its initial effects are not very noticeable. Its influence, if at all perceived to begin with, is subtle, gradual, and often indirect (typical of the innate nature of this planet). Perhaps what is suggested here is that the individual's ability to become more adept at finding outer channels suitable for the expression of Neptunian principles is further encouraged. The period of internal recapitulation he has unconsciously undertaken since birth is now technically over. His ingrained focus upon subjective ideals of being can now be redirected in a manner that allows him to bring such rare vision to the surface of his present existence, enabling him to help enrich the structure of the social matrix he is obligated to function within. He is invited by the ongoing process of life to apply his imaginative scope and social perception to serve the existing needs of his environment. Often in a manner that sparks greater collective unity and cohesion within the community. He no longer thwarts his *own* evolutionary growth by mulling over the frustration of not achieving emotional ideals of his own past in the self-absorbed manner characteristic of natal Neptune retrograde. Instead, he can better develop by now breaking away from subjective emotional attachments that he has become overly-fascinated with, and that have blocked his awareness of the unlimited avenues of needed social service. All collective, humane social concerns that now attract his interest will nevertheless require his open willingness to assert personal ideals in a manner that can foster tangible changes. He is now to make aspirations take form in society. It wouldn't be surprising if matters stemming from his past are now able to be resolved thru his compassionate attempts to heal the social ills of the present. At this point, and for the rest of his life, the individual may find himself better able to satisfactorily manifest his own unique vision of social harmony, shared understanding, and emotional unity, for he is now ready to bring to the world his own personal awareness of the basic oneness of life.

TRANSIT:

Transiting retrograde Neptune lasts about 158 days, occurring once a year. Like Uranus, its main influence can basically be related to the house it transits thru at this time. I suggest that several vital aspect contacts need to be present if Neptune in this phase is to be even somewhat consciously perceived (since it is characteristically subtle, evasive, and reluctant to manifest in well-defined material terms). Much that could be said about this retrograde transit is necessarily theoretically and speculative, since its functioning is perhaps best understood by the deeper facets of the individual undergoing it. Transiting Neptune retrograde could stir up unresolved conditions from the past (even in this present life) that can emotionally catalyze the individual's psychological make-up. What Neptune now stimulates can trigger buried, often neglected feelings within us that nevertheless run deep. Emotions unrecognized here hold much power over our conscious behavior. This retrograde period is an opportune time for reviewing all hidden undercurrents of feeling with more depth and understanding. We can and should become more reflective in this area of our lives. By being more contemplative, we are better able to receive inner guidance in regard to how we can best get in touch with these often unsettled inner feelings that normally escape our conscious attention.

When Neptune transits thru a house, matters associated with this sector are undergoing a subtle form of dissolution. Here, outer structures are continuously weakening, losing support, and are becoming less stable...regardless if outer appearances suggest otherwise (which they normally do, considering the deceptive nature of Neptune). This is typically a slow process. And we are apt to ignore this ongoing dissolution for quite some time until it has finally taken hold and undermined the structures and supports we have blindly depended upon. Neptune here only undermines that which had faulty or unrealistic structure to begin with, however. It wears down that which we have ignored or avoided for too long a time. When Neptune turns retrograde during its transit, the weak elements of these frail, unhealthy structures are better brought to our inner mind's attention. We are given a chance to re-view our blindspots and uncover the deeper reasons for our vague discomfort with the outer circumstances of this house. In doing so, we can recognize emotionally deprived parts of ourselves that now need our nurturing, compassionate concern. Previously fragmented feelings are now able to become more fully integrated with the remaining components of our psyche, but only thru the conscious effort made by an already self-aware individual. Without our conscious cooperation, very little constructive change can occur. Hopefully, retrograde Neptune enables us to feel more unified and whole from within once we have wrapped up all loose ends internally and have attended to our "unfinished business." However, one may have to experience several retrograde Neptune transits before this happens. Perhaps with each succeeding retrograde transit, deeper layers of the self are penetrated. We are encouraged to dissolve those distorted impressions accumulated from our past that have become too crystallized. And in doing so, we are able to renew ourselves spiritually.

For some, this retrograde transit could instill a greater need for privacy, seclusion, and withdrawal more than would normally be the case when Neptune is direct. Introspection is emphasized as well as increased receptivity to the stirring of the inner nature. However, on the other hand, this could also denote a time period when unrecognized escapist tendencies hold a greater fascination for the individual so inclined. Emotional vulnerability can be intensified, although in a manner that is less obvious on the surface. Aspects made at this time should give clues as to how the individual may handle these energies. On a constructive level, the individual may now take the time to explore the fertile world of his untapped imagination, allowing inspiration to lead him to greater awarenesses about his latent abilities. It can be an excellent time to further strengthen one's powers of visualization and imagery (and therefore can be very beneficial for those who want to advance their creative talents in whatever field they show promise). Self-discipline is still needed wherever Neptune is concerned if we hope to receive the emotional enrichment this planet can grant us during this retrograde phase.

PLUTO RETROGRADE

NATAL:

For those able to respond to Pluto retrograde natally, regenerative forces compelling the total re-shaping of one's awareness may be even more deeply embedded within the unconscious, and cannot be brought forth easily. Similar to both natal retrograde Uranus and Neptune, retrograde Pluto may focus its transformative powers upon conditions that have already been established within the individual from the past. In general, there can be much more psychologically guardedness than found with Pluto direct. The individual unconsciously resists having his inner negativities scrutinized by both his conscious self and others. By damming up these energies and not finding suitable channels for their release, profoundly disturbing tensions can subvert the healthy functioning of the psyche. Because this is a more internalizing Pluto, the individual can suffer a greater suppression of desire on some level. Pent-up forces here can build up awesome pressures that can dangerously bottle up, until they are unable to hold back from violent eruption. Sometimes, such high-charged emotional "debris" may be released better thru deep sleep states, vivid dream experiences, or thru various forms of altered awareness (often induced by chemical stimuli). The individual is less prone to find outer social avenues for such release. Although intensity of will can be more emphasized with this condition, it seldom exposes itself on the surface in a direct manner. The individual is more apt to eventually tear down internal structures he is at war with first before attempting to break down external social structure.

The apparent difficulty in finding proper release for Plutonian power could encourage the development of uncommon phobias, destructive emotional complexes, morbid compulsions, fixated desires, and a wide range of perversions. When Pluto retrograde is very much under stress patterns, hostility can be directed inwardly towards the self in a relentless manner, or it could manifest as *uncontrollable* social aggression. A similarly afflicted Pluto when direct would be more likely to calculate such aggressive behavior with more strategy. But since unconscious factors here seem to have more sway over the nature, retrograde Pluto suggests the individual has less control over the darker elements of himself. But for the more self-aware individual, retrograde Pluto presents an opportunity to search deeply within to uncover and investigate the root causitive factors for any hang-ups (karmic hang-overs) one may have. It may enable him to have an in-depth understanding of himself because of this, plus incredible insight into the workings of the unconscious. He can be driven to explore the hidden psychological motivations of himself as well as others easier than one with Pluto direct (who may spend too much time involving himself in circumstantial power struggles, since the need for dominance over *external* affairs here can be stronger). Psychological stamina is increased with retrograde Pluto, and probably due to the fact that this individual is in need of re-examining parts of his past that can be very threatening and overwhelming for the Ego. Without such stamina and internal endurance, he would likely avoid deep penetration into himself. Although often unconscious, he may have a fear of being overpowered by the shadowy parts of himself and can only feel more secure when actively having knowledge of their nature. Pluto retrograde is perhaps even more compulsive in its search to unlock fundamental mysteries of being.

As Pluto stays retrograde longer than the remaining planets, more people have this planet retrograde in their natal charts than any other. Yet since Pluto represents almost super-human qualities of being that are quite remote from what we have been conditioned by life to become, *very* few individuals are able to handle its inscrutable energies in a comprehensible manner. Whether retrograde or direct, Pluto's direct influence upon the conscious make-up of an individual is almost nil. It seems the only connection most individuals can have with Pluto is thru the collective effect of mass developments, and especially those of a revolutionizing nature. However, expect the charismatic and powerful leaders who spearhead such social movements to have greater access to Pluto's energy on a personal level. But for most of us, Pluto acts as as highly impersonal influence. I speculate that the group of souls who incarnate together with Pluto retrograde may collectively find themselves more concerned with retaining their own sense of power thru a willful determination to ignore external authority symbols (while those with Pluto direct are more driven to join forces in an attempt to overthrow such authoritarian pressure thru active defiance). Pluto retrograde souls are apt to be less desirous of merging with the collective whole and may express more anti-social traits. Social isolationists are more likely to be found in this group, while outer fringe rebels and social malcontents who actively attempt to undermine the Establishment may be found in greater numbers in the Pluto direct group. Perhaps the Pluto retrograde group is more intent upon *internal* revolution. Regardless, these individuals can be more remote, unapproachable (in terms of deep intimacy), and harder to really get to know well due to their accentuated secretiveness. They tend to undergo psychological eruptions and total inner purges that are scarcely observable on the surface. However, the few outstanding members of this group could help humanity make great strides in understanding the vast and unlimited *powers* of spirit, working thru the personal unconscious. These can be the courageous pioneers willing to explore the outer realms of inner space, as well as the inner realms of outer space. They are more concerned with the *source* of power that generates the enormous collective changes in the world, and are driven to find the key to mastering this primal power. (*Pablo Picasso - Marie Curie - Alan Watts - Dylan Thomas - Aleister Crowley - Howard Hughes - Richard Nixon - Timothy Leary*).

PROGRESSED:

When Pluto turns *retrograde* by progression, it remains so for the duration of one's incarnation (160 progressed years). The external affairs of the house Pluto natally occupies are apt to gradually become more complex and multi-level as time goes on. But they can also lead the individual into tapping his own regenerative powers, resulting in a greater sense of personal renewal when wisely handled. A needed psychological rebirth, transmutation of desire, or transformation of values is now more necessary than ever if he is to further benefit at all from matters of this house. He is to look within himself with greater intensity and a sense of stark reality in order to understand where and how he must further rehabilitate himself. This requires that he meet up against those darker forces that he has formerly allowed to take hold over his emotions in the past. Perhaps conditions were not suitable evolution-wise in the beginning of his life for him to best accomplish his needs here, and thus he was not to confront the retrograde import of Pluto until this appointed time (its influence was held in abeyance until conditions were ripe). Perhaps he had to first undergo experiences most suitable for Pluto direct before he was allowed to undergo this transition. Who can say for sure?

Karmically, the individual may be reintroduced to powerful obsessions or intensely willful desires that were allowed greater expression in past lives. He now may be tested once again in this life to see if he can deal with these potent inner forces and passions without allowing them to drain or consume him. One should be aware of the emergence of power-drives, manipulative urges, compulsive or irresistible desires (especially if anti-social), or drastic impulses to completely sever ties in relationships. This may give him clues about his most unlit self in past lives. He now may have to more carefully examine the contents of his unregenerative self in greater detail. Nevertheless, this progressed period could also denote a time when the individual can attune himself to a level of inner awareness where he is able to recognize and reclaim potent soul resources from the past that significantly advanced his evolutionary growth. He can re-contact those dimensions of himself where he was able to attain a degree of self-mastery that now could help him cleanse all residual personal and racial karmic negativity from within. Martin Schulman feels that retrograde Pluto allows the individual to experience "mass consciousness within himself."5 He feels the individual "experiences the struggle of mankind as a very personal struggle within himself. He personally feels the need to overcome in himself all that has been lowering the consciousness of the society he lives in."6 I couldn't agree more with Schulman's profound insight.

When Pluto turns *direct* by progression, its effect is understandably slow to manifest. Like the other Higher

Octave planets, Pluto at this point is now to direct its attention upon the more encompassing needs of society rather than isolated self-development. Ideally, the individual should now be ready for deep social commitment, for his recapitulation period is now officially over. He is now better able to offer the world the benefits of the powers he developed during his period of self-examination. This does not mean, however, that he will. But opportunities for making a greater social impact upon the world now become more evident. In most cases, the individual will simply begin to function more actively within his immediate environment and accept worldly situations as they are without undue introspection and analysis. He feels a less compulsive urge to dig into himself to understand his existence, which could be a welcomed relief for some. Hopefully, the battlefield is no longer within. He now can find external outlets allowing him to vent his concentrated inner forces in a manner that is psychologically satisfying. With his attention now being slowly conditioned to observe world processes instead of strictly subjective ones, this individual may discover that he has a broadened perspective of social matters that few share. He is able to view the human drama from its widest range and scope. He also can better understand mass motivation, even in its extreme expressions, since he has experienced similar motivations in himself. The more he has mastered the darker shadows of his own being during the retrograde period, the more he is able to tolerate the expression of similar shadows when demonstrated upon the mass level, since he is no longer fearful of them. And because he is more fully aware of their nature, he can help transform them into renewed powers that can benefit the growth of society.

TRANSIT:

Transiting retrograde Pluto lasts about 160 days, occurring once a year. Although its influence is mainly concentrated upon the house it transits thru at this time, it moves so slowly that even its house influence may seem obscure for most of us. Remember that Pluto represents that part of our psyche that is often hard to fathom. It suggests where we are often completely in the dark about the nature of internal developments we are undergoing, since its action works upon our deepest, underground levels of being. Yet it works relentlessly and sometimes even ruthlessly in accomplishing its ultimate aim. When retrograde, Pluto halts the external development of the house it passes thru (although with utmost subtlety) and instead forces us to focus upon where we have failed to adequately regenerate ourselves during past transit cycles of this planet. We are rarely aware of this at the time, yet the more aware we can become, the less soul-wrenching this retrograde transit becomes. All we seem to comprehend is that tensional matters from the past that were already disturbing enough psychologically to confront *then* are being brought once again into our direct path *now* for re-examination (even though the situational affairs presented to us at this time may seem radically different). Pluto is only concerned with confronting us with the essence of that which we have not transformed to a higher level of expression. It is less interested in the manner it brings this awareness about, at least in terms of how it threatens our ego-centered being. I guess Pluto figures that this is *our* problem to work out, not Pluto's. Resourceful Pluto will usually use whatever it can at the moment to make a deep and often disturbing impact upon our nature, according to root vulnerabilities we have allowed to run rampant.

As Pluto is a planet of extreme motivation, it is most prone to attack those parts of ourselves that have unfortunately taken on extreme manifestation. It only forces us to transform that which is in dire need of rehabilitation. At this time, retrograde Pluto will continue to hound us in a manner that may seem incomprehensible and even persecutory when viewed strictly from the shallow surface of our current mundane experiences. While some of us may try our best to obscure our inner intentions in this sector of life and try to remain innocent about the nature of our actions here, Pluto keeps a keen watch upon the real and fundamental motivations behind such actions. From a practical point of view, transiting retrograde Pluto suggests that the individual has an opportunity, according to the house involved, to retrace his steps and discover latent sources of power (hidden resources) formerly overlooked, that now can help him further his objectives in this area once properly unearthed. Much here depends upon the degree of self-discipline, emotional self-mastery, and even appetite-control (sensuality can be problematic when Pluto is prominently active in the chart). Pluto in this condition may even force us to re-evaluate our rights and values vs. those of others. Pluto now tells us that we must concentrate more deeply upon the underlying nature of current house activities rather than randomly scatter our interests according to the dictates of our emotional self-will...for to do so only brings us into more tensional self-confrontation with unresolved parts of ourselves that we feel powerless in overcoming. Like Saturn, Pluto shows us the reality of our limitations, although from a more psychological point of view. This can be a marvelous time for the self-aware individual to apply more penetrating insight towards exposing those wayward elements of one's inner self that need a sense of rebirth. These are typically those parts of the psyche that chronically resist constructive change upon the emotional level. Usually, where we have our greatest internal resistance to alterations of our inner pattern is where Pluto can do its most effective work.

Retrograde Pluto in transit can be especially adept at ferreting out hidden weak spots in whatever area it focusses its probing abilities. For when retrograde, it is even more attentive to subtle details that would normally be overlooked. Since its transiting retrograde period lasts for such a long time, the individual is gradually conditioned to delve into himself for potential growth in this area that current situational affairs alone cannot provide. A degree of psychological withdrawal is needed if one is to become more fully aware of resources coming from the inner depths. Those lacking in self-awareness are less able to seek out the subtle potentials available at this time. They simply react to the perplexing turn of events that are apt to occur without any sense of understanding, inclining them to feel victimized. But even for an individual to feel this suggests some degree of attunement with Pluto. For most, transiting Pluto retrograde passing thru a house is hardly recognized.

In closing this chapter, I would like to add that, astronomically speaking, when a planet is retrograde, it is also *nearest* the Earth during this period of its cycle. It thus appears to be at its *brightest* (with its disc seemingly *larger* at this period when viewed telescopically). In *Cycles of Becoming*, Alexander Ruperti states: "What actually happens geocentrically when a planet goes retrograde is not backwards movement so much as an apparent loop in space which the planet describes as it moves nearer to the Earth. The planet seems to go out of its regular orbital path as if pulled towards the Earth, forming a loop directed Earthwards."[7] Another interesting astronomical fact is that planets Mercury and Venus conjunct the Sun when at the midway point of their retrograde cycle, while planets Mars thru Pluto oppose the Sun at their midway point when retrograde. Note that any planet (except the Moon) in opposition to the Sun will always be retrograde in a natal chart. Ruperti interprets a retrograde planet as one allowing the individual to view the function of that planet more closely (since it is actually moving closer to the Earth), perhaps enabling us to develop new perspectives concerning that planet. Dane Rudhyar feels that the important factor of a retrograde planet is that it is moving away from the direction of the Sun and Moon, suggesting that it represents energies that go against the natural flow of life energies in order to help us go back and find better solutions to problems that naturally arise during the direct period.[8] The fact that retrograde planets appear larger and brighter to us at this time more than any other may symbolically suggest greater *enlightenment*, perhaps due to our more direct attunement with our unconscious at this time. Just as they are astronomically highlighted at this time, retrograde planets could highlight those psychological factors of our nature that need our closer examination if they are to help us find more advantageous ways of unfolding our being.

References:

(1) Virginia Ewbank, Joanne Wickenburg, *The Spiral of Life*, self-published, Seattle, 1974, p. 18.
(2) John McCormick, *The Book of Retrogrades*, Pavilion

Press, Livingston, N.J., 1973, p. 17.

(3) Tracy Marks, *The Art of Chart Synthesis*, Sagittarius Rising, Natick, Mass., 1979, p. 51.

(4) Louis Acker, Frances Sakoian, *Predictive Astrology*, Harper & Row, U.S.A., 1977, p. 91.

(5) Martin Schulman, *Karmic Astrology: Retrogrades & Reincarnation*, Vol. II, Weiser, Inc., N.Y., 1977, p. 190.

(6) *Ibid*, p. 190.

(7) Alexander Ruperti, *Cycles of Becoming*, CRCS Publications, Calif., 1978, p. 259.

(8) Dane Rudhyar, *An Astrological Study of Psychological Complexes*, Servire/Wassenaar, The Netherlands, 3rd edition, 1970, pp. 146-147.

11
Exploring the Hemispheres

The natal chart is divided into four main regions of space called Hemispheres. Each Hemisphere consists of six houses; and theoretically, each has one of the four *angles* of the chart at its midpoint. The angles in astrology represent four primary expressions of *identity* individuals adopt in coping with life. Each angle can be described as follows:

The ASC is the angle representing our conscious, immediate sense of *personal identity* or *self image*. The ASC denotes the process by which we view ourselves as we emerge out into the external world and assert our being. It depicts the nature of our continuous surface expression and response. The ASC denotes our most personalized characteristics of self-expression that uniquely describe us as separate entities, distinct and independent from all others. We readily establish a spontaneous association with these traits, and can assertively apply them towards the direct pursuit of basic self-related needs. In short, the ASC depicts our self-will in action, according to the behavioral pattern of the sign on this angle.

In contrast, the DESC becomes our angle of *reflected identity* or *other-image*. It can describe latent parts of our own nature that we do not relate to as personally or as directly, at least initially. These qualities are typically projected onto others we attract, who then mirror back such facets to us during the ongoing process of relationship. And usually, what is mirrored back to us is done in a manner that can promote greater objectivity and widened perspective concerning the intrinsic nature of these traits, plus the part they play in making us feel more whole and complete within. They are thus reflected back to us thru the open attitudes and behavior of those we interact with.

The MC is the angle representing our *social identity* or *public-image*. Unlike the ASC, the MC denotes a more impersonal identity for the individual. This image is often not one of the individual's own choosing, but instead is one he learns to structure according to the pressures and demands of his existing society. As this becomes a growingly conscious identity, the individual is better able to determine his proper place and function within the greater social scheme of things. And it is according to the nature of this public-image that the individual will be tested and judged by the world-at-large, for better or worse. It is thru the adoption of this identity that the individual establishes a degree of control and management over his existence. The MC suggests traits in our nature that urge us to aspire towards manifesting our highest potential in a purposeful manner, often resulting in the ultimate accomplishment or achievement of our life objectives.

The IC is the so-called "midnight" angle of the chart, representing our *inherited identity* or *subjective-image*. How we instinctively view our inner being at its most fundamental, security-oriented roots can be determined here. This angle describes our internal home base of operations. It reflects the subconscious role we constantly adapt to in securing a deeper foundational point within. The IC denotes our most natural way of anchoring ourselves inside before we branch out and experience our being externally. Our subjective identity is also strongly responsive to surrounding outer influences and can be subliminally conditioned to absorb and retain impressions from our early environment (usually thru our family structure). Thus, this identity is partly inherited. Of all identities shown by the four angles, the IC has the closest connection with the past. It is a subconscious image of ourselves that was likely developed in previous cycles of experience before birth (implying genetic or past life conditions).

The ASC corresponds to the *Eastern Hemisphere* while the DESC relates to the *Western Hemisphere*. Both these Hemispheres are divided by the *meridian*. The IC relates to the *Northern Hemsphere* while the MC corresponds to the *Southern Hemisphere*. Both these Hemispheres are divided by the *horizon*. In delineation, it is important to consider which particular Hemisphere is the most emphasized in the natal chart, for this can be one factor pinpointing an individual's basic orientation towards his outer life experience. An emphasized Hemisphere can usually be determined according to the number of *planets* (more than sensitive points) found within any Hemisphere. Six or more planets are necessary for a Hemisphere to be considered emphasized. When two Hemispheres hold an equal amount of planets (or 5 in each), then see which one holds the Sun plus the Moon and/or ruler of the ASC. This gives prominence, especially if that Hemisphere should contain all three. But if any two out of three are to be found in one Hemisphere, and it still is hard to determine which has greater weight, then check to see how many planets within each respective Hemisphere fall in angular houses, and/or closely conjunct one of the corresponding angles. Perhaps the signs and actual planets involved can further offer reinforcing support. I personally feel the Sun alone would take precedence over the influence of both the Moon and ruler of the ASC in this context, since the Sun also relates to one's main life objectives. The astrologer's ability to skillfully synthesize all correlating principles is required.

EASTERN HEMISPHERE

This Hemisphere begins at the cusp of the 10th house going counterclockwise and ends at the cusp of the 4th. Its foundational structure point is the ASC. Thus, the Hemisphere is centered around the expression of self-identity and the exercise of self-will. When a majority of planets are located here, the individual best unfolds his life potential by exerting much will and drive in consciously promoting personal affairs or interests that capture his direct attention. There can be indicated here a strong amount of initiative and enterprise in this person's approach towards life (particularly so when most planets in this Hemisphere are found in the three houses *below* the horizon). This person is usually prone to instigate situations in life, since the inclination here is to impress himself upon the environment rather than be influenced and moulded by the environment. As this is a Hemisphere of karmic intake, the individual is relatively free to act on his own behalf in obtaining objectives with less hinderance or interference from others. Yet because he does not tend to solicit the intimate involvement of others, people may not offer him support or assistance that could prove beneficial to self-determined goals. He is apt to resist such association in favor of independent pursuit, since there is less a sense of give-and-take implied with this Hemisphere. And thus, the individual is left alone in his efforts for the most part.

Being conditioned to be more immediately in charge of his affairs in this lifetime, the individual basically desires to have the general say-so concerning how and when he wants certain conditions to unfold. He is self-motivated to act according to his own exclusive terms. When he decides what it is that he really desires to do in this world, life may demand that he self-sufficiently work towards these goals in a decisive, single-minded manner if optimum results are to manifest. It is thru the development of self-reliance that this individual achieves ambitions that satisfy his needs. If most of the planets in this emphasized Hemisphere fall *above* the horizon, the individual's focus becomes more impersonal and universal. He can put much personal attention upon the larger issues of world experience and work towards social advancement, but normally only according to his own vision. If six or more planets are found here (particularly the luminaries and the ASC ruler), imbalance in orientation can occur. The more planets involved, the more the qualitites of any Hemisphere can become exaggerated. Under this condition, the person tends to over-emphasize his individuality to the point that he has a difficult time integrating himself with others, feeling a sense of equality, and functioning comfortably as a social (even sociable) entity. Being thus self-absorbed to a fault, he may then lack adequate objective awareness of others he becomes personally involved with. He only is interested in fulfilling his needs first and foremost in a very self-centered way. Demanding to be his own boss at all times, the individual here may push off all outside influence not directly under his control, regardless of how constructive. Positively, self-made individualists who have had to struggle against opposition to independently make their own mark in the world can often be found here. But with little inclination to cooperate or compromise with others, such people may easily alienate others, create much social distance, and choose to live out the solitary life of the lone-wolf. (*Napoleon - Joseph Stalin - Isadora Duncan - St. Teresa of Avila - Ernest Hemingway - Alice Bailey - Karl Marx - Gertrude Stein - Friedrich Nietzsche - Margaret Mead - Edward Kennedy - Joan Baez - Billy Carter - Madalyn Murray O'Hair*).

WESTERN HEMISPHERE

This hemisphere begins at the cusp of the 4th house going counterclockwise and ends at the cusp of the 10th. Its foundational structure point is the DESC. This Hemisphere is centered upon personal social awareness and the recognition of other-identity. Its basic theme concerns the expression of one's reflected image. When a majority of planets are located here, it signifies an individual who does not have as much freedom of action to exclusively determine the course of life direction he is to take, but often finds that vital issues and personal interests are more in the hands of others. This is the child (but not necessarily the pawn) of fate position. It may prove harder for this person to be recognized and accepted for his own true individuality, for he is more apt to become a creation of his social environment or a product of his own times. Relationships should be very essential for fostering the natural unfoldment of his being. This individual develops best by learning how to properly adjust to the needs of others. Actions taken here need to be mutually advantageous to all parties involved if true balance is to be established. Unlike one with Eastern Hemisphere emphasis, this person is more attuned to the process of sharing, and often acts according to the probable end-results such action may have upon others. This individual is able to receive attention from others, who can become instrumental in helping him obtain his objectives. He is less likely to resist or block their aid and support. Plus the more consideration and attentive concern he shows others, the more willing they are to pitch in and lend him a needed hand.

As this is a Hemisphere of karmic output, the individual is

more attracted to life experiences that require from him greater interpersonal involvement. He is being conditioned in this life to reach out to others directly and build constructive alliances. He is also now to learn how to effectively cooperate with life. He seldom benefits himself when he exclusively demands having his own way at the expense of others, plus he is less able to do so in most instances. Although this individual may seemingly have less control over the development of opportunities that come his way (since they are less self-initiated), he is also usually held less accountable for his mistakes, setbacks, or failures in general, as there is often someone else involved who triggers such consequences. Should six or more planets be found in this Hemisphere, the individual may show imbalance in expression by becoming too dependent upon others to further establish his sense of social identity. He may allow people to control and manage more of his destiny than is beneficial. Here is typically found a greater lack of self-determinism and self-assertion than would be indicated by one with Eastern Hemisphere emphasis. This could create a tendency to be easily imposed upon or used for the advantage of others. This may especially be so if most of the planets here fall in the three houses *above* the horizon in this Hemisphere, since these houses denote greater social focus and interpersonal activity than do the lower three houses. On the other hand, the individual may be adept at using others to his own personal advantage, since this Hemisphere can suggest one who is capable of applying strategy in his relationships. The individual could have trouble relating strictly to himself on an in-depth level, especially in terms of initiating personal action. He may show difficulty acting upon his own decisions alone, and detrimentally may lean upon others too much to accomplish those things that he instead needs to independently tackle himself. (*Adolph Hitler - Edgar Cayce - F. Scott Fitzgerald - Jean Harlow - Marilyn Monroe - Jacques Cousteau - Francisco Franco - Sigmund Freud - Joan of Arc - Vanessa Redgrave - Duke of Windsor - George Sand - Bette Midler - Sylvia Plath*).

The *Eastern* and *Western* Hemispheres are natural *polar opposites*. When we intently focus upon expressing the dynamics of one Hemisphere to the exclusion of its polarity, conflicting and sometimes distorting perspectives develop. We then need to resolve this dilemma and bring ourselves back into more balanced awareness. How? By learning to instead concentrate our attention upon integrating the positive functions of the opposing Hemisphere. Ideally, we should strive to coordinate both sectors constructively, since they are natural complements. Although few do this adeptly enough, most of us tend to swing from Hemisphere to Hemisphere until we have determined the degree of balance desirable for our development. If an individual does not seem to depict the qualities of the emphasized Hemisphere indicated in his chart, then check to see if he is attuning himself more to the dynamics of the opposite Hemisphere during this time period. All polarities (or oppositional factors in the chart) tend to do this. All the above can be said for the next pair of Hemispheres:

NORTHERN HEMISPHERE

This Hemisphere begins at the cusp of the 1st house going counterclockwise and ends at the cusp of the 7th. Its foundational structure point is the IC. Being the Hemisphere *totally* below the horizon in the chart, it represents that which is personally subjective, reflective, and in need of internal focus (at least at the start of the individual's life process). Planets here show urges that require depth of experience before the individual can utilize them openly and purposefully in his external environment. He tends to contain these urges in a self-absorbed manner for some time before he attempts to direct them towards more impersonal social concerns. Generally speaking, life is approached from an introverted viewpoint (regardless of how externally active and eventful one's participation in the world appears on the surface). The individual grows best by assimilating his life experience and relating it to the deeper reality of his inner nature. He is conditioned to get intimately in touch with his subjective identity much more here than in any other Hemisphere. He is to become aware of his root purpose for being (going beyond mere surface self-expression), and needs to seek personal meaning in his life first and formeost. By becoming increasingly attuned to that which is fundamental to his nature, the individual can tap into qualities operating at the roots of his personality.

As the individual leans towards a self-reflective and introspective disposition, he does not comfortably deal with *continuous* worldly affairs that call for direct public exposure or overt social involvement. He may even seem reluctant to attract attention to himself, at least in an assertive, obvious manner. The driving motivation here concerns the attainment of security from within rather than the temporal security society could offer him thru elevated position and status. He instead needs to find his own subjective anchor in life before he can become settled with worldly functioning. Regardless of how much he contributes to the greater needs of the world-at-large or does for the sake of ongoing social progress, he is still psychologically not a person who will put personal, gut-level needs aside. They must at all times be attended to and appeased before he advantageously furthers the potentials of his expression in the world. Detachment does not come easy for such a person. Constructively, the individual can direct his energies towards nurturing his environment with a great amount of caringness and concern. If six or more planets are found in this Hemisphere, the imbalance that can occur could denote one who is prone to becoming too focussed upon internalizing his response to life. He may choose to withdraw or turn away from active participation in the world in favor of safe retreat. Should many of these planets undergo stress aspects, then such retreat is not often healthy and may even be regressive. In this case, the urge to avoid open confrontation with the sometimes uncompromising realities of external life can be emphasized. Yet in a productive sense, such an emphasis can encourage the individual to identify himself with the less tangible, material aspects of life, enabling one to put much personal energy into unearthing psychological and spiritual realities hidden within human nature. (*Krishnamurti - Carl Jung - Helena Blavatsky - Amelia Earhart - Dane Rudhyar - Mary Baker Eddy - Gustave Flaubert - Elizabeth Kubler-Ross - Toulouse-Lautrec - Martin Luther - Duchess of Windsor -*

Albert Schweitzer - Queen Elizabeth II - Barbra Streisand).

SOUTHERN HEMISPHERE

This Hemisphere begins at the cusp of the 7th house going counterclockwise and ends at the cusp of the 1st. Its foundational structure point is the MC. As this is the Hemisphere *totally* above the horizon, it represents conscious, worldly-focussed experience. This Hemisphere directs the individual away from his private inner realm of subjective, self-contained impressions and instead propels him into the more objective, active affairs of society. It is the Hemisphere in which one's sense of public identity can be developed thru the fulfillment of socially-directed ambitions and goals. The individual is presented with impersonal, even universal, life situations that test his ability to function in a collective sense. He develops best by gravitating towards a public life where he can involve himself in the dynamic, external conditions of his existing social environment. Thus, he is likely to expend much energy dealing with the broader issues of his community. Having a greater sense of social participation than one with an emphasized Northern Hemisphere, this person often functions better on the one-to-many level. Yet one of the problems with an over-emphasized Southern Hemisphere is that the individual can become too detached or removed from himself to effectively deal with his inner needs. He tends to look outside of himself for solutions to problems that are best found within. He may not feel comfortable internalizing his urges and focussing subjective attention upon himself, and therefore may not know how to nurture and protectively support his own being. The individual might instead choose to know himself thru things he accomplished in the outer realms of experience. He tends to be more self-related and in tune with his own identity, however, if most of the planets of this Hemisphere should also fall in the upper sector of the Eastern Hemisphere.

An emphasized Southern Hemisphere suggests that the individual is undergoing a life in which he is to purposefully utilize his abilities for the sake of social development in a tangible, manifest manner. Yet if six or more planets are located here, the imbalance likely to occur can encourage this individual to become too impressed by the material end-products of his efforts, while having little comprehension of (or lasting interest in) the subtle, motivational factors underlying such efforts. By only dealing with life challenges on the surface level, he may be caught up with the superficial satisfaction of expanding his influence and power in the mundane realm. And while he may show a fuller capacity to handle life affairs in the greater social environment outside of himself, he may also fail to get in touch with the roots of his nature and view himself from a deeper perspective. Constructively, this Hemisphere when emphasized could denote a socially active personality who does much in the world to stimulate changes within the scheme of things, rather than merely reflect upon what potentially could be done. He can deal more directly with social actualities rather than idealize about such conditions, yet not take an active part in altering them. This individual does not retreat from the world at large, and is better able to confront it according to *its* own terms, for better or worse. Compare this with the individual with Northern Hemisphere emphasis, who is apt to only contend with the outer environments according to *his* own terms. (*John F. Kennedy - Marilyn Monroe - Benito Mussolini - Lillian Carter - Galileo - Pearl S. Buck - Nelson Rockefeller - Eleanor Roosevelt - Martin Luther King - Zelda Fitzgerald - Henry Kissinger - Lenny Bruce - Margaret Trudeau - Queen Victoria*).

12
Understanding the Quadrants

Although a study of Hemispheric emphasis can indicate an individual's overall life orientation, the introduction of the four Quadrants of the chart may help pinpoint and define more sharply how and where the individual further concentrates his attention. Each Quadrant is a unique mixture of a horizon-based *and* a meridian-based Hemisphere, encompassing three houses of the chart:

1ST QUADRANT

This Quadrant is a composite of both the *Northern* and *Eastern* Hemispheres. It begins at the 1st house cusp going counterclockwise and ends at the 4th. As previously stated, the Eastern Hemisphere deals with the exercise of individual freedom of action, leading to the development of self-identity. It is quite self-motivated. The Northern Hemisphere concerns itself with highly personal, subjective interests. It stimulates an individual's awareness of his deeper identity. Thus, this Quadrant can understandably be interpreted as a specialized life sector fostering a high degree of personal involvement and self-concern. When this Quadrant is the most emphasized, the individual relates to himself primarily as an independent entity, yet one somewhat psychologically disconnected from social involvement in the larger world around him. His need for inner security is here linked with his ability to direct his self-will and execute action in personal affairs as he sees fit. He tends to be intent upon managing his own life, which constructively could suggest self-reliance and self-assurance. Yet if this person cannot find effective ways of resolving personal conflicts that keep him at war with himself, self-management can be difficult to attain. Plus he may be too bundled up inside himself to let others guide him towards more fulfilling ways of expressing his energies.

Note that the initiating element of the 1st Quadrant is *fire*, and that the absent element is *water*. This suggests the psychology of the Quadrant. Fire symbolizes the vital, spontaneous drive for independent self-expression. Yet its inclination towards self-interest also renders it an egocentric influence. Thus, planets within this Quadrant express a driving urge to immediately experience oneself thru activities exclusive to one's current interests. A majority of planets found here (notably the fire planets) could denote much self-concern, or one with a strong sense of "I am." If such planets are very much under stress aspects, the potential for self-centeredness increases. And most so if the individual already has an emphasized *Eastern* Hemisphere. Although often markedly individual, this person can become highly self-absorbed in his personal affairs, and tends to be alienating due to his lone wolf disposition. He is at least not one who encourages intimacy with others easily. Constructively, this Quadrant could also reveal the self-made individual whose intent, personal focus and effort enables him to succeed in his endeavors in a vitally independent manner.

The only element not represented in this Quadrant is water, which is the natural element of deeper synthesis and assimilation of experience. Water is greatly sensitive to the unifying processes of life, and thus is a universal, socially connective element. Its absence (in reference to the natural wheel) suggests that the basic psychology of this Quadrant emphasizes self-reliance, not other-dependency. If water signs and planets (Moon, Neptune, Pluto) happen to be found here in the chart, they are indicative of *self*-support in which the individual first nurtures and protects his own needs rather than those of others. All water values are directed towards the self and experienced subjectively before the individual directs them towards the general environment. But since this Quadrant innately lacks water motivation, the individual with planetary emphasis here may need to learn how to become more sympathetic and understanding of others, more sensitized to *their* personal concerns, and thus more nurturant and caring in his response to external conditions not directly under his management. Even his own sensitivity towards himself may still be focussed upon the surface level of concern, implying that he is less inclined to probe deeply into the realm of his own being where subtler motivations operate (unless there is also found an emphasized *Northern* Hemisphere). In general, the 1st Quadrant type is more reactive than reflective. The polar opposite of this Quadrant is the 3rd Quadrant. When 1st Quadrant conflicts create too great an imbalance in the life pattern, directive solutions can often be found in this complementary upper Quadrant. (*Catherine the Great - Emily Dickinson - Karl Marx - George Eliot - Louis Pasteur - Mark Twain - Oscar Wilde - Toulouse-Lautrec - George Wallace - Barbra Streisand*).

2ND QUADRANT

This Quadrant is a composite of both the *Northern* and *Western* Hemispheres. It begins at the 4th house cusp going counterclockwise and ends at the 7th. The Northern Hemisphere tells us that this Quadrant still centers upon experiences more personal to and internalized by the individual. Inner security remains an important need. However, with the Western Hemisphere now involved, the individual is more drawn towards active interpersonal involvement. He is more deeply affected by the behavior and circumstances of others than the relatively immune 1st Quadrant type. He is motivated to find personal security thru relationships and tends to have a strong subjective link with others, which can make him more vulnerable to their feelings and attitudes about him. This may not always be obvious on the surface, however. Especially if this Quadrant type also has an emphasized *Northern* Hemisphere, being highly reflective. He is less likely to color relationships according to his own personal needs if the *Western* Hemisphere is emphasized, since planets above the horizon allow for more objectivity in evaluating others. The 2nd Quadrant type is prone to want response from others and cannot live in a vacuum. His sensitivity towards people helps him understand his own inner being with greater depth.

Note that the initiating element of the 2nd Quadrant is *water*, and that the absent element is *air*. Water symbolizes the ability to be highly receptive to undercurrents and subtle changes. Its instinctual nature operates readily to "feel out" the mood and underlying substance of any environmental condition. Thus, should a majority of planets be found here (especially the water planets), the individual can be highly sensitive to the inner, less obvious nature of others. The emotional impact of social interaction is a vividly felt reality for this person. Unlike the more self-contained and seemingly self-secure 1st Quadrant type, this individual tends to be more psychologically dependent upon others in his search for self-meaning. He feels he needs close association with others to give him a sense of personal purpose in life. Because this Quadrant is both water-motivated *and* below the horizon, it suggests an ability to tune into facets of a relationship (being also a Quadrant of the *Western* Hemisphere) that are not exposed or realized on the surface...or that may be still in the form of undeveloped potential. This can result in heightened perception of interpersonal needs. It gives the individual the capacity to view unions from a less superficial standpoint.

The only element not represented in this Quadrant is air, which is the natural element of social involvement and mental objectivity. It is distinctly impersonal and detached in its external evaluations of life and needs to create a sufficient degree of distance in order to develop broadened perspective. Its lack here can denote that this Quadrant does not innately promote detachment within the nature. If emphasized, the individual normally is more ruled by the heart than the head. Human warmth, closeness, and the sharing of deeper needs are more important for the individual's basic growth than are a comprehension of abstract ideals or personal freedom of expression. Instead of rationally observing relationship from a non-commital view, this person tends to become actively rooted in the center of unions and personally identifies with their development. A lack of air-motivation, however, can also indicate one who does not readily recognize and/or assimilate different viewpoints than his own without feeling a threat to his established security needs. He may have to learn to develop greater tolerance and acceptance of varied attitudes that do not necessarily reinforce his own. In general, he seeks the support of people to help fulfill his inner needs first before he can comfortably function in the greater world. The polar opposite of this Quadrant is the 4th Quadrant. Tensions and imbalances formed in this 2nd Quadrant can be worked out by the adoption of the constructive values of this complementary upper Quadrant. (*Mozart - Mary Shelley - Edouard Manet - Duke of Windsor - Anais Nin - Marlene Dietrich - Richard Nixon - Marlon Brando - Duchess of Windsor - Robert Redford*).

3RD QUADRANT

This Quadrant is a composite of both the *Southern* and *Western* Hemispheres. It begins at the 7th house cusp going counterclockwise and ends at the 10th. The Southern Hemisphere denotes impersonal involvement with social objectives and external affairs in the world at large, where the needs of a collective unit or goal outweigh the private, exclusive needs of the individual. The Western Hemisphere requires shared experiences with others, plus adjustments and compromises made for the greater purpose of any union, and not just for self-fulfillment. When this Quadrant is the most emphasized, the individual is likely to express an open interest in the wordly affairs of life that benefit the growth and development of others. Relationships in their more broadened sense attract his attention, especially when the *Southern* Hemisphere is also emphasized. This is perhaps the most mundane (i.e., "of the world," not necessarily "commonplace") of all Quadrants. The individual is inclined to concentrate upon dealing with the objective realities of his environment. This is the only Quadrant in which contact with the personal self is not emphasized, and very much so if most planets fall above the horizon in the *Southern* Hemisphere. The individual is less impersonal in his life approach should the *Western* Hemisphere also be emphasized, since planets below the horizon denote personal security urges needing nurturing attention. The individual is encouraged by life to fully participate in society. Constructively, he may show an active concern in promoting public causes or advancing social welfare in some manner. Yet one drawback with this Quadrant is that the individual can become too caught up in the larger issues of outer life and doesn't find time to know and nurture himself. This is particularly so if the planets of this Quadrant primarily fall in the gregarious 7th and 9th houses. However, since this is the sector containing the 8th house, inner transformation of values is necessary for growth. This will normally come about thru interior struggle in coping with the demands of the social pace one has set into motion for himself. In general, the individual can attract much public attention to himself in regard to his external efforts and activities.

Note that the initiating element of this Quadrant is *air*, and that the absent element is *earth*. Air is the element that denotes a clear social perspective and the ability to formulate broad-minded, although abstract, plans for ideal collective progress. It is the element of freedom of circulation, seeking to function upon ever-widening mental levels involving a multiplicity of activities and interests. Thus, a majority of planets here (especially the air planets...Mercury, Venus, and Uranus) describe one who wants to move about in his community and become more consciously aware of the variety of interchanges happening around him. He may be especially drawn towards joint efforts, collective ventures, and compromising alliances... and is often the "voice-of-the-people" type of personality. His destiny in life is almost totally in the hands of the public. He can be chosen to fulfill their needs and almost become their personal property to some extent. The only element not represented here is earth. This is the natural element of form, structure, consolidation, and practical reality. Its lack here implies that one with this Quadrant emphasized needs to approach social ideals from a more down-to-earth, workable level. Although the potentialities of society interest this person, he must become more methodical in his approach and more accepting of routine. Ambitions here need to be reasonable and realistic if he is to succeed. This Quadrant is better suited for one who likes to deal with immediate problems calling for quick response rather than those social matters requiring careful, long-range planning. A lack of earth also means that the individual is often not well-grounded within himself and has a harder time resisting pressures from the outer environment to carry out its demands. He is perhaps too open and receptive for his own good in this regard. The virtues of the 1st Quadrant, as the complementary polar opposite, can help to alleviate the tensions created by a mismanaged 3rd Quadrant. (*John F. Kennedy - Margaret Trudeau - Ronald Reagan - Sylvia Porter - Jean Paul Sartre - Marilyn Monroe - Sigmund Freud - Brigitte Bardot - F. Scott Fitzgerald - Bette Davis*).

4TH QUADRANT

This Quadrant is a composite of both the *Southern* and *Eastern* Hemispheres. It begins at the 10th house cusp going counterclockwise and ends at the 1st house. With the Eastern Hemisphere involved, the focus is back again on self-determinism and concern about personal control and direction over life affairs. However, due to the added influence of the Southern Hemisphere, the individual is inclined to make great personal efforts to contribute something of universal value to the world-at-large. Yet even when supporting important social causes or collective ideals, the individual is still able to keep his personal identity intact (unlike the 3rd Quadrant type). And this is especially so when an emphasized 4th Quadrant is also combined with an emphasized *Eastern* Hemisphere. By now, it should be clear that each Quadrant forms one half of two inter-connected Hemispheres, and that a Quadrant's expression is further colored according to which of these two Hemispheres dominates. An emphasized 4th Quadrant combined with a dominant *Southern* Hemisphere denotes one who is less independently self-involved in the pursuit of worldly aspirations, and who is more prone to compromise with others in manifesting his social vision. The emphasized 4th Quadrant type tends to personally identify with some larger-than-life activity. He wants to sense himself functioning on a grander scale in the outer environment, and often in a field of public service or social duty.

Note that the initiating element of this element is *earth*, and that the absent element is *fire*. Earth is an element interested in productivity and desires lasting security. It wants to realize in concrete terms its efforts and is driven to build and preserve organizational frameworks in society that are durable and workable enough to last the test of time. Thus, a majority of planets located here (and especially the earth planet Saturn) can denote an individual who wants to ground himself securely in the larger affairs of the world thru self-initiated efforts that influence the welfare of the masses. But he can be resistant (earth) to worldly development he has no personal management over. He can be somewhat detached from public opinion concerning his activities and does not need the degree of approval and acceptance from others typical of the 3rd Quadrant type (since his sense of self-identity is better preserved). He can also be a tower of strength or a stabilizing force for many, even though he is not personally influenced by them (unlike the 2nd Quadrant type). However, many planets here under stress patterns can indicate one who can become personally disruptive in his social efforts to have an impact upon the world, due to a lack of cooperative enterprise. Unlike the more self-focused and self-contained 1st Quadrant type, this person may seek to impose his demands upon others for the sake of some ideal cause, expecting them to help him fulfill his impersonal interests upon a larger range of influence without altering his plans or taking partial control over them.

The only element not represented in this Quadrant is fire. Although motivated by essentially personal impulses and needs (being a Quadrant of the *Eastern* Hemisphere), the individual paradoxically expresses the lack of fire thru his inability to view himself as just another separate entity with his own exclusive approach towards the world. In other words, he may regard his own needs and desires as basically those of everyone else. He is apt to universalize his own personal interests and attempt to relate to himself thru the agency of broader collective situations. He is able to initiate activities for others and is inclined to direct such affairs, but only shows a dynamic interest in making such an effort as long as his actions are given momentum by the collective support of others. His own self-will is harder for him to recognize, since he oftens acts on the behalf of others

in a seemingly unselfish, humane manner. He does appear
to have the stamina and persistence to work with important
social conditions until he has achieved his sought-after
goals. (*Clara Barton - Albert Einstein - Maria Montessori -
Alexander Graham Bell - Queen Victoria - George Bernard
Shaw - Evangeline Adams - Ernest Hemingway - Alice
Bailey - Pope John Paul I - Madalyn Murray O'Hair - Henry
Kissinger - Germaine Greer - Martin Luther King*).

QUADRANT SYSTEM OF MOTIVATIONAL ANALYSIS

The following is a speculative method given to aid the
astrologer in determining the *focal strength* of any
emphasized Quadrant. I have found it personally helpful in
disclosing further clues about the underlying dynamics of
the Quadrant. It seems to indicate (at least to me) those
principles which are most essential to the Quadrant's
expression. Test it out and see what you gain from it:

First, calculate the *midpoint* of the Quadrant that
dominates. In other words, determine the midpoint of the
ASC/IC for the 1st Quadrant if emphasized. Find the
midpoint of the IC/DESC if the 2nd Quadrant dominates.
Should the 3rd Quadrant be highlighted, determine the
midpoint of the DESC/MC, or the MC/ASC for an
emphasized 4th Quadrant. I refer to this as the *Primary
Quadrant Midpoint*. Next, see what planet, if any, makes
the *closest conjunction* to that Midpoint. I suggest using an
orb no wider than 7°, and especially if the birth time is
reasonably "exact." If a planet of this Quadrant *does* form a
close conjunction aspect, I interpret this to mean that the
Quadrant's basic function of operation can be brought to the
individual's objective awareness thru *circumstantial*
experiences according to the fundamental nature of that
planet. The overall natal condition of this accented planet
(its sign position, aspects to other planets, etc.) may help to
reveal the general *external* viewpoint the individual is
conditioned to assume as time goes by when learning to
deal with objectives and challenges natural to this
Quadrant. Such conditioning will normally come from
outside situational sources (people as well as events). It
describes what the environment demands of the individual.

If no planet conjuncts this Midpoint within the orb suggested, then this person may be less able to directly connect his *inner* nature (symbolized by the planets) with the external conditions that nevertheless influence his behavior; they may seem like something apart from what the individual recognizes himself to be. And thus, he may have a harder time understanding the purpose of such conditioning. In this case, added information about such external conditioning may have to come from the *sign* the Primary Quadrant Midpoint occupies and, to a lesser extent, the natal position of that sign's ruler. This Quadrant should be even more significant if the Sun, Moon, or ASC ruler happens to conjunct this Midpoint.

There can also be determined a more subtle, indirect Quadrant influence operating which can reveal the individual's own subjective attitudes adopted when coping with the challenges of this sector. It describes an individual's more internalized needs that may or may not be adequately satisfied thru the outer conditions the individual attracts to himself. I refer to this as the *Secondary Quadrant Midpoint.* In this context, the term "secondary" is not to imply that which is less important or essential for development, but instead that which is merely less obvious or apparent on the surface level. Unlike the Primary Quadrant Midpoint, this Midpoint is to be calculated according to the *planets* of the emphasized Quadrant. Simply calculate the midpoint of the two outermost planets of the entire grouping (in other words, both the first planet of the group going counterclockwise or clockwise, as well as the last planet). This Secondary Quadrant Midpoint may not always have a planet conjunct it within the group (and the suggested orb is 4°). If this Midpoint, however, does conjunct a planet, then that planet can reflect an urge or drive which indicates the individual's psychological reaction to those experiences natural to the emphasized Quadrant. It hints at this person's inner response to such outer experience. However, since a planet conjunct the Secondary Quadrant Midpoint is actually conjunct the midpoint of the two outermost planets, the nature of these planets needs to also be considered. Their combined influence modifies the expression of that planet more directly than does its sign position or natal aspects in most cases. If no planet makes a conjunction to this Midpoint within the grouping, then note the sign in which the Midpoint falls, and then check out the activity of that sign's ruler. Subjective attitudes in a case like this can become more complex and even somewhat troublesome. This condition seems to at least denote a special problem or challenge that one needs to meet up against psychologically and resolve to some extent before being able to inwardly accept the nature of experience typical of this Quadrant. Perhaps this is because without a planet at this Midpoint, the individual may have a harder time connecting himself with other parts of his *own nature* (i.e., the planets that create this Midpoint) rather than just the external environment. The Secondary Quadrant Midpoint tends to describe what the individual demands from the outer environment plus himself. It generally reflects one's less obvious desires, securities, fears, frustrations, etc. concerning the situations presented to us in this sector.

Example: If the *2nd Quadrant* is emphasized (subjective dependency upon others for inner security, plus personal awareness of one's purpose for being) and *Saturn* conjuncts the Primary Quadrant Midpoint, the individual is likely to be conditioned thru early circumstances to feel rejected, neglected, emotionally frustrated, or highly sensitive to any expression of disapproval and judgement from others (especially authority figures); he seems to have to work harder to earn acceptance and recognition. He may then eventually approach all future personal relationships with a certain degree of timidity, cautiousness, self-criticism, or a sense of inadequacy (which is no surprise, since Saturn here should normally fall somewhere in the 5th house, giving one a serious and sometimes awkward approach to matters in this sector of self-love, personal pleasure, and self-display). And should this Saturn be heavily under stress patterns, then expect an increase of self-doubt, fear of consequences, general uncertainty, and self-blockage, which may further intensify the potential interpersonal frustration indicated. This could result in the avoidance or even resentment of all intimate relationships that could put one in closer touch with Saturn lessons, often leaving the individual quite unfulfilled and insecure about his own worth in the eyes of others. Yet, constructively, he is being conditioned (albeit the hard way) to develop a stronger inner foundation from which to build a sturdier sense of self-esteem. He also needs to manifest thru structure and organization that which he feels to be his personal source of security in his life. This normally requires sufficient discipline and self-control, plus a sense of patience and earnest commitment. The individual is being pressured by the demands of his life to define himself in a manner that insures a vital, creative sense of self-recognition.

At the same time, should the *Moon* happen to conjunct the Secondary Quadrant Midpoint, the individual's inner urge from a most basic and instinctual level is to cherish human closeness, to yearn for interaction of a nurturing nature, and to sensitively reflect upon his personal purpose for living. He psychologically may grow and flourish best when able to become intimately attached to another and/or the public upon a securely rooted basis. Instead of being guarded and self-protective, this person inwardly desires to be warm, comforting, and caring of those he shows a strong attraction for. His inner reactions to outer experiences are much more emotional and deep than they appear on the surface. He is not as aloof and distant as he may seem. Yet the contrast felt between his inner and outer disposition may prove quite frustrating for him. Since the outermost planets of this Secondary Quadrant Midpoint further color the nature of the planet contacted, it would be quite beneficial if the Moon here was also at the midpoint of *Sun/Venus, Sun/Jupiter, Mercury/Venus, Venus/Jupiter, Venus/Uranus,* or *Venus/Neptune*...since all these midpoints basically have a friendly, sociable, and/or emotionally responsive nature. Thus, they would help to encourage the Moon to flow with its urges easier and manifest its true nature. However, should the Moon be found at a more tense planetary midpoint (such as *Mars/Uranus, Mars/Neptune, Mars/Pluto,* or *any Saturn*-involved midpoint in this Quadrant), and/or should it receive powerful stress aspects from other areas of the chart, then hypersensitivity and personal insecurity (already shown by the Primary Quadrant Midpoint conjunct

Saturn) could be even more problematic. If no actual planet conjuncts this particular Secondary Quadrant Midpoint, but the Midpoint itself occupies the sign *Cancer*, the interpretation would be similar (although not identical). Remember, under this condition, there could be suggested a problem with Cancer principles. Perhaps reinforcement here could also be found according to the condition of the natal Moon and 4th house. And here, the combined influence of the outermost planets of this Quadrant cluster does not operate, since no planet is here to actually trigger their midpoint degree into expression.

If a planet at either Midpoint is *retrograde* or *intercepted* (or both) it may pose less obvious yet more complicated situations and psychological challenges. This can also hold true when no planet is involved but the sign occupying either Midpoint is intercepted. Sometimes, you may find that *both* the Primary and Secondary Quadrant Midpoints conjunct the *same* planet. Perhaps this suggests that the individual is able to integrate the outer and inner expression of that planet in a manner that allows for a greater degree of personal transformation. The planet involved is at least highly accentuated for better or worse. Anne Frank had *Jupiter* conjunct both her Primary and Secondary Quadrant Midpoints in the mass-conscious *4th Quadrant* (plus she also had *Eastern* Hemisphere emphasis). Regarding the Primary Quadrant Midpoint, Jupiter could denote her *outer* conditioning during her life (suggesting an emphasis upon religious, ethnic, political, and morality concepts in relation to the larger world around her). Being a victim of the Nazi oppression, she certainly was brought into direct contact with mass-involved social issues (all beyond her personal volition). Yet also being an Eastern Hemisphere type, Anne Frank was driven to attempt to personally control and manage the structure of her precarious existence in the only immediate, self-involved manner available to her...thru the outpouring of her private revelations in the most publicized diary known to the world in this century. Her Secondary Quadrant Midpoint, also conjuncting Jupiter, indicated that her inner nature was humanitarian, understanding, wisdom-seeking, inspirational, and freedom-loving in both a personal *and* universal sense (4th Quadrant emphasis). This indicates to me that her outer conditions (as horrific as they were) also provided her the impetus to find a psychological way to transcend the catastrophic time period she was forced to live thru, and instead find a way to rise above the existing mass consciousness in an almost saintly manner. And perhaps because, in her inner heart, she was rich in benevolence, compassion, and unconditional acceptance of humanity.

CRCS PUBLICATIONS

ASTROLOGY, PSYCHOLOGY & THE FOUR ELEMENTS: An Energy Approach to Astrology & Its Use in the Counseling Arts by Stephen Arroyo
.... $7.95 Paperback; $14.95 Hardcover
An international best-seller, this book deals with the relation of astrology to modern psychology and with the use of astrology as a practical method of understanding one's attunement to universal forces. Clearly shows how to approach astrology with a real understanding of the energies involved. Awarded the British Astrological Assn's. Astrology Prize. A classic translated into 8 languages!

ASTROLOGY, KARMA, & TRANSFORMATION: The Inner Dimensions of the Birth-Chart by Stephen Arroyo .... 264 pages, $9.95 Paperback; $17.95 Deluxe Sewn Hardcover
An insightful book on the use of astrology as a tool for spiritual and psychological growth, seen in the light of the theory of karma and the urge toward self-transformation. International best-seller.

CYCLES OF BECOMING: The Planetary Pattern of Growth by Alexander Ruperti
.... 6 x 9 Paperback, 274 pages, $9.95
The first complete treatment of transits from a humanistic and holistic perspective. All important planetary cycles are correlated with the essential phases of psychological development. A pioneering work!

AN ASTROLOGICAL GUIDE TO SELF-AWARENESS by Donna Cunningham, M.S.W.
.... 210 pages, Paperback $6.95
Written in a lively style by a social worker who uses astrology in counseling, this book includes chapters on transits, houses, interpreting aspects, etc. A popular book translated into 3 languages.

RELATIONSHIPS & LIFE CYCLES: Modern Dimensions of Astrology by Stephen Arroyo
.... 228 pages, Paperback $7.95
A collection of articles and workshops on: natal chart indicators of one's capacity and need for relationship; techniques of chart comparison; using transits practically; counseling; and the use of the houses in chart comparison.

REINCARNATION THROUGH THE ZODIAC by Joan Hodgson ..... Paperback $5.50
A study of the signs of the zodiac from a spiritual perspective, based upon the development of different phases of consciousness through reincarnation. First published in England as *Wisdom in the Stars*.

LOOKING AT ASTROLOGY by Liz Greene .... 8½ x 11, $5.95
A beautiful, full-color children's book for ages 6-13. Illustrated by the author, this is the best explanation of astrology for children and was highly recommended by *School Library Journal*. It emphasizes a healthy self-acceptance and a realistic understanding of others. A beautiful gift for children or for your local library.

A SPIRITUAL APPROACH TO ASTROLOGY by Myrna Lofthus ..... Paperback $12.50
A complete astrology textbook from a karmic viewpoint, with an especially valuable 130-page section on karmic interpretations of all aspects, including the Ascendant & M.C. A huge 444-page, highly original work.

THE ASTROLOGER'S GUIDE TO COUNSELING: Astrology's Role in the Helping Professions by Bernard Rosenblum, M.D. .... Paperback $7.95
Establishes astrological counseling as a valid, valuable, and legitimate helping profession, which can also be beneficially used in conjunction with other therapeutic and healing arts.

THE JUPITER/SATURN CONFERENCE LECTURES *(Lectures on Modern Astrology Series)* by Stephen Arroyo & Liz Greene .... Paperback $8.95
Transcribed from lectures given under the 1981 Jupiter Saturn Conjunction, talks included deal with myth, chart synthesis, relationships, & Jungian psychology related to astrology.

THE OUTER PLANETS & THEIR CYCLES: The Astrology of the Collective *(Lectures on Modern Astrology Series)* by Liz Greene .... Paperback $7.95
Deals with the individual's attunement to the outer planets as well as with significant historical and generational trends that correlate to these planetary cycles.

THE PRACTICE & PROFESSION OF ASTROLOGY: Rebuilding Our Lost Connections with the Cosmos by Stephen Arroyo .... late 1984, Paperback $7.95
A challenging, often controversial treatment of astrology's place in modern society and of astrological counseling as both a legitimate profession and a healing process.

A JOURNEY THROUGH THE BIRTH CHART: Using Astrology on Your Life Path by Joanne Wickenburg...168 pages, Paperback $7.95
Gives the reader the tools to put the pieces of the birth chart together for self-understanding and encourages creative interpretation of charts by helping the reader to think through the endless combinations of astrological symbols. Clearly guides the reader like no other book.

THE ASTROLOGY OF SELF-DISCOVERY: An In-Depth Exploration of the Potentials Revealed in Your Birth Chart by Tracy Marks....... 288 pages, Paperback...................................$8.95
A guide for utilizing astrology to aid self-development, resolve inner conflicts, discover and fulfill one's life purpose, and realize one's potential. Emphasizes the Moon and its nodes, Neptune, Pluto, & the outer planet transits. An important & brilliantly original new work!

THE PLANETS & HUMAN BEHAVIOR by Jeff Mayo...180 pp, Paperback $7.95
A pioneering exploration of the symbolism of the planets, blending their modern psychological significance with their ancient mythological meanings. Includes many tips on interpretation!

ASTROLOGY IN MODERN LANGUAGE by Richard B. Vaughan...340 pp, $9.95
An in-depth interpretation of the birth chart focusing on the houses and their ruling planets--including the Ascendant and its ruler. A unique, strikingly original work! (paperback)

THE ART OF CHART INTERPRETATION: A Step-by-Step Method of Analyzing, Synthesizing & Understanding the Birth Chart...by Tracy Marks Paperback $7.95
A guide to determining the most important features of a birth chart. A must for students!

For more complete information on our books, a complete booklist, or to order any of the above publications, WRITE TO:

CRCS PUBLICATIONS
Post Office Box 20850
Reno Nevada 89515-U.S.A.